BUSHMEAT

T0386689

/ AFRICAN
/ ARGUMENTS

African Arguments is a series of short books about contemporary Africa and the critical issues and debates surrounding the continent. The books are scholarly and engaged, substantive and topical. They focus on questions of justice, rights and citizenship; politics, protests and revolutions; the environment, land, oil and other resources; health and disease; economy: growth, aid, taxation, debt and capital flight; and both Africa's international relations and country case studies.

Managing Editor, Stephanie Kitchen

Series editors

Adam Branch
Alex de Waal
Alcinda Honwana
Ebenezer Obadare
Carlos Oya
Nicholas Westcott

THEODORE TREFON

Bushmeat

*Culture, Economy and
Conservation in Central Africa*

HURST & COMPANY, LONDON

IAI International African Institute

Published in collaboration with the International African Institute.
First published in the United Kingdom in 2023 by
C. Hurst & Co. (Publishers) Ltd.,
New Wing, Somerset House, Strand, London, WC2R 1LA
Copyright © Theodore Trefon, 2023
All rights reserved.

The right of Theodore Trefon to be identified as the author of
this publication is asserted by him in accordance with the
Copyright, Designs and Patents Act, 1988.

A Cataloguing-in-Publication data record for this book
is available from the British Library.

ISBN: 9781787388147

www.hurstpublishers.com

CONTENTS

PREFACE

People in Central Africa have traditionally eaten most species of wildlife – commonly referred to as bushmeat – for thousands of years. From hamlets to megacities, there is hunger – literal and otherwise – for bushmeat. Bushmeat is a luxury for some and a basic subsistence protein for others. It can, therefore, be trivial or extraordinary depending on where and when it is eaten, and by whom. Although Central Africa is transforming rapidly, the appetite for bushmeat continues unabated, and has created what is widely considered to be a bushmeat crisis. The shift from subsistence rural consumption to highly commercialised urban use can be explained by a number of factors, including newly developed trade networks, demographic evolution (including rural–urban migration), cultural attachment, and political and institutional deficiencies. These overlapping realities have led to soaring bushmeat consumption throughout the region – be it at home, as street food or in restaurants. Meanwhile, bushmeat consumption and trade have direct and indirect consequences on people's well-being, biodiversity, local economies and public health. The Covid-19 pandemic has brought bushmeat to the fore as a global issue that extends well beyond Central Africa.

Bushmeat: Culture, Economy and Conservation in Central Africa tells the story of this multifaceted issue, which is largely unknown outside expert circles, and which is often animated more by emotion and ideology than by science or respect for cultural realities. This book delves into the craving for the meat of wild animals in a culturally sensitive way – without taking sides – while giving voice to the hunters, transporters, traders, consumers, conservationists and other protagonists in the spreading bushmeat political economy. My research and writing are an attempt to balance the multiple layers of difference between conservation and development, and between conservation and Central African world views, without pitting one against the other. Some readers may wonder about the timeliness of a book about bushmeat when veganism and vegetarianism are trending. One reason for its timeliness is that food remains the root of culture, and the very word 'meat' derives from the word 'food'.[1] Another reason relates to the sixth mass extinction. Also known as the Anthropocene extinction, it is an ongoing process that is provoking the extinction of millions of plant and animal species. The publication of this book will hopefully also serve to bring attention to this process.

I'm aware that my critical assessment of conservation policies may appear harsh, but I'm also fully aware of – and have tried to nuance – the evolution in the conservation mindset since the 1980s. Some readers coming from a donor or conservation background may want to dismiss some of my analysis, while some social science academics may think it is not as critical as it could be. These divergences point to the highly contentious and politicised nature of wildlife use and management. By emphasising the extent to which bushmeat fills the hearts, minds and stomachs of the region's population, this book humanises what has turned into a bushmeat crisis discourse by looking at wildlife through people's attitudes and behaviours. The need to consider their lived relationships with wildlife is paramount. While this book does not have an explicit policy objective, it may be useful to the decision-makers, public donors and philanthropists, and other experts who are constantly struggling to cope with the seemingly incompatible priorities of human development and the design and implementation of sustainable wildlife management strategies. Without underestimating ecological factors, my portrayal of the problem is inspired by an anthropological and cultural approach that puts the human factor at the heart of the analysis. Ethno-anthropological studies, based on listening to people, provide crucial information for the design of behaviour change initiatives, aimed at making hunting more sustainable, while encouraging Central Africa's city dwellers to consume less bushmeat. This book also respects an interdisciplinary approach because bushmeat is the subject of numerous research priorities that need to be studied in an integrated way. These include food security, cultural identity, gender relations, public health, political economy, demography and the youth bulge, urbanisation, biodiversity, deforestation, forest ecology, wildlife crime and governance.

Telling this story required reading thousands of pages of articles and books, government and international agency reports, non-governmental organisation documents, and a vast quantity of grey literature. While there is an abundance of such scholarship published in the form of specialised scholarly articles, largely written by conservation biologists, there is no book that looks at bushmeat through a social science lens in a holistic way. This not-for-experts book fills that surprising gap. It is written for a general readership interested in contemporary Africa, wildlife, culture, nature and the environment, and conservation. But because of its holistic approach, experts will also be able to find interest in it: someone working in the area of infectious diseases, for example, could learn from the chapter on cultural drivers of consumption; an expert specialising in legal frameworks and law enforcement could find the chapter on hunting useful. Given the individual concerns of readers, there is consequently no need to proceed from chapter to chapter in the order published here. Readers can feel free to skip from one chapter to another according to their own interests. I deliberately allowed for some slight overlap and repetition in chapters, so each can be read independently.

Where possible, I consulted the most recent sources available, while looking at older sources, which was also necessary to account for the shifts in the themes addressed. This book, therefore, is part synthesis of documentation and part summary of original ethnographic data accumulated thanks to multiple assignments in the region. These trips gave me the opportunity to observe how bushmeat is hunted, traded and consumed while carrying out formal interviews and engaging in hundreds of informal conversations. These took place primarily in the Democratic Republic of the Congo (DRC) where I have extensive experience, but also in the Republic of Congo and the Central African Republic (CAR). Interviews and discussions were conducted mostly in French, but my conversational knowledge of Lingala greatly facilitated exchanges, especially in rural areas where people are sometimes not comfortable speaking French. I've eaten my fair share of duiker, porcupine, cane rat, red river hog, crocodile, and monkey on a few rare occasions. Doing so was in part a research strategy to get hunters, restaurant owners and traders to speak openly to a white foreigner about his activities. At the same time, it was an opportunity to experience first-hand the importance of bushmeat in people's hearts and minds.

The main geographic focus of this work is the Congo Basin where the problem of unsustainable wildlife consumption is particularly acute. The area is also home to some of the world's most notoriously undemocratic regimes, adding a host of wildlife management difficulties. The Congo Basin extends into Cameroon, the Central African Republic, the Democratic

Republic of the Congo, Equatorial Guinea, Gabon and the Republic of Congo. With a total area slightly larger than Nigeria (or 1.4 times larger than the US state of Texas), the Congo Basin is home to the world's second-largest contiguous tropical rainforest after Amazonia. This represents 70% of all of Africa's forests. Although there are various interpretations of how to define 'Central Africa', I use that term and the countries of the Congo Basin interchangeably. The space was previously referred to as 'Equatorial Africa' but that label is rarely used today.

This book comprises nine chapters, including two background chapters. They are intertwining threads that converge to construct my threefold central narrative: bushmeat is culturally and economically important; wildlife is under severe pressure; and current management strategies to mitigate unsustainable hunting are largely inefficient. Each of these chapters could be books in themselves – but those volumes will be for someone else to write. My ambition has been to present these important topics as chapters in a single volume to promote an integrated, holistic approach to the study of bushmeat – holistic, yes, but with particular emphasis on social science research methods and analysis. Despite my efforts to be as thorough as possible, there is at least one gap in this book: a designated chapter on bushmeat and gender. To fill this gap, at least in part, I've added whatever information I have been able to discover on the role of women in the bushmeat trade, both from my own interviews and from the literature. The ethnographic story of Mama Régine in Chapter 7 provides a clear understanding of one facet of the gender and bushmeat issue, specifically the role of a female bushmeat restaurant owner.

The introduction – Chapter 1 – sets the stage by outlining people's reliance on bushmeat, why there is a bushmeat crisis, local perceptions and international responses to it, and a discussion about wildlife sustainability and major threats. The first background chapter – Chapter 2 – explains deforestation drivers and trends. It is a necessary starting point because wildlife habitat is under serious pressure. As the forest area shrinks, wild animals find it increasingly difficult to reproduce, survive and thrive. The second background chapter – Chapter 3 – offers a historical analysis of conservation efforts in Africa with a focus on protected areas. These spaces have become highly politicised arenas in which actors with different visions and agendas compete with one another over access and resource rights. Chapter 4 presents the hunter's universe – his motivations, world views, constraints and opportunities. It also addresses the paradox of hunters being empathetic with the animals they kill. This chapter highlights both change and continuity in the hunting realm. Chapter 5 presents the drivers of consumption by responding to the question 'why eat it?' The response is complex, sometimes contradictory, and gives no overriding motivation. Tradition, taste, availability, cost and lack of alternative proteins are some of the intertwining reasons. While other chapters focus on bushmeat as nourishment for the soul as well as sustenance for the stomach, Chapter 6 looks at bushmeat as money. It presents a discussion of how to manage open access resources, a price-cost-earnings commodity chain analysis, and an overview of supply and demand drivers. Chapter 7 is the most ethnographic chapter and recounts the personal story of Mama Régine, who runs a bustling bushmeat restaurant in one of Kinshasa's most populous districts. Before delving into her narrative, it presents some of the problems of food insecurity that the urban poor have to grapple with. Chapter 8 makes the connection between consumption of wild animals and zoonotic diseases – or diseases that are transmitted to humans from wild animals. Although there are thousands of them, this chapter looks at three case studies: Covid-19, the origins of which remain unclear, and HIV and Ebola, which both emerged in Central Africa through human–wildlife contact. Instead of delving into the medical and biological complexities of zoonotic diseases, this chapter focuses on the social and cultural dynamics connecting people, wild animals and disease. Finally, Chapter 9 argues that the legal frameworks adopted by the governments in the countries of the Congo Basin are unable to sustainably manage wildlife for a host of reasons – one of which is the persistent problem of poor public service provision. It analyses the legality–legitimacy dichotomy and points out the overwhelming obstacles to enforcing laws, concluding that despite important advances in designing alternative livelihood strategies and launching behaviour change campaigns, laws without social take-up cannot be effective. 'Game over?' is the question addressed in the book's short general conclusion. These chapters make up the book's main focus: bushmeat is food for the heart, mind and soul just as much as it is money and food for the stomach.

ACKNOWLEDGEMENTS

The research and writing of this book have been a collective effort encouraged by lots of friends, colleagues and experts from academia, the development sector and conservation organisations. They have contributed to this work indirectly through inspirational conversations and directly by commenting on draft chapters. Four anonymous readers helped improve the manuscript, each of them contributing in different ways, in a spirit of congeniality. There was a division between the expectations of one anonymous reader who encouraged me to make the book more academic and the views of two other readers who explicitly welcomed the manuscript's readable flow, style and structure, thus making for an accessible presentation of the bushmeat crisis to a general non-expert readership. I revised the draft in a way that struck a balance between the two perspectives.

I'm particularly thankful to Barbara Avelino, Idriss Ayaya, Filip De Boeck, Thierry De Putter, Kevin Dunn, Meredith Gore, Olivier Igugu, Dan Ingram, Noël Kabuyaya, Anne Laudisoit, Guillaume Lescuyer, Louisa Lombard, Jacky Maniacky, Germain Mavah, Krossy Mavakala, Daniel Mpoyi Mpoyi, Mutambwe Shango, Patricia Teixidor, Patricia Van Schuylenbergh, John Waugh, Patrick Welby and Juliet Wright. The significant investment of these individuals is an indication of their genuine

ACKNOWLEDGEMENTS

interest in the book's value. I'm especially happy to be able to pay tribute to those who have encouraged and supported me in my career as a researcher over the past four decades: my mother and father of course, Ken Barlow, Edouard Bustin, Pierre de Maret, Pierre Englebert, Guido Gryseels, Samy Mankoto, Baudouin Michel, Diane Russell, Filippo Saracco and Nicodème Tchamou. Two stars who deserve very special acknowledgement are my daughter Lea and son Basil for their unwavering moral support.

Two women have staunchly provided the encouragement needed to transform a vague idea into the present volume. Stephanie Kitchen, managing editor of the African Arguments series with whom I've worked to publish two previous books, *Congo Masquerade* (2011) and *Congo's Environmental Paradox* (2014), deserves special thanks. The other is Michelle Wieland, director of rights and communities, Africa, at the Wildlife Conservation Society. Michelle, you've been more of an inspiration to me – and to many others – than you probably realise.

The Royal Museum for Central Africa has been paying my salary since 2006 to carry out interdisciplinary research into environmental governance in the DRC. I feel extremely lucky to have had such an amazing career opportunity and am grateful to the museum for its sustained support. It is unlikely that I would have been able to write this book over the past three years without my museum salary. The fact that wildlife is peripheral to the museum's core research focus is proof of its respect for academic freedom, which is increasingly under threat in many institutions. My teaching and research association with the ERAIFT graduate school (École Régionale Post-universitaire d'Aménagement et de Gestion Intégrés des Forêts et Territoires Tropicaux) in Kinshasa since 2000 has been a formative experience in helping me to understand natural resource management through an integrated perspective, inspired by UNESCO's Man and the Biosphere (MAB) programme. ERAIFT and MAB seek to improve the relationships between people and their environments based on scientific research. Additional support came from the UK Research and Innovation's Global Challenges Research Fund (UKRI GCRF) Trade, Development and the Environment Hub, via ERAIFT. The Wildlife Conservation Society provided a generous grant for book purchases and distribution.

I haven't cited the names of all the people interviewed while researching and writing this book but they are credited in endnotes when their information was used. Everyone interviewed agreed to have their real names appear in this book except for a few individuals who are referred to as anonymous respondents. I was sensitive to human subject ethics guidelines and was governed by the 'do no harm' principle to avoid putting anyone at risk. People were quite willing to talk about bushmeat, generally without reservations.

The manuscript was submitted in the form of an advanced draft to African Arguments in January 2022. After I responded to reviewers' extensive comments, production started in November 2022. Alice Clarke and Daisy Leitch at Hurst, supported by the International African Institute/African Arguments, oversaw the subsequent production steps, such as copyediting, page layout, indexing and getting endorsements. Miles Irving drew the book's two maps. Russell Martin meticulously copyedited the text which was checked and re-checked by Ross Jamieson.

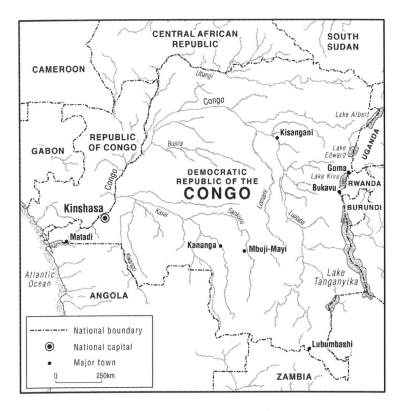

Map 1: Map of Central Africa

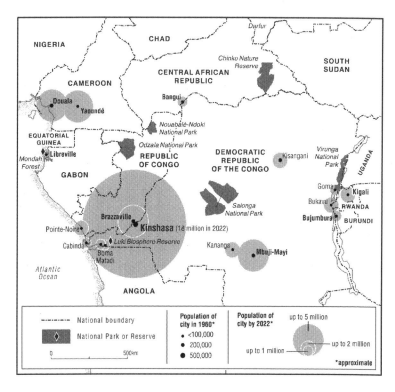

Map 2: Cities and selected national parks and reserves

LIST OF TABLES

LIST OF ABBREVIATIONS

CAFI	Central African Forest Initiative
CAMPFIRE	Communal Areas Management Programme for Indigenous Resources
CAR	Central African Republic
CARPE	Central Africa Regional Program for the Environment
CBFP	Congo Basin Forest Partnership
CIFOR	Center for International Forestry Research
COMIFAC	Council of Ministers in charge of the Forests of Central Africa
DRC	Democratic Republic of the Congo
ECOFAC	Écosystèmes Forestiers en Afrique Centrale
EVD	Ebola virus disease
FAO	Food and Agriculture Organization
FARDC	Armed Forces of the DRC
GIS	Geographical Information Systems
HIV	Human immunodeficiency virus

LIST OF ABBREVIATIONS

ICCN	Congolese Institute for Nature Conservation
ICUN	International Union for Conservation of Nature
LAGA	Last Great Ape Organization
NGO	Non-governmental organisation
PETA	People for the Ethical Treatment of Animals
RAPAC	Réseau des Aires Protégées d'Afrique Centrale
SIV	Simian immunodeficiency virus
SMART	Spatial Monitoring and Reporting Tool
TEK	Traditional Ecological Knowledge
TRAFFIC	Wildlife Trade Monitoring Network
UKBWG	UK Bushmeat Working Group
USAID	United States Agency for International Development
WWF	World Wide Fund for Nature

1

MEAT FOR SOME, WILDLIFE FOR OTHERS

If it scampers, slithers, swims, walks, crawls, burrows or flies, there is a good chance someone will want to eat it. Practically all forms of wildlife, from the largest emblematic mammals (such as gorillas, hippos, elephant, okapi) to small insects (such as grasshoppers, termites, caterpillars, larvae) are avidly consumed in Central Africa. A general rule of thumb is: 'whatever wildlife can be eaten, will be eaten'.[1] The craving for the flesh of wild animals, in conjunction with the absence of domesticated livestock, is ground zero in what has become known as the 'bushmeat crisis'. There are some variations from country to country and from region to region, but the most commonly consumed and affordable bushmeat species in Central Africa are porcupine, duikers (also named forest antelopes) and small monkeys, in contrast to prestige animals such as leopard, gorilla and elephant, which are less frequently available in restaurants and at markets and far more expensive.

'Bushmeat is everything: it's money and food, it's what makes me feel good' were the words of Séphora, a market seller in the Republic of Congo.[2] Variations on her expression – such as 'it tastes good, it's traditional, it's African' – were frequently heard during interviews. Eating bushmeat throughout much of Central Africa is quite simply normal, desirable and commonsensical, which explains why it is such a complex challenge to conservation efforts. This ordinary embeddedness is captured in the first part of the present chapter's title: 'meat for some'. Accounting for the human factor in the broader wildlife conservation effort is this book's main objective and, in doing so, it examines culture, economy, belief systems, urban sociology and normative frameworks. This converges with the individual narratives and analysis that humanise the culture and economy of bushmeat hunting, trade and consumption.

Bushmeat, a term used synonymously with 'game meat' or 'wild meat', is defined in wildlife conservation circles as 'non-domesticated terrestrial mammals, birds, reptiles and amphibians harvested for food'[3] or 'wild animal protein that is hunted for human consumption'.[4] 'Wild meat' is the term increasingly used in conservation circles as 'bushmeat' appears to be less politically correct. In Africa, the word 'bush' is used to describe forest or wilderness; so, animals hunted or trapped there become bushmeat. Bushmeat is also the literal translation of the widely-used French term *viande de brousse*, which is close to the Lingala *nyama ya zamba* (meat from the forest).[5] Although there is some linguistic debate about the meaning of *nyama*, in popular language in much of the Bantu-speaking world, *nyama* is the same word for both live animals and meat.[6] *Musuni* (flesh, in Lingala) is also sometimes used to refer to meat but less frequently than *nyama*, and it also applies to the flesh of fish and fruit. *Nyama* (or *nyama na yo!* – you animal!) is an insult exchanged by drivers in Kinshasa's notorious traffic jams and applied to mischievous children. This shouldn't be surprising to English speakers, who similarly use the term 'meathead' to refer to a rough or stupid person. *Nyama* is also a lascivious compliment for a woman's plumpness.

Eating wild animals – usually smoked, stewed, grilled or roasted, and served with a larger portion of rice, cassava, taro or plantain – is a way of life in Central Africa. Eating wild animals is so paramount in some societies in the African rainforest that people distinguish between two types of food shortage: one, hunger; the other, craving for meat.[7] The Lele of DRC have the word *ihiobe* to describe a particular form of hunger resulting from 'meatlessness'.[8] Bushmeat is first of all food, but it is likewise a cultural reality with profound cognitive associations. Once at the centre of complex ritual and symbolic relations between hunter and wild animal (see Chapter 4), bushmeat today is a desired ingredient in the diets of rural and urban communities. African food and gastronomy expert Igor Cusack fittingly grasped that 'a national cuisine is just a symbol of national identity, like a national anthem or flag'.[9] In Central Africa, bushmeat is an essential ingredient in that identity. Not only do people think they have the right to eat these wild animals, they also believe that they have a duty to do so. I've heard multiple variations of this (admittedly self-serving) sentiment in conversations in villages and towns: 'God filled our forests with animals for humans, he gave them to us, so we have to eat them to respect His plan. We have the duty to transform these animals into food. Why would we just leave them there?' This attitude is closely related to the basic teachings of Genesis and the belief in the Garden of Eden. Even the cartoon character Homer Simpson contemplated the topic: 'If God didn't want us to eat animals, why did he make them out of meat?'[10]

People from around the world consume animals in ways that may be surprising – or even repulsive – to people outside a given environment. Their choices, based on cultural attachment, biological needs and psychological perceptions, may nevertheless make sense for them in specific contexts for certain events and at certain times. Culturally and traditionally, bushmeat is somewhat similar to an American hamburger or English fish and chips. South Koreans are notable consumers of dog meat; Japanese, Icelanders and Norwegians eat whale. Americans visiting France can be disconcerted to see horsemeat steak on a restaurant menu. Despite a total ban on hunting, authorities in Ecuador found evidence that Galapagos tortoises were hunted and eaten.[11] This emblematic reptile with a lifespan of more than a hundred years was central to Charles Darwin's work on the theory of evolution. These are just a few examples of culinary idiosyncrasies. Cannibalism is an extreme example of idiosyncratic consumption and was practised – essentially for ritual purposes – in the DRC during the conflict of the late 1990s.[12]

A pioneering quantitative exercise published in 1999 claimed that 1.1 million tons of bushmeat was harvested annually in Congo Basin countries.[13] In 2002, however, that amount was dismissed as an underestimation, indicating a figure four times higher.[14] Today, it is estimated that Central Africans consume between 5 and 6 million tons of bushmeat annually (compared with 1.3 million tons in the Amazon Basin).[15] In both basins, bushmeat provides somewhere between 60% and 80% of daily protein needs.[16] Five or six million tons is a staggering amount when put into comparative perspective. That equals approximately half of Brazil's annual beef production, Brazil being the world's second-largest beef producer after the United States. At least 50 million people in the Congo Basin depend on wildmeat for their food security and daily subsistence.[17] Based on a synthesis of 16 studies from Congo Basin countries, Robert Nasi and colleagues put forward an annual per person consumption of 51 kg (all wildlife species combined).[18] This compares with a US annual per capita meat consumption of 124 kg – with the US topping the list of the world's meat intake.[19]

The hunting of wild animals precedes recorded history. It has been an uninterrupted subsistence activity for at least

100,000 years.[20] Hunting scenes figure in the oldest known artistic representations – notably the Palaeolithic cave paintings of Altamira in northern Spain and Lascaux in south-western France.[21] It is significant that in these paintings, animals are portrayed while trees, vegetation or other environmental markers are not, revealing the central place animals occupied in the world views of the artists. There is a plethora of common English surnames that derive directly or indirectly from hunting and hunting or warring implements. Archer, Arrowsmith, Bowman, Chase, Fletcher, Fowler, Gore, Grosvenor, Harrier, Hunt, Hunter, Huntington and Spear are but a few examples. Hunting and the art of warfare, moreover, are ancient complementary activities.

The Anthropocene's impact on the natural environment and its contribution to global climate change form a hotly discussed problem today. Although less widely known and discussed outside of expert circles, the human impact on wildlife is overwhelming. Habitat loss and deforestation (discussed in detail in Chapter 2) are a significant driver of human-induced wildlife loss. Unsustainable hunting of wild animals is another driver. It is relatively recent in Congo Basin countries and has been a gradual process – exacerbated in the past few decades by commercial hunting for urban markets. What is clearly at risk is not only biodiversity but cultural diversity too. In simple terms, sustainable hunting would allow for the relationship between hunter and wild animal to continue indefinitely. Unsustainable hunting, conversely, forecloses the possibility of future generations continuing to access the meat of wild animals. Nevertheless, sustainability is a very complicated reality to grasp, in part because bio-monitoring data is not always up to date and is, in some cases, incomplete. Moreover, there is no comprehensive regional monitoring system in Central Africa (unlike in southern and eastern Africa where monitoring systems are somewhat more advanced). It is more difficult to monitor animal populations in dense forests than in the savannahs.

In theory, it can be assumed that as the number of hunters increases in a given forest space, their returns (in terms of catch per unit effort and time spent in the forest) diminish. But individualistic economic determinism means the number of hunters will continue to increase 'until a period of absolute diminishing returns is reached'.[22] Only then will hunters shift away from hunting, but the damage to wildlife populations will already have taken place. While data from Gabon indicating that a hunter can harvest 3 kg of meat in six hours is anecdotally interesting, taken as an isolated fact it is of only marginal significance from a conservation perspective.[23] The amount of wildlife harvested is, nevertheless, an excellent example of a research question that merits replication in other hunting sites. Influenced by species-based factors such as reproduction rates, biomass distribution and extraction, biological models of sustainability do not include social and economic sustainability.[24] This absence exacerbates the challenges to conservation.[25]

Before being able to conclude that hunting is unsustainable in a specific geography, one would have to calculate reproduction rates and biomass levels (i.e. how many animals are in the forest). This is an exercise that requires funding, professional fieldworkers and meticulous methodological design. Unlike in savannahs and grasslands where aerial counts of large herbivores provide reliable information, the closed tree canopy of rainforests and the resulting poor visibility make this method impractical. There are consequently two preferred ways of carrying out censuses in rainforest environments: direct visual observations (sightings of single animals and sightings of groups) and indirect monitoring (counting dung and nests).[26] Recent developments in Geographical Information Systems (GIS) technology are increasingly used in modelling and mapping wildlife distribution at large spatial scales. Drones, camera traps and the Spatial Monitoring and Reporting Tool (SMART) are other new tools that combine innovative software, capacity-building and site-based protection to address the challenges of wildlife conservation.

In the early 1990s concerns about unsustainable hunting in Central Africa led conservationists to coin the expression 'bushmeat crisis'. With increased awareness of the problem, a group of scientists and conservation organisations created the Bushmeat Crisis Task Force in 1999 in the US and the UK Bushmeat Working Group (UKBWG) in the UK around the same time. Their aim was to promote conservation of wildlife populations threatened by commercial hunting. Related work has been constantly gaining momentum in an effort to design and implement creative responses. A constellation of well-respected conservation and research organisations, universities and international agencies have invested heavily in trying to identify creative, socially acceptable and environmentally realistic solutions. The International Union for Conservation of Nature (IUCN), the Food and Agriculture Organization of the United Nations (FAO) and the Center for International Forestry Research (CIFOR) are a few noteworthy examples. All of the major conservation non-governmental organisations (e.g. the Wildlife Conservation Society, Conservation International, the World Wide Fund for Nature, the African Wildlife Foundation, the Zoological Society of London, the Jane Goodall Institute, and the Dian Fossey Gorilla Fund) have all made some effort at setting up and supporting similar programmes. Other organisations, such as the International Fund for Animal Welfare[27] and the Humane Society, seek to curb hunting, but in this case from a more ideological 'end all forms of animal cruelty' perspective.[28] Early initiatives aimed at addressing the unsustainable commercial trade in bushmeat include a resolution passed in 2000 at the World Conservation Congress and discussion of the problem at the Conference of the Parties to the Convention on International Trade in Endangered Species the same year. All of these initiatives require massive amounts of money and commitment.

International donor agencies have accepted the challenge to deal with the bushmeat crisis and are therefore investing heavily every year in the region to improve wildlife management in and outside national parks. They have also started to implement actionable ideas about the drivers and obstacles to behaviour change regarding bushmeat consumption (see Chapter 8). Millions of tax dollars and euros (principally but not exclusively from the US, the UK and the European Union and member countries) and well-endowed philanthropic grants are spent annually on trying to understand and act on the socio-economic, political and ecological contexts that could contribute to more sustainable wildlife management.

Marshalled by wildlife conservation experts, activists and policy-makers, high-level summits have been convened and international conventions signed. A bevy of the world's rich and famous – from Hollywood heavyweight Leonardo DiCaprio to media mogul Ted Turner or investor billionaire Warren Buffett – have also supported wildlife conservation efforts in Central Africa. Kung Fu actor Jackie Chan, in partnership with the African Wildlife Foundation, created the *Kung Fu Pangolin* video to raise awareness in Asia about the illegal wildlife trade. In the video, Chan trains pangolins to ward off poachers by using kung fu. *Indiana Jones* star Harrison Ford is vice-chair of Conservation International. Actress Uma Thurman supports the South African Rhino Rescue Project. Unlike former King Juan Carlos of Spain, who was repudiated by ordinary Spaniards for indulging in a lavish elephant hunt in Botswana in 2012, King Charles III and Prince William (the latter created United for Wildlife and was the impetus for the London Declaration, which led to the Illegal

Wildlife Trade Challenge Fund and the Earthshot Prize while also teaming up with former football superstar David Beckham under the WildAid banner) are also wildlife protection activists. Their engagement is not dissimilar to the way some Western celebrities are taking part in other facets of the appropriation of Africa, such as George Clooney's and Madonna's humanitarian advocacy.[29] Super-rich Amazon founder Jeff Bezos committed $10 billion 'to help preserve and protect the natural world' by setting up the Bezos Earth Fund.[30] (It is significant that he chose the word 'protect' instead of 'conserve' in such a high-profile declaration, implying that conservation strives towards the sustainable use of nature by humans, while preservation seeks to protect nature from humans.) Multi-billionaire aviation businessman Richard Branson pledged billions for nature, including support for the African Wildlife Foundation (but his airline profits dwindled owing to the Covid-19 pandemic, which put a dent in his ability to make good on his intentions).

Celebrity support, nevertheless, is far from universally encouraged – even less accepted. Resource Africa, for example, an advocacy group for people's rights to use their natural resources sustainably, has called for a stop to the meddling with a powerful open letter addressed to UK-based celebrities. Operating in southern Africa, Resource Africa was inspired by what was then the ground-breaking CAMPFIRE model, which helped communities benefit from conservation.[31] Because it is rather unusual, Resource Africa's perspective is an important contribution to the global conversation about conservation.

> As representatives of millions of rural Africans, the majority of whom live below the poverty line, we are urgently appealing to you, as celebrities with status, to stop undermining our globally recognised conservation efforts and our basic human right to sustainably use the natural resources on which our communities' livelihoods depend. In recent months you have lent your names to campaigns to stop hunting

in Africa. We acknowledge that you are doing so with the best of intentions and we welcome your interest in our wildlife. But you have expressed these views without full appreciation of the implications for our people or wildlife, and without consulting us, who live with and manage African wildlife and who will ultimately determine its future.[32]

Greater public awareness and better understanding of the problem of community and wildlife sovereignty – based on the best scientific research and innovative methodologies – have not translated into workable conservation strategies with demonstrable results. We know what the problem is, but we don't know how to fix it. The debate over trophy hunting is a relevant example. Some African countries tolerate trophy hunting because it is a source of revenue and can be welcomed by local communities. However, it is unclear if it leads to tangible conservation benefits, especially in countries with poor governance performances.

The Convention on Biological Diversity gives a concise but compelling summary of the bushmeat crisis, which is associated with the issues of wildlife sovereignty: 'The loss of wildlife will impact the availability of animal protein and fat sources for countless numbers of people and also initiate cascading alterations of ecosystems as species that play important ecosystem functions (e.g., seed dispersers, seed predator, control of prey species) are eliminated through overhunting.'[33] While the bushmeat crisis is real, it is also still 'oversimplified' in some policy and conservation circles, especially with respect to 'its important livelihood and welfare dimensions'.[34] The level of knowledge and degree of sophisticated analysis are constantly improving, but the hunting, trade and consumption of wild animals go on unabated. There is therefore legitimate concern and a broad consensus among experts that time is running out, encapsulated in assessments such as 'local extinctions of hunted species are widespread, with West and Central Africa being particularly hard hit'[35] and 'the unrelenting decline of mammals suggests many vital ecological and socio-economic services that these species provide will be lost, potentially changing ecosystems irrevocably'.[36] Although the two dynamics are closely intertwined, in many areas of Central Africa it has been suggested that hunting is a greater threat to wildlife than deforestation.[37] As that view is admittedly controversial and is certainly site-specific, one would need to carefully analyse factors such as human population density, forest ecology, hunting techniques, proximity to urban areas, and trade networks and law-enforcement capacity to confirm it.

Unsustainable wildlife management is a problem that can be looked at from various overlapping perspectives. Despite the absence of exhaustive data, there are numerous studies documenting the inexorable decline of many wildlife species. Large, slow-reproducing mammals such as elephants and gorillas are particularly vulnerable because they are less resilient to current threats than smaller, more rapidly reproducing animals such as cane rats or duikers. Forest fragmentation is more of a threat to large mammals than smaller animals. Hunters using firearms, moreover, prefer to target large game first and smaller animals afterwards. Overhunting, however, is not a recent trend. In some cases, species extirpation dates back at least a hundred years – for elephant in the Cameroon Highlands, for example. The same area is now empty of other large mammal species which once roamed there such as gorillas, lions, leopards, buffaloes and chimpanzees.[38] Interviews with hunters in central Gabon revealed that large mammals had disappeared over the second half of the last century due to overhunting.[39] In northern Central African Republic there was a 65% decline in large mammal populations from 1985 to 2005.[40] The okapi population declined by at least 43% in north-east DRC in just over a ten-year period.[41] Populations of large-bodied wild animals have also been wiped out of the Bombo Lumene hunting reserve by the twofold reality of hunting and habitat loss.[42] Between 10,000 and

14,000 elephants were slaughtered annually in the Congo Free State between 1885 and 1908).[43] These are just a few examples that allowed a team of researchers who carried out a survey based on the International Union for Conservation of Nature's Red List to determine that 301 species of terrestrial mammals are being hunted out and are now threatened with extinction.[44]

There are, conversely, some site-specific studies that suggest hunting is sustainable. This is the case among agricultural communities of Kiliwa in north-eastern DRC[45] and around Takoradi, Ghana's third-largest city: 'Following the historical depletion of those species most vulnerable to overhunting, the remaining terrestrial mammals in the Takoradi market (84% of trade volume) appear to be harvested sustainably at present.'[46] These counter-examples indicate that sustainable hunting may be possible in some circumstances. This is also noteworthy from a methodological and ideological perspective because conservation researchers tend to carry out studies where hunting is unsustainable, as demonstrated by most publications. There are large parts of Central Africa where cane rats or probably even blue duikers are not under severe hunting pressure. Many conservation biologists agree, however, that the hunting of some species of primates and large-bodied mammals that reproduce slowly is unsustainable.

Unsustainable wildlife management is also very much a human tragedy. Communities who live in forest areas and depend on bushmeat for sustenance are victims. As wildlife levels diminish, obviously people's food supply does too, as does their possibility of earning money through bushmeat trading. Children are particularly hard hit because those who consume forest foods have a higher nutrient density than children who do not.[47] The nutritional benefits of bushmeat and the negative consequences of its decline are enormous and have been observed throughout Central Africa.[48] At the global level, one survey estimated that more than one billion poor people depend on bushmeat for protein, most of the B-vitamin complex, and the minerals of iron and zinc.[49] While forest-dwelling peoples consume lots of other types of foods, be they farmed, fished or foraged in the forest (such as caterpillars and grubs, which are important high-protein seasonal foods), bushmeat is a significant contribution to nutritional balance. As a general rule, the closer people live to rivers, the more fish they eat; the further their villages are from rivers, the more meat they traditionally consume.

Bushmeat is important not only for protein and iron but for healthy fat too, which is often scarce in forest environments.[50] Many studies have shown how reduced access to bushmeat impoverishes rural populations and negatively impacts on their nutritional status. According to a good summary of this situation: 'the direct cost of wildlife loss falls most heavily on the rural poor, directly reducing the amount of animal protein available to them, and eroding one of the few commodities that they can sell'.[51] A dramatic trend in Cameroon, for example, shows that 'new nutritional troubles like anaemia, obesity, hypertension, high rates of cholesterol and diabetes, are commonly reported among recently sedentarized hunter-gatherers.'[52] Decreased access to bushmeat, along with increased access to inferior-quality domestic meats and other commercial foodstuffs, is a direct cause of these downward trends in public health.

The development of commercial networks for urban markets reduces access to meat because full-time and part-time hunters prefer selling meat for money instead of putting it into the household pot: the perception that eating meat is tantamount to eating money frequently comes up in conversations. A farmer-hunter in a village close to a main road in the Luki Biosphere Reserve (DRC) told me that if he caught a cane rat, he could sell it for enough money to buy cheap imported chicken and fish, rice, oil and condiments, to feed his family of six for nearly a week.[53] This is an understandable paradox because if the family were to eat the cane rat, they wouldn't have money to buy other foodstuffs. It comes down to selling a relatively small quantity of quality meat to a commercial trader to be able to buy a much larger stock of lower-quality food that could last longer and feed more family members.

Hunting, gathering and fishing (along with farming) are complementary activities carried out by numerous communities in Central Africa. But fish stocks also suffer with the increasing rarity of wild animals – and vice versa. As bushmeat availability declines, communities tend to fall back on fish for healthy protein.[54] But this shift is also unsustainable and contributes to a downward spiral: overhunting inexorably leads to the depletion of fish stocks, which in turn exacerbates pressure on wildlife. Throughout Central Africa, the average fish size is smaller than before and catch volumes are diminishing. In all types of waters – fresh, brackish and ocean – fish are under threat. Waters are overfished, poorly managed and largely unregulated, and increasingly polluted. The practice of catching large fish with harpoons on the Congo River was common in the late 1970s.[55] Today, it is quite rare. People tend no longer to respect spawning seasons and now use fine-mesh nets, even mosquito nets, which seriously impede regeneration. The use of toxic chemicals (such as soap and pesticides) is also on the rise, a technique that kills fish, which float to the surface of the water and which can then be easily collected. Smaller streams are particularly vulnerable. The environmental and health costs of these detrimental practices as they expand in scale are obviously high. As with animals, some fish species mature quickly, produce large quantities of eggs, and spawn more than once a year. Others do not reach reproduction for at least two or three years and produce far fewer eggs.[56]

Most communities who live near water fish, in addition to carrying out subsistence farming. There are numerous techniques and practices with different kinds of paraphernalia, but a dugout canoe and a net are the basic gear along the region's large rivers. As most people in the Congo Basin countries live near water, this translates into millions of fishermen and fisherwomen. There are consequently far too many people harvesting from a vulnerable fish base. Overfishing, however, is an understandable predicament – similar to hunting – because satisfying hunger today is considered a more urgent priority than securing one's potential future well-being. Popular perceptions about sustainability are problematic. When asked if they thought stocks could disappear in Lake Mai-Ndombe, a group of adult fishermen responded that such a situation was unimaginable because of the quantity of sand around the lake; they claimed to believe that the grains of sand would metamorphose into fish.[57] Like bushmeat, eating fish is culturally ingrained and a major source of sustenance for the region's population. Also, as with bushmeat, selling surpluses contributes to family incomes.

This introductory chapter ends with the transcription of an interview with a man who grew up in a village in a dense forest area in DRC's Sankuru Province; he now lives almost one thousand miles away in Kinshasa. Casimir describes himself as a village boy turned urban hunter. His narrative teaches us that conversations about bushmeat can be very emotional while suggesting that they need to be decoded with finesse. His story is a good reminder of the need to pay careful attention to the discrepancies between what people think, what they say, and what they do. That anthropological rule of thumb applies to all kinds of subjects the world over but it is particularly relevant to bushmeat. Casimir hints at shared collective patterns about meat, while also portraying a quite idiosyncratic relationship with it, which should caution us about drawing blanket – and judgemental – conclusions.

BUSHMEAT

Bushmeat takes up a lot of room in my universe; it is wired into my DNA. I grew up fishing, farming and hunting in Kole, learning about forest life from my father, who was a teacher at the Catholic mission school. As he had a salary, he was able to purchase a shotgun and buy cartridges even though we mostly hunted with bows and arrows, liana snares and sometimes metal cables. Many village hunters avoid the shotgun today because authorities tax them.

At home we ate meat just about every day with vegetables and cassava – and piles of different kinds of caterpillars – but lots of people in and around our village just ate meat and cassava. Gout is a public health problem in Kole because it comes from eating too much meat. If they didn't have meat, they'd say they hadn't eaten, especially hunter-gatherers.

Some things in the hunting universe have changed, others have stayed the same. Growing up (I was born in 1986) I learned about what today you call sustainable hunting. My friends back in Kole don't pay attention to that anymore. We nevertheless continue to pay tribute to the village elders by giving them their share of an animal: the head, intestines and, if it's a large animal like a wild boar, a leg. I never bothered with fetishes because I never had problems catching lots of animals. I returned to Kole a few years ago and was heartbroken to see a housing settlement in what was once a forest where I hunted.

I wouldn't have been able to complete my studies without the money we earned from hunting. When I got a scholarship to study in Kinshasa my mother cried her eyes out. She was so used to me bringing healthy forest food home for her to cook. When I came to Kinshasa in 2005, it was difficult to be in touch with the family other than by bush radio and letters sent and received through the Catholic priests' network. I didn't get much meat then. But today thanks to our mobiles, I know exactly when a boat from my village will dock in Kinshasa so I pick up the smoked meat I ordered from friends and family. I also arrange to have meat sent to me by the Caritas flight organised by the Catholic mission.

Kole people thrive on the meat they hunt, but they sell some too. Traders come from Kinshasa by boat with money and goods to barter; locals buy smoked meat at our market and take it to Kinshasa – they are like small-scale wholesalers. Boats come to Kole fairly regularly, about once a month. The journey takes around five days. A friend from Kole lives in my neighbourhood. He is a semi-professional trader in fresh bushmeat and live animals which he brings to Kinshasa by road through Bandundu. Sometimes I buy meat from him.

My wife grew up in the city so she doesn't have the same need for meat as I do. I taught her how to cook it and she has come to savour it. When I joke with her that my whole body is in Kinshasa except my stomach which stayed back in the village, she gets it. I love the taste of meat and the fact that it tastes like the forest; it's healthy and organic. Meat also helps me forget my woes.

With my small salary as a university assistant I make the effort (it's not a sacrifice) to buy meat on a fairly regular basis, every month or so. In 2020 I bought smoked crocodile, python, antelope, wild boar and porcupine. Many people in Kinshasa say that bushmeat is a luxury food. But for people like me who have connections back home, it's not a luxury. I just think about it as ordinary food that we can have at any meal. This differs from other people who need a special occasion to put their hand deep in the pocket to buy it at the market.

Yesterday I was a village hunter, today I'm an urban hunter. When I leave the house in the morning, I tell my wife I'm going hunting. That means hunting for money and opportunities. I hunt in the city to bring something home at the end of the day just like my father hunted to feed me meat. As a university assistant, the library is my new forest, providing me with intellectual sustenance. When I enter the library, I respect the rules of silence; that reminds me of the need to be quiet in the forest too, not to frighten animals. Before, I literally trapped animals in the forest. In Kinshasa, I feel like the city is a big metaphorical trap where you are bound to get snared if you're not careful. If you neglect social rules, you'll be trapped like an animal. If you want to catch an animal, you need to know its habits; if you want to avoid being trapped by humans, you have to know what makes them tick.

Meat is a big part of my past and present. It will certainly be part of my future too: I'll share it to maintain good relations with my friends and family, and will pass its cultural and nutritional value down to my children. Yes, meat is my alpha and omega. God, family and bushmeat – those are the things that really matter to me.[58]

BUSHMEAT

Casimir's narrative deserves being reproduced here because it sets the tone for the style and content of subsequent chapters. It opens this book by touching on multiple central themes such as hunting, bushmeat trade, food choices, deforestation, nostalgia, urban dynamics, and social and family relations. With its original ethnographic data, it indicates to readers how my cultural approach to the study of bushmeat will unfurl.

2

A SHRINKING FOREST HABITAT

Deforestation impacts on wildlife

This chapter provides essential perspectives on the multiple, intersecting factors that affect rates of bushmeat consumption, emphasising the point that the best way to analyse the bushmeat crisis is through a holistic approach. This is important because many of the challenges facing wildlife lie well beyond the realm of conservation. Among the factors that must be taken into account are urbanisation, demographic pressure, climate change, deforestation and habitat loss. From a conservation perspective, these notable and uncontrollable factors raise some very daunting challenges. How can conservation efforts keep up with the looming threat of wildlife extinction due to diminishing habitat – particularly in areas of seemingly unending rural poverty and low development indicators? Increasing the size and number of protected areas, as outlined in the next chapter, is a controversial option that raises significant social and political problems. Creating and enforcing a realistic legal framework (Chapter 9) is an institutional challenge that is still very much work in progress, with few successful outcomes. How sustainable can wildlife management actually be, given the seemingly irreversible disappearance of animals' natural habitat? This chapter delves into the deeply troubling problem of trying to strike a balance between the real economic needs and expectations of people living in forests and the ecological needs of forest animals.

Subsequent chapters in this book explain how commercial hunting and bushmeat consumption dramatically threaten the sustainability of Central Africa's wildlife while negatively impacting on people's subsistence and well-being. This chapter deals with another overwhelming threat: habitat loss induced by deforestation. Deforestation refers to the destruction, fragmentation or degradation of natural ecosystems, which in the Central African context are caused predominantly by human activities. Deforestation can be triggered, for example, by logging, mining, clearing land for food production (primarily for agriculture but also grazing), infrastructure development such as road-building, or urban expansion. Deforestation, in other words, results from exogenous capitalist economic activities as well as local subsistence ones.

As forests shrink, wild animals face greater challenges to thrive. Habitat destruction is among the most common causes of defaunation – the conservation term for the extinction of animal populations or species from an ecological setting. As natural spaces decrease in size or are degraded, these animals find it proportionately more difficult to find food, water, and protection to reproduce and raise their young. The degradation of an animal's habitat can be stressful, especially if it is in increased contact with predators or finds itself in greater competition with other animals for the resources it needs to thrive. Climate change from deforestation threatens the well-being and survival of wild animals by increasing the risks of wildfires, which is another source of stress. A further ominous risk – addressed in Chapter 8 – is the spread of zoonotic diseases, because deforestation creates unprecedented contacts between wild animals and humans. Stress in wild animals is not only an animal rights preoccupation but a public health problem too. Stressed animals are more vulnerable to diseases which may be passed on to humans. Covid-19 (discussed in Chapter 8) has sharpened awareness about how the destruction of natural habitats creates opportunities for zoonotic disease outbreaks.[1]

The Congo Basin (also referred to as the Congo River Basin) extends into Cameroon, the Central African Republic (CAR), the Democratic Republic of the Congo (DRC), Equatorial Guinea, Gabon, and the Republic of Congo. It has a total land area of 5.3 million square kilometres[2] – which is more than five times the size of Nigeria. The Congo Basin is home to the world's second-largest tropical rainforest after Amazonia, representing 70% of all of Africa's forests and 91% of the continent's dense rainforests.[3] A mosaic of rivers, forests, savannahs and swamps, the basin is uniquely rich in biodiversity. In the DRC alone, there are an estimated 1,000 species of birds and the same number of freshwater fish, 421 types of mammals,[4] and 302 reptile species.[5] There are dozens of primate species, a number of emblematic creatures such as elephants, gorillas and chimpanzees, and endemic species such as bonobos and okapis. From this biodiversity perspective alone, the Congo Basin is one of the most important wilderness frontiers remaining on earth.

These forests are essential to the approximately 122 million people (Table 2.4) who live across the Congo Basin. Forests provide agricultural land, fuelwood, building materials, fish, bushmeat and non-timber forest products. Culture and ecology – or site specificity – determine the value of these assets, so it is impossible to rank them for the Congo Basin as a whole. Forests also provide essential ecosystem services such as climate and water regulation and carbon sequestration. Meat has been and remains a major source of animal protein for the people, especially as the region's ecology is not conducive to cattle-breeding. People living in these countries have low levels of human development and endure moderate to high levels of political corruption, which means that they would be far worse off without these vital resources in such fend-for-yourself situations. This applies to their livelihoods and also to their well-being. In addition to the strictly pragmatic subsistence priorities, many people perceive their forests as mystical places where the living and the dead rendezvous in ritual ceremonies, providing the cosmic link between their ancestors and future generations.

The world's largest tropical peatland complex – crucial for carbon sequestration – straddles the DRC and the Republic of Congo.[6] This peatland is also home to the world's densest concentration of gorillas.[7] Despite very low human population density (around two inhabitants per square kilometre), those gorillas are threatened by commercial poachers. When a well-to-do man in Brazzaville wants his pregnant wife to give birth to a strong healthy baby, he makes sure to arrange for her to eat gorilla meat. (Cultural perceptions such as this one are addressed in detail in Chapter 5.)

These precious forests, and the wildlife they support, are vulnerable. Worldwide, up to one million plant and animal species are threatened with extinction in the coming decades.[8] There has been a nearly 10% loss of tree cover worldwide between 2001 and 2019, and much of it is in the Congo Basin.[9] Pressure on forest ecosystems is constant and has a strong cumulative effect. We have therefore become quite familiar with comparisons of the equivalent of 'x number' of football pitches of tropical forest being lost every minute. There are multiple interconnected causes, which can be grouped into two main categories: proximate causes, or specific human activities (agricultural practices, the development of roads, and the cutting down of trees), and social processes (demographic pressure, urbanisation, trade, governance and culture).[10] Another way of framing these interconnected causes of deforestation would be to say that Congo Basin forests are entangled in multiple competing values.

Table 2.1 shows deforestation rates per country. Although it sounds dramatic, according to well-respected experts, by the end of this century the forests of the Congo Basin may well be gone if current trends continue.[11] This eventuality would have a significant impact on human health, political dynamics and development, and wildlife. To express this in more human terms, a child born today in the dense tropical forest will very likely witness the loss of that forest by the end of his or her life. After having lived in Kinshasa for more than a decade before returning to his village of origin, a Congolese graduate student lamented to me: 'I shed real tears when returning home after an absence of a few years and seeing a housing settlement in a forest where I hunted as a young man.'[12]

Another dimension of this forest vulnerability was analysed in a seminal journal article by Kent Redford in 1992, referring to the concept of the 'empty forest' – a forest that has large old-growth trees and a healthy canopy but is devoid of its large mammals.[13] Kent was pioneering in his emphasis on the mutual dependence between forests and wildlife – the plant–animal nexus – including the vital ecological role of seed dispersal. Many tree species rely on large mammals for seed dispersal and so, as populations of these mammals decline, biodiversity suffers.

Table 2.1: Deforestation rates (2010–2020)

Country	Deforestation rate
Cameroon	0.27
Central African Republic	0.13
Democratic Republic of the Congo	0.83
Equatorial Guinea	0.34
Gabon	0.05
Republic of Congo	0.06

Source: Adapted from Global Forest Resources Assessment 2020 (www. fao.org), Annex 2, Table A1.

Forest loss and population growth appear to go hand in hand. Tables 2.2 and 2.4 show that the DRC has a high population growth rate and a high rate of deforestation; they reveal too that Gabon has a low population growth rate and little to no forest loss. Table 2.1 indicates the main drivers of deforestation in the six countries of the Congo Basin. Although drivers vary from country to country, subsistence agriculture is the dominant cause of deforestation in the region as a whole (see Table 2.3). Only Gabon, where industrial logging was the main driver, bucks this trend. This contrasts with the situation in South America and Southeast Asia where the production of globally traded commodities (mainly beef, soy and palm oil) is the main driver of deforestation. Satellite imagery reveals that throughout the region, deforestation is most visible in proximity to urban settlements, roads, and other areas with high population density.[14]

Table 2.2: Main deforestation drivers by country (%)

Country	Subsistence agriculture (rotational and semi-permanent)*	Large-scale commercial agriculture	Industrial logging	Road-building and infrastructure development	Mining	Other (including natural forest disturbances)
Cameroon	58.0	5.4	21.8	2.9	n/a	–
Central African Republic	94.8	–	1.1	–	0.2	–
Democratic Republic of the Congo	93.3	0.3	0.9	1.0	n/a	–
Equatorial Guinea	75.1	3.1	–	18.7	3.1	–
Gabon	32.2	2.3	61.6	4.2	n/a	–
Republic of Congo	49.2	1.0	45.7	1.2	n/a	–

* This category includes charcoal production.

Source: adapted from Tyukavina et al. (2018).

Table 2.3: Aggregate regional deforestation drivers (%)

Subsistence agriculture	68.85
Industrial logging	22.42
Road-building and infrastructure development	5.60
Large-scale commercial agriculture	2.42
Mining	1.65

Source: adapted from Tyukavina et al. (2018).

Population growth

In the Central African context, it's probably safe to assert, given the linkages between population growth and deforestation, that more people means less wildlife. The DRC is the country that matters most in the habitat loss discussion because 60% of the Congo Basin's tropical rainforests are located there. With an annual population growth rate of 3.2%, the number of Congolese will double in 22 years. Population data through the region needs to be considered as estimates because of relatively poor data collection and reporting systems. Other than the Central African Republic, which presents an anomalous case of low population growth (most probably because of prolonged civil conflict), all five other countries have a rate higher than 2.5%. At 2.5%, populations double in 28 years. One important social factor throughout the region that could reduce population growth is the time girls spend in school. 'Numerous studies have documented the importance of increasing women's education as a key variable contributing to fertility decline in the developing world.'[15] In other terms, women with no or only primary education have more children than women with secondary or higher education.

The DRC is expected to be the world's sixth most populous country by 2100.[16] High population growth in this country of abundant biodiversity is the result of continued high fertility rates and falling mortality rates. Demographic trends and forecasts for the DRC, therefore, do not bode well for wildlife – nor for the millions of Congolese who depend on forest resources for their nutrition, survival and well-being. Nor do they bode well for the international community's efforts to combat climate change.

Having many children is an important cultural reality in the DRC, as elsewhere in Africa. Most Congolese men and women believe that producing large families is normal and desirable. Family planning is culturally anathema and birth control options are not only disavowed but largely unavailable, particularly in rural areas. Socially influential Catholic and Protestant religious groups are ideologically opposed to limiting fertility through family planning. The fact that these religious groups discourage family planning dovetails with Congolese reluctance to curtail fertility. International agencies that try to promote family planning, moreover, are often accused of being insensitive to Congolese values. Pride in having large families is part and parcel of being Congolese. This applies to both men (for reasons of economy, social status and masculinity) and women (motherhood is a cherished socio-cultural value). The more children one has, the greater the social capital one accumulates.[17] Children, often perceived as a form of labour, are also regarded as the equivalent of a social security system; they are born to take care of their parents in old age. Economic constraints in urban areas tend to diminish the number of children in low- to middle-income families, but this choice is made reluctantly. Children are equated with school fees and medical expenses, and mothers who stay at home could instead be working outside to earn money. Better-off urban families are less subject to this constraint. Urban centres are experiencing rapid population growth, particularly Kinshasa, whose present population of around 17 million is projected to increase to 35 million by 2050.[18] By then, scarcely a generation away, the Congolese capital will be the world's fourth-largest megacity.[19]

Congolese social norms expect a young girl to become a *mama* – meaning a wife and mother. Ideally this should come through marriage, but motherhood – in or out of wedlock – is the first of these two priorities for most Congolese women. Moreover, being a mother is a prerequisite for being considered a 'real woman'. Female sterility is a socially 'legitimate' reason for a husband to take a second wife. These generalities may appear controversial but they are even supported by popular language. For example, when a man introduces his partner to people, saying *mama na bana* (mother of my children) has more value than introducing her as *mwasi na ngai* (my wife). Pride in large families is even institutionalised in the national anthem: 'Congo: we shall populate your soil and ensure your greatness.' The anthem was co-authored by the Jesuit priest Simon-Pierre Boka, who was inspired by the biblical injunction 'Be fruitful and increase in number; fill the earth'. The Bible is the most widely owned book in the country (and increasingly listened to on the faithful's smartphones). Congolese are deeply devout and nearly all adhere to some form of Christian church. The fact that John and Mary are the most commonly given names is an indicator of this.[20] This discussion about family and population growth is central to the bushmeat crisis because, depending on the community, institutional frameworks, resource rights and ecology, it is probably safe to assume that in many situations in Central Africa, as human population numbers increase, wildlife numbers decrease.[21]

Table 2.4: Population dynamics of Central Africa

Country	Pop. 2018[1] (in millions)	Pop. 1960[1] (in millions)	Growth rate	Rural–urban ratios	Major cities	Human development rank[14]
Cameroon	24.7	5.2	2.61[2]	44/56[2]	Yaoundé, Douala, Garoua[8]	153/189
Central African Republic	4.7	1.5	1.51[3]	59/41[3]	Bangui, Bimbo, Mbaïki[9]	188/189
Democratic Republic of the Congo	84.0	15.2	3.2[4]	56/44[4]	Kinshasa, Lubumbashi, Mbuji-Mayi, Kananga[10]	175/189
Equatorial Guinea	1.3	0.255	3.6[5]	28/72[5]	Bata, Malabo[11]	145/189
Gabon	2.0	0.499	2.6[6]	11/89[6]	Libreville, Port-Gentil, Franceville[12]	119/189

Country	Pop. 2018[1] (in millions)	Pop. 1960[1] (in millions)	Growth rate	Rural–urban ratios	Major cities	Human development rank[14]
Republic of Congo	5.4	1.0	2.6[7]	33/67[7]	Brazzaville, Pointe-Noire, Ouesso[13]	149/189
Total	122.1	23.6	–	–	–	–

Sources: 1. http://www.fao.org/faostat/en/#data/OA; 2. https://www.worldbank.org/en/country/cameroon; 3. https://data.worldbank.org/country/central-african-republic; 4. https://data.worldbank.org/country/congo-dem-rep; 5. https://data.worldbank.org/country/equatorial-guinea; 6. https://data.worldbank.org/country/gabon; 7. https://data.worldbank.org/country/congo-rep; 8. https://www.citypopulation.de/Cameroon-Cities.html; 9. https://www.citypopulation.de/CongoDemRep-Cities.html; 10. https://www.citypopulation.de/Centralafrica.html; 11. https://www.citypopulation.de/EquatorialGuinea.html; 12. https://www.citypopulation.de/Gabon-Cities.html; 13. https://www.citypopulation.de/Congo.html; 14. https://hdr.undp.org/content/human-development-report-2020.

Cities consuming the forest

This section argues that urbanisation has significant impacts on the trade and consumption of wild animals. Urban settlements are relentlessly gnawing away at a fragmented forest mosaic comprising secondary forests, degraded forests, remnants of primary forests, and fallow areas. Peri-urban space is particularly vulnerable to over-exploitation and biodiversity loss.[22] 'The city is a huge open mouth, always hungry and never satiated,' according to a sociologist from Brazzaville.[23] The dominant factors that determine the trade and consumption of bushmeat in these landscapes are the size of the settlement, purchasing power, culture, institutional norms and frameworks, and proximity to forest spaces. The future of tropical forest areas in Central Africa – so necessary for the future of the region's wildlife – depends to a very large extent on city dwellers. Conservation and wildlife management have a hard time keeping up with rapid urbanisation. In 1960 Johannesburg was the only African city with a population exceeding one million;[24] in 2021 there were 52.[25] In her encyclopedic study of how cities 'are bound by their appetites to the natural world', Carolyn Steel argues that 'to understand cities properly, we need to look at them through food'.[26] This section is inspired by that claim, but inverts cities and food: thus, to understand bushmeat consumption properly, we need to look at urban sociology.

Rural–urban migration has been a relentless post-independence process in Central Africa. Many rural people do whatever they can to leave their villages or arrange for their children to do so. Despite the difficulties in finding work, food and housing in the big cities, people perceive them as offering more hope for the future than their villages. Migrants are forced to depend on family support networks, live by their wits and develop resilience strategies because access to health clinics and schools, water and electricity, technology, cold beer, entertainment and elegant dress is more often than not, more a dream than a reality. Young men and women prefer the relative anonymity of even the urban slum to escape from the strict kinship codes that dictate village life. The fear of witchcraft sanctions is another motivation to break away from what is seen as a place with no future and few economic opportunities.[27] The city is equated with money in the minds of young dreamers and as a stepping stone to Europe or America. As a consequence, there has been steady outward rural migration since independence in the 1960s. As it is mainly youth in their years of high fertility who migrate, villages depopulate, leaving behind young children and the elderly as the dominant demographic groups. The combination of urban pull and youth fertility accounts for why four out of the six countries in the region now have populations that are more than 50% urbanised (Table 2.4).

Subsistence agriculture

As subsistence farming is the overwhelmingly dominant driver of deforestation in the Congo Basin, and therefore a direct threat to wildlife, it merits some explanation, particularly of its linkage with bushmeat consumption. Slash-and-burn agriculture, also referred to as itinerant, shifting or swidden farming, is the principal agrarian system. Although there is no dominant 'traditional' version of agriculture in the countries of the Congo Basin, there are patterns. Men clear a new field of around two or three hectares every year with machetes and axes. Chainsaws are sometimes available but the use of rudimentary tools prevails. It seems incongruous in the 21st century, with all its technology and sophistication, that the axe and machete remain such major threats to the well-being of the planet. After clearing, men set fire to the felled trees and stumps, producing as a result a thin layer of fertile ash on the topsoil. Women take over with the longer processes of tilling, planting, weeding and harvesting. Having many children is an investment strategy in this labour-intensive form of farming. African farmers are well versed in rainfall patterns, planting seasons, soil fertility, and crop rotation methods. Multiple crops are grown simultaneously to ensure seasonal diversification and to avoid risks from disease and pests (cane rats and other rodents can wreak havoc in farm plots, which is another reason why they are trapped and eaten). Newly cleared plots are farmed for two or three years. Then, as fertility decreases, they are abandoned to remain fallow for up to ten years before being re-farmed. The observance of fallow periods is crucial in this type of system because it contributes to the reconstitution of forest cover and the ecosystem's nutrient cycle. Fallow contributes to reforestation, which is often neglected in doomsday forecasts and calculations about deforestation.

Slash-and-burn agriculture has been decried in recent years by agronomists and environmentalists, who claim that it destroys tropical forests. While this is not entirely false, the argument needs to be nuanced. Slash-and-burn has been practised for centuries in the region. Not only did it not destroy the forests, but it contributed to maintaining and enriching their fragile webs of biodiversity. Human diversity and biological diversity can be mutually supportive. This connection is sometimes referred to as 'biocultural diversity', which is an emerging field of study in anthropology. Biocultural diversity is defined as the 'diversity of life in all its manifestations – biological, cultural, and linguistic – which are interrelated within a complex socio-ecological adaptive system'.[28] 'Both people and their habitats are part of a single reciprocal system,' according to Jan Vansina, writing in his historical analysis of Equatorial Africa.[29] Wild animals are part of this system. So too is fire, managed by people over centuries to achieve the right balance between savannah and dense tropical forest.[30] Without people setting fires, much savannah land – and the wild animals that live on it – wouldn't exist.

The real problem with slash-and-burn agriculture is unsustainable demographic pressure. While it works well in low-population density areas like the DRC's central basin, once the threshold of 20 to 30 people per square kilometre is surpassed, soil fertility declines as fallow periods become shorter. Where land rights are poorly defined and poorly regulated – which is the case throughout most of Central Africa – the problems of conflict over farming space, poaching, illegal small-scale logging, and outward migration are exacerbated. These are the direct consequences of more people on finite land space. Critiques of slash-and-burn tend to underestimate the importance of seasonality and time management integrated in the world views of tropical forest peoples. These considerations are significant for development and conservation efforts because they could help guide the need to harmonise agricultural activities with hunting, fishing, gathering, and social activities. On the basis of time-proven needs and respect for these natural cycles, tropical forest peoples in Central Africa have co-evolved with traditional resource management systems that are 'slow and cyclical'.[31]

In high-population density areas such as Cameroon's western regions and the eastern DRC, these traditional patterns, which encompass slash-and-burn, have reached the limits of sustainability. Table 2.4 shows that high population density contributes to making slash-and-burn unsustainable. Agriculture, as it is currently practised, is intimately connected to forest degradation. From a policy perspective, this means that there is an unassailable need to integrate the two sectors to mitigate their impacts on people and their environment. It is impossible to have viable forest management systems without somehow harmonising them with agricultural practices. Pressing this point further, it could be argued that food production has a direct impact on conservation and protected area management efforts throughout the Congo Basin.[32]

Strategies to mitigate deforestation and its suite of environmental and social consequences need to be designed in an integrated way because all key environment sectors are connected – and not only forest management and agriculture.[33] Associating agriculture and energy with forest management is a prerequisite not only for environmental sustainability but also for poverty reduction. Forest management cannot be sustainable without taking into account agricultural practices, water management, and energy supply and demand. Forest management is also closely related to infrastructure development, land tenure, protected area conservation, and social and cultural practices and governance. This raft of problems is exacerbated by the way the relations of local populations with their natural resources are embedded in centuries-old historical processes that some influential partners, such as donors and international environmental NGOs, tend to misconstrue or arrogantly underestimate.

Logging and mining impacts on wildlife

Logging and mining are both extractive businesses contributing to unsustainable hunting and wildlife depletion. Industrial logging is the primary source of deforestation in Gabon and a major driver in the Republic of Congo and Cameroon. Logging, both industrial and artisanal, has a direct influence on hunting intensity and is therefore a threat to wildlife.[34] Remote forest areas that were previously difficult to penetrate by outsiders have been opened up by loggers through road-building. This has a direct impact on wildlife because it enables actors along the hunting–marketing chain to exploit remote forests and protected areas. Men working in the logging camps and migrant men and women are drawn to these places of real and perceived economic opportunities in hopes of finding employment. They are, moreover, consumers of bushmeat themselves despite the fact that logging company policies require the companies to provide alternative foods to their workers. Respect for such policies is important for those companies that are certified or are in the process of seeking certification.[35] The workers, who have relatively strong purchasing power, also make arrangements with local villagers to hunt for them by supplying guns and ammunition, cables for snares, and transportation. Road-building and lorries are not a good combination for wildlife; they also lower the transaction costs for hunters to get their quarry into commercial networks and urban markets. Men working in these camps therefore participate in the commercial bushmeat networks that supply urban areas. Logging thus constitutes a double threat: it is a major driver of deforestation and it intensifies hunting.

There are, however, emerging dynamics in the industrial logging sector that can reduce pressure on wildlife. New policies and partnerships are being designed and implemented to control hunting in some of the region's large logging concessions operated by companies that are sensitive to their international reputations. This applies essentially to those that export to the European and North American markets.[36] National governments, private companies and conservation organisations have made some progress in developing sound wildlife management by prohibiting the use of metallic snares, preventing trade, and cracking down on the hunting of endangered species in logging concessions. These policies appropriately advocate working with communities and promoting development initiatives. The International Tropical Timber Organization champions these partnerships.[37] While these policies may be sound, enforcing them in the Central African context is difficult. A European manager in one of the Republic of Congo's largest forest concessions outlined the company's strict rules and regulations aimed at controlling workers' involvement in the bushmeat trade while also confessing that African managers and foremen choose not to sanction workers in the case of violations.[38] He also mentioned that while the company has a long-term forest management vision – and conservation objectives fit into that vision – the main motivation for respecting best-practice guidelines about bushmeat is the need to maintain the company's Forest Stewardship Council certification, as some of their timber is exported to the European market. Strict guidelines regulating access to meat in logging concessions raises an ethical quandary: companies restrict access to meat for their workers but at the same time are satisfying the appetites of wealthy Western consumers for tropical timber.

Artisanal gold and diamond mining provokes similar kinds of threats to wildlife, both in and outside protected areas. Mining disrupts forests' ecological balance and can be catastrophic when dynamite and mercury are used. There are various other reasons why artisanal mining is a threat to wildlife. Diggers consume bushmeat themselves because there is often scarce food production on mining sites, which are magnets for migrant labourers who either dig themselves or provide services such as petty trade, restaurants, leisure and other activities. A study of the links between artisanal mining and bushmeat consumption and trade carried out in eastern DRC confirms this situation, concluding 'that bushmeat hunting to supply meat to mining sites is widespread'.[39] Artisanal digging is significant in DRC's provinces of Ituri, Haut Uélé and the Kivus, where commercial bushmeat trading networks are run or protected by militias and the national army.[40] The abundance of firearms in these sites is not conducive to good wildlife management either. In 2008, the World Bank estimated that there were some 10 million artisanal miners in the DRC.[41] Given socio-economic trends, this figure has certainly increased significantly. Just the sheer number of miners consequently has an impact on bushmeat consumption. Formal industrial gold mining has its own range of impacts. One of Africa's largest gold mines is in the DRC's Haut Uélé Province, operated by Barrick Gold. Before the mine opened in 2010, the town of Watsa had a population of around 10,000 inhabitants. Today it is a settlement of approximately 500,000, having expanded rapidly and without urban planning or service provision. The mine is in close proximity to the Garamba National Park, which is under serious threat because this massive migrant population is responsible for the illegal extraction of bushmeat, charcoal and building materials.[42]

Artisanal digging of all sorts of minerals vital to the high-tech sector took off in DRC in the twilight of the Mobutu dictatorship. At around the same time the state was relinquishing what little control it had of the activity. The genocide in Rwanda, the Congolese civil wars, and the ensuing chaos and insecurity in much of eastern Congo in the late 1990s to early 2000s provided significant economic opportunities for diggers – in addition to offering resources to the multitude of armed militias and rebel groups operating in the region.[43] A study of 265 mining sites in eastern DRC conducted between 2016 and 2018 concluded that Congolese soldiers of the national defence force (FARDC) were heavily involved in 66% of them.[44] The political dynamics of conflict coincided with the twofold process of de-agrarianisation (people abandoning farming) and income diversification in poor rural areas. This is the kind of situation that led Deborah Fahy Bryceson to coin the term 'multiplex livelihoods', a description which captures the move away from farming to digging. Digging for diamonds and gold became an attractive activity for young rural men yearning for change in environments where opportunities for wealth creation are rare.[45] Commenting on the reality that farming no longer allows families to satisfy their needs and desires, Stefaan Van Bockstael and Koen Vlassenroot argue that diamonds have become 'a farmer's best friend'.[46] Artisanal mining requires physical stamina but, other than that, entry barriers are low, tools are rudimentary, and no particular knowledge is necessary.

Charcoal

Charcoal production in Central Africa is a significant cause of forest degradation and habitat loss, thereby creating another problem for wild animals. Table 2.5 reveals a considerable divergence in urban access to electricity in Central Africa. The DRC is the country with the poorest comparative record, followed by the Central African Republic. Urban needs for charcoal in the DRC are the second most important cause of forest loss and degradation after agriculture. City dwellers throughout the DRC have a vital dependence on charcoal for cooking. Charcoal supplies at least 81% of urban domestic energy. In addition to mothers who need charcoal to cook for their families, enterprises such as brick-making (for house construction), bakeries, restaurants and artisanal alcohol distilling also depend on charcoal and fuelwood. In some cases, the wood used to make charcoal is a by-product of land cleared for agriculture, but most trees are cut down specifically for charcoal production, thereby leading to habitat loss. As people have no energy alternatives, charcoal production is turning peri-urban space into devastated biodiversity vacuums. Just as with the bushmeat economy, well-organised trade networks have developed to link producers (often young urban unemployed men) with consumers.[47]

Kinshasa exerts pressure on forests well beyond its immediate hinterland. Cars, pick-ups and lorries transport bags of charcoal from the Kongo Central Province 500 kilometres away. Bandundu also supplies Kinshasa via road and river. Some charcoal comes

Table 2.5: Urban and rural access to electricity

	Urban	Rural
Gabon[1]	97%	38%
Equatorial Guinea[2]	93%	43%
Cameroon[3]	88%	18%
Republic of Congo[4]	62%	16%
Central African Republic[5]	34%	0.4%
Democratic Republic of the Congo[6]	19%	1%

Sources: 1. https://2012-2017.usaid.gov/powerafrica/gabon; 2. https://wedocs.unep.org/bitstream/handle/20.500.11822/20489/Energy_profile_EquatorialGuinea.pdf?sequence=1&isAllowed=y; 3. https://2012-2017.usaid.gov/powerafrica/cameroon; https://documents1.worldbank.org/curated/en/361311498151364762/pdf/116642-WP-PUBLIC-P150241-20p-Detailed-Case-Study-Cameroon-20151204-No-Logo.pdf; 4. https://2012-2017.usaid.gov/powerafrica/republic-of-congo; https://www.afdb.org/en/documents/document/congo-rural-electrification-appraisal-report-30233; 5. https://www.se4all-africa.org/seforall-in-africa/country-data/central-african-republic/; 6. https://2012-2017.usaid.gov/powerafrica/democratic-republic-congo.

from the distant Equateur Province by barge along the Congo River. Tree-harvesting is also affecting protected areas such as the Kisantu Botanical Garden, the Luki Biosphere Reserve and the prestigious Virunga National Park, where militias have taken control of the profitable charcoal network to supply the city of Goma as well as Rwanda.[48] Ituri's charcoal helps fuel Kampala and Nairobi, proof that unsustainable wildlife management in the DRC is exacerbated by the lack of forest and energy management efforts in neighbouring countries. Again, as with the bushmeat business, there are a multitude of cultural, family and commercial incentives and actors (producers, transporters, retailers and wholesalers) involved in the charcoal commodity chain. Entry costs are low (tools are rudimentary) and no particular technical *savoir faire* is required. In areas where wealth creation options are limited, charcoal production is a logical short-term choice in the fend-for-yourself economy, despite loftier considerations about environmental impacts.

3

CONSERVATION, DEVELOPMENT
AND WILDLIFE

Irreconcilable global priorities

Forest dwellers in Central Africa have at different points in time been seen both as threats to wildlife conservation and, conversely, as conservation champions. This profound incoherence is more than an existential debate for these people whose basic human rights have been neglected and sometimes even brutally violated. This chapter argues that sovereignty over space and resources has been usurped by conservation schemes. Depending on the prevailing paradigmatic winds – usually decided by outsiders – local inhabitants can be excluded or included in conservation schemes.

Who owns these forests so important for biodiversity conservation and climate change mitigation? For the state, the forest is a national asset and the government has the sovereign right to conserve, exploit, grant concessions, sell and decide who has legal claims. For international NGOs, forests constitute a global heritage that justifies external management intervention.

Local populations have yet another view – forests belong to them and constitute a legacy handed down by their ancestors to be husbanded for their children's use and well-being. Forest-based communities have indeed had a very long conservation tradition. The opinion of a Congolese rural sociologist in this context makes sense: 'Conservation and natural resource management are just new words for attitudes and practices that my grandmother knew all about.'[1]

This chapter presents historical and current trends relating to the relations between development and conservation to support my main argument about usurped sovereignty. A timeline is developed to highlight these trends without arguing that it shows a clear linear evolution, because conservation has many actors who have different agendas, approaches and ideologies, all of which change over time. This chapter also shows how conservation is a paradox: its foundations are romantic, its implementation brutal. Are development and conservation reconcilable global priorities? For some the answer is yes; for others, it is not so clear-cut. Individual experience and geographical area of expertise determine how people respond to the question. Boots-on-the-ground fieldworkers and project implementers are often at loggerheads with theorists, decision-makers and other policy designers.

While there is a broad consensus that development and conservation are indeed both urgent global priorities, there is less agreement that they are necessarily reconcilable priorities. The debate – which is in a state of constant discursive and policy flux – is fierce, ideological and unresolved. Failure to look at the bigger picture is part of the problem: 'because participants in the debate are often busy arguing with each other – in terms of biocentric vs anthropocentric arguments – they lose the ability to see how both conservation and development are heavily influenced by wider political economic trends'.[2]

CONSERVATION, DEVELOPMENT AND WILDLIFE

At least at the discourse level, the past few decades have seen significant efforts in reconciling development with improved environmental management. But these efforts tend to overlook the fact that conservation can be regarded just as much as a consequence of modernity as a reaction against it. In this sense, it could be argued that modern conservation is a creation of the development agenda.[3] This is related to a fundamental consideration flagged by Bram Büscher and Webster Whande: 'The global political economy determines how both policy issues inherent to the conservation and development debate need to continuously be re-operationalised in order to remain politically acceptable.'[4] This shifting progress, moreover, is geographically and thematically selective: it has been less successful in Central Africa, where concrete results lag far behind policy discourse, than in southern and eastern Africa.

Environmental problems that influence the conceptual design of conservation policies include species distribution and extinction, soil degradation, pollution, deforestation, habitat loss and the effects of climate change. Conservation policies are also influenced by human development indicators, which in Central Africa testify to stubbornly entrenched poverty, particularly in rural areas but in urban settlements too. There has been little success in resolving the rural poverty trap and other traps, which development economists and sustainability science experts describe as 'persistent, self-reinforcing and undesirable situations'.[5] Rural poor and urban elites in Central Africa have heard – to borrow from Jean and John Comaroff – the 'crusading creeds'[6] of modernity and development but without benefiting from the kinds of results they perceive as desirable. The social, political, demographic, cultural, technological and economic conditions that existed when subsistence hunting was sustainable have evolved dramatically. What has happened to the small isolated hunting, gathering, fishing and farming communities on

45

large expanses of natural lands? One would be hard put to find any such communities that are not in some way familiar with – and covetous of – the trappings of modernity. Enduring poverty helps explain why some sceptics voice the opinion that the West has developed at the expense of its natural environment. African intellectuals perceive Western efforts to nudge African governments to sacrifice development for the sake of mitigating global climate change and protecting biological diversity as a kind of redemption for the layers of environmentally unfriendly mistakes made in the past.

'Conserving nature while providing water, food and energy for a growing human population is possible. It is not an either-or proposition.'[7] Such bold declarations as this, made by the World Economic Forum, are nevertheless far from being universally shared and are even further from being scientifically proven. Policy discourse about conservation should be considered with scepticism. Despite the enthusiasm and good intentions, the rationale behind such declarations is flawed by a mishmash of hubris, naivety and wishful thinking. Given the debate's ideological underpinnings relating to responsibilities and sovereignty, it is difficult not to be drawn to comparisons with the Christian civilising mission. Robert Nelson's opinion on these underpinnings is compelling: 'Like Christianity historically, current environmentalism is possessed of a strong missionary spirit. In this respect and others, the rise of environmental colonialism is not unrelated to Christianity in defending forms of colonialism.'[8] Nelson's opinion is relevant to the conservation debate because of the way it emphasises solutions emerging from the outside, ones based more on belief than scientific research.

Parties from both sides of the fence advance partly convincing doctrines which can be crudely summarised as follows: It is unrealistic to expect developing countries with weak institutions, inadequate infrastructure, social insecurity, poverty, and democratic deficits to embrace the kind of green economy and sustainable development discourses encouraged by high-income democracies. Conversely, if these governments do not adhere to a green sustainability vision, their vital resources will be depleted; wildlife species will be extirpated, agricultural lands will become infertile, and climate change will disrupt rainfall patterns while provoking all kinds of apocalyptic natural disasters. Environmental degradation will motivate hungry, unskilled rural people to flock to overpopulated urban slums and migrate to greener pastures in Europe and the United States. The problem surrounding these platitudes is that neither is entirely true or false. This chapter gives nuance to these opposing doctrines by tracing some of the major historical trends of conservation and development paradigms, showing how they have a direct impact on wildlife management and an indirect impact on the urban bushmeat trade. The shift from exclusionary conservation to sustainable development narratives and policies may seem somewhat peripheral to the main focus of this book on bushmeat consumption. Its centrality, nevertheless, lies in the way it places hunting, trading and eating wild animals in the broader context of Central African socio-environmental systems and the way these have been affected by powerful historical realities.

Understanding bushmeat commodity chain dynamics entails delving into the myriad linkages, technologies, places, actors, constraints and opportunities of getting meat from the forest to the urban cooking pot. As forest habitat shrinks – and national park surfaces expand (or even stay the same) – it is reasonable to assume that there will be increased hunting and poaching in and around these parks. The future of a number of wildlife species in Central Africa could therefore lie in these parks – if, of course, management reality can keep abreast with policy ambitions, which is another reason why the discussion about sovereignty and access to land and resources contributes to our understanding about the future of bushmeat hunting and trade. The tension between management reality and policy ambitions – a main theme in this chapter – is far from being resolved because of the diverging views, needs and expectations of conservation's vast array of local and foreign stakeholders.

Policy initiatives about sustainable wildlife management are central to the conservation–development dichotomy. Despite donor funding and the tenuous optimism of some wildlife conservation NGOs, sustainable wildlife management schemes in Central Africa that have an impact and that can be scaled up seem more like pious wishes than ambitions that are objectively verifiable. Real urgency and the perceived need to do something at all costs prevail over the acknowledged risk of failure. Like so many other examples of international development schemes in Africa, well-intentioned policies are far from achieving expected results. International donors and NGOs are often unable to grasp the subtleties of local culture and sensibilities, designing programmes that are not necessarily accepted by government authorities and ordinary people. These international partners also have difficulty in recognising the power of state and non-state actors, kinship communities and trade networks. There is little reason to expect that sustainable wildlife management initiatives will be more successful. An evaluation of Central Africa's most ambitious internationally promoted conservation and biodiversity programme, CARPE, or the Central Africa Regional Program for the Environment, pointed to 'lackluster' overall results, in part because its implementing partners failed to establish relationships of trust with local populations.[9] Trust is an absolutely essential requirement for externally funded conservation initiatives to succeed.

While donors and conservation experts behind new sustainable wildlife management schemes are trying to be innovative – by working more closely with government partners, promoting participatory zoning and behaviour change campaigns, for example – some of their other policies are reminiscent of fortress conservation and social engineering meddling.[10] Banning the hunting of large slow-reproducing species, rethinking the long-standing challenges of income diversification, and tightening legislation for protected areas management have been on the agenda for decades. Policy discussions are ongoing about how to certify bushmeat for sale, but there is a serious lack of clarity about licences, species, seasonality and quantities. When I requested information about how these policy choices were taking shape from a coordinator of a multi-million euro grant for sustainable wildlife management being implemented by four prestigious institutions (the Food and Agriculture Organization of the United Nations, the Center for International Forestry Research, the Wildlife Conservation Society, and the French Agricultural Research Centre for International Development),[11] I was told that these partners do not fully agree about strategies. One bone of contention was whether to allow the controlled sale of non-endangered species or not. Some of the partners who are pushing for a total ban of bushmeat sales argued that allowing even some selective sales of certain species would open the floodgates to chaotic, uncontrollable trade. Poor governance in Central Africa, low levels of trust, and the insufficient meaningful involvement of local populations in the decision-making process plunge this sustainable wildlife management approach into a quagmire of powerlessness and uncertainty.

From fortress conservation to sustainable development

The fantasy of preserving wildlife in the African Garden of Eden in a supposedly pristine condition was one facet of the colonial mission in Africa, essentially for the benefit and enjoyment of white hunters.[12] This quest to preserve the Holy Grail was to turn into a grandiose social engineering enterprise that led to the creation of a network of national parks all over the continent. The first was the Albert National Park in the then Belgian Congo (today's Virunga National Park). Founded in 1925, it was the initiative of a circle of aristocrats and upper-class men who shared an interest in the great outdoors, big-game hunting and scientific exploration.[13] They were the crusaders who tasked themselves with the mission of saving 'the vanishing frontier', a mission that was influenced by the late 19th-century American fascination with wilderness at a time of booming industrialisation.[14] (Be it historical continuity or random coincidence, Virunga's current chief warden is a charismatic Belgian prince.) 'Guided by notions of the sublime, a sort of beauty that evoked both awe and terror,'[15] these nature lovers wanted these spaces to correspond to their own perceptions of natural beauty, transforming them both socially and ecologically, with little concern about local people.

These values governed the pattern that other park architects would follow, all with the ultimate aim of protecting African wilderness from Africans themselves.[16] Forced displacement and resettlement of people was one brutal strategy in this crusade, which provoked extraordinary social, cultural and economic hardship. This widespread situation of usurped sovereignty was based on a spurious understanding of how people were integrated with their environment. This injustice was also inspired by powerful ideologies, sometimes based on racist views.[17] Forest dwellers throughout Central Africa are integral elements of their ecosystems and have contributed to the way in which their environments have evolved for centuries. Jan Vansina sums this up cogently: the virgin rainforest – a place without men and women – is as much of a myth as Tarzan.[18]

From an ethical perspective this raises serious concerns for both the development community and conservationists. In a way that reveals how the protection-at-all-costs aim has survived the turbulence of paradigm shifts, the World Wide Fund for Nature (WWF) mission statement still explicitly declares that the charity was established 'to protect places and species threatened by human development'.[19] The argument that conservation and development are imposed on Africans to accommodate Western interests and imagination might seem outdated and unsophisticated, but the WWF statement reveals that there is still an element of truth in it.

The idealised sites for the newly created parks were perceived as 'remote' and 'isolated', places where population density was low and human impacts on the environment minimal. The perceived backwardness of these outlying spaces – derived from a misunderstanding of or disregard for land use practices – was a colonial justification for claiming dominion. Ethno-ecological considerations essential to local populations, such as fallow periods to let land fertility regenerate and seasonality in hunting and fishing areas, were either misunderstood or disregarded by colonial conservationists. Moreover, as Louisa Lombard points out in her work on the Central African Republic, ethno-ecological factors were important for 'social and economic innovation'.[20] When people were present, they were to be resettled – sometimes through force, sometimes through political accommodation with traditional authorities. Table 3.1 indicates the number of parks in Central Africa and the percentage of land mass gazetted for conservation. The table is relevant here because it reveals the magnitude of land use change and exclusion (even though some of these parks are 'paper parks', meaning that there may be little or no real conservation implementation taking place). Industrial logging concessions cover approximately twice as much land mass as protected areas in the region. Both of these usurped spaces create similar types of social problems relating to local communities' expectations of development infrastructure, employment and social services. Some parks in the region still have strict 'integral protection' policies which are designed to keep wilderness and biodiversity out of reach of human action. Integral protection policies are increasingly criticised because of the detrimental impacts they can have on rural livelihoods.[21] Even in the parks that have adopted a sustainable management approach – one that is more tolerant of human activity – there are still numerous obstacles that weaken the effectiveness of protected area management. Obstacles range from the lack of funding, poorly conceptualised community development initiatives, shortage of qualified personnel, institutional weakness, lack of political support, and weaknesses in the legal framework and enforcement capacity.

Table 3.1: Protected areas in Central Africa's rainforest nations (2010)

Country	Number of protected areas	Percentage of landmass
Cameroon	223	17
Central African Republic	16	11
Democratic Republic of the Congo	79	11
Equatorial Guinea	13	21
Gabon	21	13
Republic of Congo	19	10

Source: https://rainforests.mongabay.com/congo/conservation.html.

Even many years after parks were created, descendants of resettled people complain of an enduring feeling of injustice which stubbornly persists in poisoning relations between community and park managers. The Salonga National Park in the DRC is one of the most notorious examples of management gone wrong from the beginning. Created during the heyday of the Mobutu dictatorship in 1970, Salonga has an indisputable biodiversity value. Managed jointly by the WWF and the Congolese Institute for Nature Conservation (ICCN), it is Africa's largest tropical rainforest park (36,000 square kilometres, or the size of Belgium and Luxembourg combined) and the third largest on the planet. I conducted interviews there in 2009 and again in 2017 and 2019, and heard a litany of grievances that remained constant over the years. 'Blood of my elders was spilled because of the park. It's almost impossible to think we'll ever be able to accept park authorities telling us what we can and cannot do.'[22] Populist politicians harangue villagers with claims that if elected, they will abolish the legal status of the park. There is much smouldering resentment and frustration over broken promises of compensation, social services, infrastructure development, employment and respect. The absence of trust and mutual disdain were voiced in multiple conversations I had with people in the Salonga Park. William Faulkner's aphorism 'The past is never dead. It's not even past' applies perfectly to the Salonga situation because people are not prepared to forgive and forget.

There have been severe human rights abuses perpetrated by rangers against local populations in Salonga.[23] Abuses stem from the legacy of exclusion and resettlement; they may also result from complicated community and family relations. The point here is that jumping to a cause-and-effect conclusion may be unfounded. Rainforest Foundation UK uncovered a series of serious allegations, including testimony that park rangers whipped and raped four women carrying fish by a river. Two of the women were pregnant and one later had a miscarriage. Rainforest Foundation also found that rangers had tortured male villagers by tying their penises with fishing lines.[24] Human rights defenders sent in to investigate these claims were allegedly intimidated by the park's anti-poaching unit head. The credibility of these allegations led one of the park's major donors, the German KfW Development Bank, to freeze its contributions. Donors – the European Commission and the United States Agency for International Development (USAID) are the park's two other main funders – were justified in being concerned that public funding could be used to train armed rangers who may have committed human rights violations. Because of widespread access to information, largely thanks to social media, donors are under pressure to ensure that they are carrying out due diligence, in the spirit of making sure that outside funding does not lead to negative repercussions. The United States Fish and Wildlife Service launched a teaching model on human rights in protected areas for park rangers, to inculcate in them the need to respect human rights in their daily work.[25]

In fairness to park rangers, it needs to be added that they risk their lives to secure large swathes of the park, providing safety to people and wildlife even though Salonga's eastern zones are still the main sources of the bushmeat found in the urban markets of Kananga and Mbuji-Mayi. ICCN mourns a long list of fallen rangers, especially in the volatile Virunga Park. The commitment of some rangers who are prepared to die for conservation while others perpetrate human rights violations is an additional argument for those emphasising the complexities of protected area management.

This troubling state of events leads to at least four ethical and management questions, none of which can be easily resolved. Are international donors responsible for human rights violations committed by their implementing partners and project beneficiaries? How can donors improve their due diligence in a context of overwhelming security problems in a country characterised by centuries of human rights violations? Should unacceptable individual actions be allowed to undermine collective institutional priorities? Can human rights violations committed by park rangers be considered as a lesser evil than the acknowledged brutality of commercial poachers? The severity of these problems leads to another key policy challenge which is gaining momentum: that of avoiding the delegitimisation of conservation because of bad behaviour. In the framework of this delegitimisation, A. T. Ford and colleagues have developed a concept they refer to as 'misplaced conservation', which 'focuses on activities where conservation resources are expended on an improper, unsuitable, or unworthy activity'.[26] This is a concern to which conservation donors and NGOs need to pay careful attention.

Another problem for donors relates to financial management and absorption capacity: Salonga's average annual operating budget is approximately $5 million. Even though Salonga's international donors are sceptical of WWF's management performance, they are also aware that there is not a long line of other implementing partners able to manage a financial package of that size. WWF therefore has a lot of leeway in deciding how to use these public funds. This perverse economic dependency recalls a hypothesis formulated by the economist John Maynard Keynes: 'If you owe your banker a hundred pounds, you are at his mercy. But if you owe a million, he is at your mercy.' Donors, in other words, need WWF just as much as WWF needs donor support.

Unlike Salonga, which is still remote and sparsely populated, many other parks are now close to cities and roads. The following examples come from multiple sites in Central Africa, which is proof of the broad geographical scope of urban sprawl. In 1925 few people were present in and around the Albert National Park (now Virunga National Park). Today, 4 million people live within a day's walk of its borders.[27] Extensive road development in the Republic of Congo in the past two decades (funded by the country's oil exports) connects the capital, Brazzaville, with the northern forest areas that are home to the Odzala and Nouabalé-Ndoki parks. The road network, despite multiple roadblocks, facilitates the bushmeat trade to the country's big cities. When the Mondah Forest was gazetted outside Libreville in 1934, the town was little more than a colonial outpost – at independence in 1960 it had 32,000 inhabitants. Today the forest is cut through by a main road and has shrunk to 60% of its original size.[28] The city's 800,000 inhabitants continue to gnaw away at it for housing, farming and resource extraction. Similarly, a main highway stretching from the port city of Boma to Kinshasa runs through the Luki Biosphere Reserve, which creates illegal economic opportunities for commercial farmers, charcoal producers, artisanal loggers and poachers. These demographic patterns are common in and around many other protected areas in Central Africa. Although the Chinko Nature Reserve in the Central African Republic is considered by many conservation experts to be one of the wildest corners of Africa, it has another kind of challenge: transhumant pastoralism (the regular movement of pastoralists and their livestock to exploit seasonally available grazing resources). These Sudanese pastoralists from the Darfur region are, incidentally, heavily armed poachers, shooting or poisoning lions to protect their herds, many of which are owned by wealthy Khartoum elites.[29]

Through media and NGO campaigning, we are increasingly aware of calls to increase the percentage of the earth's surface for protection. Protected areas, however, 'are not permanent features, but are instead dynamic and shifting governance constructs'.[30] Protected areas can be downgraded (the level of protection is reduced due to the authorisation of increased human activity), downsized (the protected surface area is reduced) and de-gazetted (legal protection is eliminated). These processes are influenced by a wide range of drivers such as infrastructure development, urbanisation, demographic expansion, and the granting of extractive industry and agro-industrial concessions. At a UN Summit on Biodiversity, numerous heads of government endorsed the proposal by the World Wide Fund for Nature and Wildlife Conservation Society to declare 30% of the earth as protected areas by 2030.[31] In an important article published in the journal *Nature*, based on a survey of 1,500 protected areas in 68 countries, H. S. Wauchope and colleagues show that wildlife within protected areas does not necessarily fare better than wildlife outside. Their findings are important from the perspective of both sustainable wildlife management and protected area management. They argue that protected areas with successful community development policies matter more than their size.[32]

Is protecting 30% of national territory protection *from* the people or *with* the people? It could prove to be profoundly reckless and hints at the potential threat of eco-fascism (authoritarian governance forcing people to sacrifice their individual interests for the greater good of the environment) and green wars (conflicts caused by environmental issues such as biodiversity loss and climate change). The increasing militarisation of park protection is epitomised by the likes of National Park Rescue, which conveys the message (but without saying so explicitly) that a good poacher is a dead poacher.[33] Others more blatantly claim that 'parks are war zones' and that if you live by the gun, you die by the gun.[34] Obviously in contradiction to participatory approaches, this militarisation is evidence of the radicalisation of conservation. Rosaleen Duffy's work documenting the upsurge in militarised conservation and anti-poaching takes a critical look at its dangers for both people and conservation, proving how slight the shift has really been from fortress conservation towards participatory conservation.[35]

Communities living in and around protected areas have been deprived of what they perceive – probably rightly in many cases – as their legitimate stake in subsistence hunting and the bushmeat economy. Acknowledging misdeeds of the past features in new conservation narratives. References to local land claims and local land pressure increasingly explain why the borders of protected areas are being redrawn.[36] The need to consider local claims for social justice in rethinking the logic of protected area management is consequently voiced more and more by the conservation community.[37] As pointed out by Daniel Ingram, 'this framework is relevant for wild meat governance and management because of the diversity of levels of need and desire for wild meat and, thus, the potential for injustice is great in some circumstances'.[38]

Racist principles were part and parcel of colonial domination in Central Africa – as elsewhere around the globe. Resource extraction, control of people's movements, land use and social engineering were governed by racist principles.[39] Colonial administrations likewise steadily institutionalised exclusion and resettlement by usurping sovereignty for conservation. Throughout most of the 20th century, top-down fortress conservation was the dominant ideology for park management. Fortress conservation is the model advocating that biodiversity protection is best achieved in spaces isolated from human activities. Exclusionary in practice, it considers animal rights to be more important than those of humans. 'Suppressive colonialism' was the system that enabled fortress conservation to function.[40] Although fortress conservation survived decolonisation for a decade or so, African governments timidly attempted to take control over their sovereignty and natural resources, for one thing by shifting conservation approaches.

By the 1980s, idealistic ambitions for the inclusive community-based participatory management of Africa's national parks gradually replaced exclusionary fortress conservation strategies. The fencing, fining and seizing approach to curtailing hunting was recognised by donors and conservation NGOs as being unenforceable owing to the very complex web of social, institutional and economic factors. Commercial hunters tend, moreover, to be better armed and equipped than rangers, who operate on limited budgets and with insufficient institutional support. International environmental NGOs promoted the shift in paradigm, partnering with national governments by offering technical assistance and co-managing the parks, which these governments were unable – and hardly motivated – to manage on their own. 'Partnering' here is a deliberate euphemism for the renewal of usurped sovereignty in the name of world heritage.

The 1980s was a particularly pivotal decade in rethinking relationships between conservation and development. It was also the decade of renaming these relationships because sustainable development, as it is understood today, has roots that go back as early as the 17th century with forest policies designed by Jean-Baptiste Colbert, Louis XIV's finance minister.[41] By the 1980s the cracks in the dominant theories of development (based on resource extraction, growth, the market, mass production, and consumerism) and fortress conservation had become apparent. These trends coincided with the implementation of the World Bank's structural adjustment programmes, which imposed strict neoliberal monetary policies on low- and middle-income countries, constituting another layer of controlled sovereignty in Africa and elsewhere. The architects of structural adjustment argued – admittedly armed with robust evidence – that leaders in sub-Saharan Africa were more interested in consolidating their own political power than promoting national macroeconomic interests. Structural adjustment policies – often critiqued as financial colonialism – are widely perceived as having failed in sub-Saharan Africa, in part because growth in the 1980s and 1990s was lower than in previous decades. Agriculture and industrialisation both suffered in the process. Structural adjustment was also found to 'significantly increase forest loss' in a survey of 62 low- and medium-income countries.[42]

In 1980, the International Union for Conservation of Nature (IUCN) published its pioneering *World conservation strategy: Living resource conservation for sustainable development*.[43] In 1987 (shortly before the collapse of the Soviet Union and the advent of 'neoliberal conservation'[44]), the United Nations World Commission on Environment and Development was set up and produced the Brundtland Report, officially entitled *Our common future*.[45] It was that seminal report which defined sustainable development as 'development that meets the needs of the present without compromising the ability of future generations to meet their own needs'. It is an oft-repeated mantra that continues to inspire government officials, NGO activists, academics, enlightened corporations and development practitioners, while constituting a fountainhead for stimulating international awareness and shaping opinions. Separating development from conservation has consequently become a conceptual thing of the past – at least for the time being. The first Rio Earth Summit of 1992 validated this new conceptual stronghold. The United Nations' Millennium Development Goals launched in 2000 and the Sustainable Development Goals launched in 2015 were to become the logical outcomes of this new approach.

Local ownership and co-management of conservation space according to participatory governance values formed a compelling concept that emerged in the wake of Rio with major donor support and buy-in from international organisations. One example was community-based conservation initiatives which capitalised on the perception that respecting local people's needs is good for conservation – and conservation is good for people's needs. Successful rainforest conservation, it can be argued, is contingent upon addressing the rights and needs of forest-dependent communities, especially with respect to land tenure.

Another variation on the theme is community-based natural resource management which according to USAID, 'aims to create the right incentives and conditions for an identified group of resource users within defined areas to use natural resources sustainably. This management approach seeks to enable resource users to benefit economically from resource management while also consolidating strong rights and tenure over land and the resources.'[46] These rights-based approaches have spawned community-based forest concessions which also seek to improve local populations' tenure claims.[47] Despite such promising rhetoric, co-management approaches are not without their flaws because they are predicated on consent and understanding by local populations of their rights and responsibilities. One problem is that programme designers (who are frequently expatriate consultants or NGO staff) tend to adopt unrealistic assumptions about stakeholder capacity to change resource management practices and their motivation to do so. The complexity of social organisation and power structures in these communities makes these problems for project managers even more unsolvable.

The implementation of participatory strategies in Africa further coincided with the design of integrated landscape approaches (also known as ecosystem-based conservation). Integrated landscape approaches recognise the need to balance different user priorities.[48] Landscapes are a matrix of protected areas, undeveloped but unprotected areas, and areas developed for habitation and economic activity. The idea is to use a systems approach that takes into account the dynamic interplay of the natural, socio-economic and political forces at play – the essential factors that cannot be dealt with by fortress conservation. The ambition is to strike a balance between multiple land uses such as conservation, subsistence and industrial-scale agriculture, wealth creation in the form of alternative livelihood strategies, resource extraction (including bushmeat hunting), ecotourism and logging. The underlying reasoning, which makes sense theoretically, is that sectoral approaches cannot respond to today's global challenges. These challenges have been analysed by Michelle Wieland, who argues: 'Contemporary conservation theory draws from social, economic, and ecological disciplines, but in spite of the varying themes on this newer model, many conflicts between stakeholders remain ...'[49] Andrew Nelson and Kenneth Chomitz have reached a similar conclusion: 'Multiple use protected areas, which allow some sustainable use by local inhabitants, might potentially achieve both social and conservation goals – or fail at both.'[50] The assumption we can make based on these opinions is that the landscape approach may be a step in the right direction socially and environmentally but it is still insufficient as an efficacious management model.

Investing in regional initiatives is now big on the forest management agenda and can be considered to be successful conservation diplomacy. The European Commission and USAID have been involved in many regional and national conservation initiatives along with French, Norwegian, German and British partners. These initiatives range from strict conservation programmes to research and capacity-building. Some notable regional initiatives are Écosystèmes Forestiers en Afrique Centrale (ECOFAC), Réseau des Aires Protégées d'Afrique Centrale (RAPAC), Congo Basin Forest Partnership (CBFP), Central African Forest Initiative (CAFI), the Central Africa Regional Program for the Environment (CARPE), and the convergence plan of the Council of Ministers in charge of the Forests of Central Africa (Commission des Forêts d'Afrique Centrale, or COMIFAC). While these initiatives are successful diplomatically at a high level, the challenges relating to effective outcomes remain.

Interest in traditional ecological knowledge (TEK) and indigenous natural resource management systems was prominent in some conservation circles (advocated largely by anthropologists) and coincided with the promotion of inclusive approaches. TEK can be generally defined as a body of knowledge built up over generations by people whose lifestyles are intimately embedded in the natural world. Passed down orally, it combines empirical environmental observations with beliefs (such as taboos) about managing resources. 'With its roots firmly in the past, traditional environmental knowledge is both cumulative and dynamic, building upon the experience of earlier generations and adapting to the new technological and socioeconomic changes of the present.'[51] The Brundtland Report acknowledged its merits for being able to 'offer modern societies many lessons in the management of resources in complex forest, mountain and dryland ecosystems'.[52] The optimism about TEK as a conservation tool was short-lived, however. Naysayers came to the fore arguing that TEK was unable to keep up with the local implications of global climate change. Market dynamics and perceptions of new needs, social stigmatisation of traditional values (especially directed against hunter-gatherers), exposure to Western values, rural–urban migration, and outside forces more broadly became real impediments to the continued promotion of TEK approaches.[53]

Two other trends deserve brief mention, both of which have implications for concerns about nation-state sovereignty and local people's rights and access to resources. One is transboundary conservation, based on the idea that nature has no borders. As ecosystems are divided by political boundaries, they are subject to national laws and policies and different social, economic and cultural factors, all of which impact on conservation efforts. Transboundary conservation has emerged as a solution to foster wildlife migration and international cooperation according to the landscape approach. Its advocates claim that it provides 'ecological benefits alongside enhanced socio-economic resilience and strengthened political relations'.[54]

The other trend is public–private partnerships, which promote, among other things, conservation through economic empowerment. Private agencies or NGOs, with funding from private philanthropists or government donors, enter into long-term contractual agreements with national governments (usually around 20 years) to manage protected areas on behalf of the state. For these arrangements to work, governments have to carry their fair share of the financial investment, so that they can't be a disguised form of donor support. Government take-up has to be proven by transparent funding. Negotiating a strong operational mandate and full financial control at the outset is part of the arrangement. The logic is that African governments do not have the financial, administrative and managerial means to deal with conservation challenges alone. They therefore need assistance in combating the illegal wildlife trade, protecting wildlife and habitats, promoting regional security, and providing economic opportunities for local communities. The anti-poaching units of these private agencies are comparatively more draconian and effective than national ones, perhaps because they are better resourced. African Parks Foundation is in the vanguard of public–private partnerships for conservation. Its promises of 'revitalizing important landscapes, restoring iconic species, and improving local welfare through tourism and other sustainable enterprises'[55] will, nevertheless, need to be proven in the long term. If national governments can derive benefits from their private sector partners, the model could have a future. A survey of protected area management options for francophone Central Africa concludes that 'with improved capacities and a more conducive legal framework, Central Africa should be able to draw upon a diversified set of management models and access funding beyond the presently dominant development cooperation sources'.[56] The implication is that delegated management is such a model, despite critiques related to infringements of national sovereignty.

A poisoned chalice

Full of inspiring beauty, emblematic fauna and mystery, the region's protected areas are clearly battlegrounds where competing stakeholders vie for power and control. As resentment and mistrust reign, their management challenges are essentially social and political. Despite official discourses to the contrary, management tends to be top-down and dismissive of the real and perceived needs and expectations of local populations. This chapter has analysed a number of paradigms, narratives, management structures and initiatives, most of which suffer from a lack of efficiency and coherence. It has shown that beliefs and understandings that propel seemingly well-intentioned conservation initiatives can prove with hindsight to have been reckless. Donors and management partners are well aware that the risks of failure are high, because their actions are far from perfect, but they are motivated by the pragmatic opinion that something has to be done urgently. Nevertheless, there does not seem to be a vision shared by all stakeholders of what the countries of the region want their parks to look like in the coming decades or how they could contribute to sustainable development. A Cameroonian researcher who studies conservation strategies has reached the following unequivocal conclusion:

> A group of conservation scientists, including faculty members from respected universities in the Central African subregion and abroad, representatives of protected areas management units, law enforcement organizations (LAGA), rangers, and international organizations (TRAFFIC, WWF) met in Yaoundé, Cameroon, in October 2019 to assess the current status of conservation in the area and discuss ways forward to solve what is considered to be a conservation crisis. Based on their combined experience, which encompassed both the social and the ecological sciences, and the data presented, it was clear that in many ways conservation in the Central African subregion is failing.[57]

The international conservation goal is important and needs to be supported by improved strategies. Nevertheless, the quest for the preservation of the Holy Grail a century ago has become a poisoned chalice for a large majority of the people living in and around today's protected areas. Conservation areas without people have clearly proven to be an unrealistic ambition, often provoking catastrophic impacts on local populations. Decision-making power about how they should be able to use their resources has escaped them, and they have not developed economically despite years of development schemes. This assessment, and other analysis presented in this chapter, have direct implications for wildlife management. Without real development options that make sense to them, people in these communities will design their own versions of development by taking charge of their destinies with their hunting shotguns and snares – and their linkages with urban bushmeat trade networks.

4

HUNTING IN TRANSITION

A glimpse from the past

The African proverb popularised by the Nigerian writer Chinua Achebe, 'Until the lion learns to write, every story will glorify the hunter',[1] is a powerful statement about unequal social relationships. It is also an appropriate epigraph to this chapter on the hunter's role in contemporary Central Africa. This book, however, does not take sides – not for the hunter, not for the prey, nor for any other actor. It gives equal consideration to all of the actors in the bushmeat sector, while delving into their challenges, opportunities, world views and motivations. Depending on the individual and context, the main motivations for hunting relate to food security, commerce, prestige and tradition. The statement 'I don't kill wild animals for the fun of it' encapsulates hunters' general sense of pragmatism.[2] Another motivation, one not frequently expressed, is simply the emotional thrill of the experience, an example that comes from Hilary Solly's research in Cameroon's Dja reserve.[3]

Better understanding of the socio-economic determinants of bushmeat consumption depends in large part on figuring out the hunter's universe. He – and, indeed, hunting is usually a gender-specific activity carried out mostly by men – is the first link in the bushmeat commodity chain. Women do, however, lay traps along the paths to their fields and in proximity to their crops at harvest time to deter predators and to supplement the evening cooking pot. Even though hunting is very much a man's world and has historically defined the very basis of masculinity, these men are strongly influenced by their wives, mothers and sisters, who are the main protagonists in feeding the family, managing resources, and maintaining family cohesion.

Conversations with hunters and conservation experts, and perusal of the many books and articles about their activities, techniques, social relations, professional challenges and world views, reveal a fascinating universe of economic opportunism, rapid change, evil, benediction, magical energy, prestige, jealousy, secrecy and survival. The hunting universe is in these respects a microcosm of Central African society. Hunting is also a universe of power, both real and perceived. The flamboyant president of Zaire, Mobutu Sese Seko, exploited the myth of having slain a leopard with a spear to account for his mystical greatness. Adolescent males in some societies are expected to kill an antelope or other animal as a rite of passage towards manhood. The Lingala word for hunter is *boma nyama*, which translates literally as animal killer. Having the reputation of being a good hunter in a village is an asset when looking for a wife or girlfriend.[4] 'You go into the forest, get meat, sell it, get money, invite friends to drink.'[5] Hunting, therefore, is a source of 'strong social legitimacy'.[6]

In most parts of Central Africa, the forest is believed to be inhabited by malevolent spirits, and it is widely assumed that successful hunters have made accommodations with these spirits for luck and protection. The implication is that hunters have divided allegiance between the human and spirit world and therefore have a somewhat dubious social status, being both respected and feared. On a more grisly note, hunting has not only been a relationship between humans and animals: human beings were hunted during the slave trade, rebels and political rivals hunt their enemies, and eastern Congolese militias hunt women, using rape as a weapon of war and resource exploitation.

Hunting is a very old practice in Central Africa, whose first occupants were hunter-gatherers,[7] also referred to as indigenous people; their traces go back 120,000 years.[8] Hunting and eating wild animals is an ongoing way of life with ancient origins. Julia Fa and colleagues have concisely summarised this historical trajectory by affirming that 'wildlife and humans are interdependent'.[9] There is, however, a very crucial distinction to be made between past and present: while hunting had been largely a subsistence activity until relatively recently (essentially until the early years of post-colonialism, which coincided with rapid urbanisation), today it is increasingly a commercial opportunity to satisfy the appetites of city dwellers. Conservation icon Jane Goodall is at pains to make this distinction clear: 'Bushmeat trade is the commercial hunting and selling of wild animals for food. It is very different from subsistence hunting, which comprises killing animals for food for a family or village. Once money is involved, anything goes.'[10] Even forest-dependent hunter-gatherers are co-opted into commercial networks, swapping bushmeat for food (cassava, for example) and goods (alcohol, used clothing, and machetes) with bushmeat traders connected to urban markets.[11] The involvement of hunter-gatherers in the commercial bushmeat trade is part of the centuries-old interdependent relationship they have with their neighbours (usually but not exclusively Bantu), albeit an unequal interdependency that benefits the latter to the detriment of the former.[12]

There is a related distinction between poaching and hunting, one characterised by significant ambiguity and uncertainty in terms of legislation and application. A man who goes into the forest to find meat for his family is a hunter in one context, but if he kills an animal in a protected area or when the state-imposed hunting calendar prohibits hunting, then he becomes a poacher. This poacher is often an impoverished opportunist, or even a desperate one, who plays a part in a long value chain. The poacher–hunter distinction is discussed in detail in Chapter 9, where the differences between legitimacy and legality are analysed.

Although commercial hunting is not new, its scale and intensity are. Today, bushmeat hunting has become 'opportunistic and therefore non-selective, depleting species indiscriminately'.[13] Moreover, in the past, hunters adhered to certain rules of sustainability – based on respect for and an intimate knowledge of their natural surroundings and ecological dynamics. They would fish during animal reproduction phases and hunt during fish spawning periods. Hunting was also selective: older males were slain first, leaving younger males and females to reproduce. The transition from traditional hunting to non-traditional hunting has been gradual.

Traditional hunting was both individual and collective. The types of species hunted and the pursuit times depended on hunting methods and tools.[14] According to Jan Vansina, forest peoples at the time of the Bantu expansion from West to Central Africa 'loved gadgets for fishing, hunting, and gathering, and they seem to have frequently invented more efficient tools'.[15] Implements and paraphernalia such as nets, crossbows, spears and liana snares were made by hand out of natural materials. Dogs played an important role in chasing game into the nets. Setting land ablaze to flush out and slaughter game, usually at the end of the dry season, was another common technique that is now on the wane. Communal hunts with fire were observed in Lower Congo (today's Kongo Central Province) in the 1960s by Wyatt

MacGaffey.[16] The practice is gradually being abandoned today because of social change, declining game abundance, and forest degradation. During the time of his research, MacGaffey observed that these forests were 'plundered rather than cultivated'.[17] All the same, hunters in and around the Luki Biosphere Reserve reported in 2020 that they still hunt with dogs even though finding quarry is increasingly difficult.

Numerous ethnographic and socio-economic studies document the complementarity of hunting, farming, fishing and other subsistence activities throughout the intercontinental tropical rainforest belt.[18] Hunting activities tend to decline when the agricultural calendar requires greater labour (for land-clearing, planting and harvesting) and intensifies when less effort is needed for farming. In the DRC's heavily forested Sankuru Province, for example, the great prevalence of men laying traps is an indication of how they combine trapping with other forest activities, primarily farming but harvesting non-timber forest products as well. Other research similarly shows that rattan harvesting and the commercialisation of wildlife are complementary and mutually supportive activities for villagers in Cameroon.[19] In Sankuru, 91% of hunters lay traps, 52% hunt with dogs, 42% use shotguns and 29% use bows and arrows.[20] These hunters collectively admit that 'any comestible animal seen is killed'.[21] Evidence of the continued use of dogs for hunting comes from the Kole region of Sankuru where dogs are still included in bridewealth packages, along with cloth, salt, goats and palm wine.[22]

Meat from traditional hunting was distributed according to strict hierarchical norms, with choice morsels going to the village chief. Collective net hunting also served a ceremonial purpose within communities. Research from southern Cameroon found that it was organised to celebrate births, marriages, funerals or the lifting of a curse or to welcome a special guest to the village.[23] Vansina's vivid description of collective net hunting in the Dja area of Cameroon emphasises its social, ecological and symbolic dimensions:

> Collective hunting ... with nets ... was a dry season activity, usually carried out in the weeks before the farming cycle began ... In the nineteenth century hunting with nets was widespread in the dry season. It was a cooperative and exciting endeavour, usually involving all men of the village. One-day hunts were organized from the village, usually on special occasions such as an initiation, a funeral, a marriage. Longer, more intensive expeditions occurred when the villagers left for hunting and gathering camps. Like restricted war such hunts were a major occasion for manifesting the esprit de corps of a village; great feats of hunting were remembered for a long time, and hunts, like wars, were hedged about by ritual.[24]

Although this form of hunting has largely disappeared, there are some continuing examples. Billy Kabala observed the practice in the DRC's Salonga National Park in 2016.[25] The Mbuti in DRC's Ituri Province continue to hunt with dogs and nets. The Baka of the Central African Republic still practised net hunting in the early 1990s, according to Andrew Noss.[26] I was told by village-based Baka in 2021 in the northern Republic of Congo that they have lost the requisite skills, ability and interest in net hunting. Although it is quite difficult to establish the veracity of such statements, the fact that the Baka don't own dogs is an indicator that in fact they probably have ceased this form of hunting. The example of net hunting, which has community importance in helping maintain social cohesion, serves to reinforce the argument made throughout this book that wildlife is much more than meat.

Smoking meat is one of the skills hunters need to master. The terms *viande fumée* and *viande boucanée* are used interchangeably to refer to smoked meat in Central Africa. Unlike biltong and jerky, which are dried with salt and spices, the Central African conservation process entails slow drying over a smoky fire without additives. While 'buccaneer' is an English word that is commonly associated with the pirates of the Caribbean, it derives from the Arawak word *boucaner*, which means to smoke meat or fish. The original buccaneers were 17th-century European hunters who smoked wild meat on Hispaniola Island for sale to passing ships.

The smoky taste of bushmeat is very much part of its appeal to the palate. The smoking process is a crucial cooking and conservation step that takes place in the forest at hunting camps. Without refrigeration, smoking is the optimal solution. Smoking also diminishes the problem of carrying heavier fresh meat from forest to village while it gives the taste that people love. Once an animal is captured (whether shot, snared or trapped) it is prepared for smoking at a forest hunting camp. This is a happy moment for hunters who have successfully captured animals and can now think about it as food, money, and occasion for a hearty welcome back in the village. The first step is removing the intestines, which the hunters eat themselves, prepared as boiled stew, while sometimes sharing intestines or head with their dogs. Duikers, small primates and cane rats are smoked whole; larger animals with denser flesh such as wild boar or gazelle will be butchered into pieces before being smoked. Again depending on the animal, its fur may be seared off with fire. Once cleaned and butchered, the meat is then placed on wooden racks suspended over a slow-burning smoky fire for a period of between a few days and over a week. To ensure the desired kind of smoke, a mix of dead wood, freshly cut branches and brush is used. Depending on whether the meat will be destined for sale in a far-off city or eaten sooner in the village, the smoking process will be longer or shorter. *Moto moko* is the Lingala expression for the technique of lightly smoking meat for just a couple of days: it isn't appropriate for long-term conservation but is preferred for meat that will be eaten quickly because it gives the meat a nice blend of smoky taste while preserving the basic taste of the animal. Meat is kept in smoky kitchen huts once carried to the village, while waiting to be bought or to be eaten. Kept in a dry, well-aired environment, smoked meat can last for months. Even though the smoky taste is generally associated with wild meat from the forest, people also appreciate smoked domestic animals such as rabbit or goat. A Kinshasa colleague told me that his family gave him a smoked rabbit, which he found to be 'as delicious as a smoked cane rat in terms of taste and texture'.[27]

The hunter's universe

Hunting practices that are now variably referred to as non-traditional, modern or commercial are essentially individual – as opposed to traditional or collective (as described above). Hunters lay wire snares and use 'the definitive symbol of the hunter', the shotgun.[28] 'Going into the forest without my shotgun would be like going to church without a Bible.'[29] When asked what other symbols are identified with the modern hunter, hunters indicate the headlamp (used for jacklighting, or stunning an animal at night with the light) and cartridges. The symbolism of the cartridge reveals a fascinating association with the hunter and his prey. The anthropologist J. G. Frazer, in his encyclopedic *The Golden Bough* (a comparative study of mythology and religion), mentions hunters in New Guinea who, as a way of anticipating good luck, put bullets in their mouth prior to a hunt.[30] Doing so was a symbolic ritual step: a bullet in the mouth was like a first course before tasting the meat they would eat thanks to the same bullet. Although the example is dated and comes from far afield, it indicates the comparative and, perhaps, universal importance of hunting beliefs and rituals.

Shotgun and wire-snare hunting have eliminated the relationship of physical and symbolic proximity between hunter and prey that existed when spears, crossbows, and bow and arrows were used. Although contemporary hunting often includes both traditional and modern techniques, the material culture of hunting is evolving, making the slaughter more efficient[31] – and, in some cases, market-oriented, as highlighted by the following observation from Gabon. 'The reasons given for gun hunting trips suggested that gun hunting was often undertaken when a hunter wished to make money immediately, for a specific need, compared with trapping, where the timing and type of catches could not be predicted, and the use of the meat was decided on after, rather than before, it was caught.'[32] These techniques evolved as new needs and expectations crept into the rural mind. A traditional chief in the Lake Télé Community Reserve (in the north of the Republic of Congo) laments:

Today isn't yesterday. The cash economy came to us like a lightning bolt. In the past, it was forbidden to sell animals from a collective hunt. The meat was distributed throughout the village and the choice cuts were offered to the chief. Today, money confounds our relationship between humans and animals. Yes, really, modernity has hit us with brutality.[33]

A village elder in the same area – half-proudly, half-remorsefully – showed me two hunting spears which belonged to his late father, padlocked safely in a storage hut. 'My papa used these during collective hunting expeditions. They were already remnants of the past when I became old enough to hunt. I keep these spears to show my grandchildren. They are like old books to teach them about our heritage.'[34]

Despite the adoption of new world views about hunting, sustainability, family and the attraction of personal possessions, some lessons from their fathers still govern hunters' relations with wildlife. They pray to their ancestors for benediction and protection against accidents, ferocious animals, evil spirits and magic spells. While this reality still has some currency, it is shifting and not as well respected as when it was recorded by the pioneering social anthropologist Evans-Pritchard in the 1930s. The following passage is a good example of the need to maintain good relations within the community for successful hunting.

> A witch may enjoy a certain amount of prestige on account of his powers, for everyone is careful not to offend him, since no one deliberately courts disaster. This is why a householder who kills an animal sends presents of meat to the old men who occupy neighbouring homesteads. For if an old witch receives no meat he will prevent the hunter from killing any more beasts, whereas if he receives his portion he will hope that more beasts are killed and will refrain from interference.[35]

Bonne chasse in French (good hunt) is the equivalent of good luck in English. It colloquially refers to luck in finding anything from a partner to groceries at the supermarket. Without exception, hunters say hunting is largely about luck. If they have a clear conscience and respect the rules imparted to them by their elders, they can get lucky – which translates into finding a spoor and bagging lots of game. Lack of respect leads to an unsuccessful day. *Lupemba*, which is the Lingala word for 'luck', also has a variety of related meanings such as destiny, success, blessing or talent.[36] All of these notions, which can be achieved by hard work or magic, are part and parcel of the hunter's cognitive universe. There is, of course, nothing uniquely African about these beliefs. Admittedly dated and disconnected from the Western world today, the following example reveals the universality of certain beliefs. In the late 1700s the German poet Gottfried August Bürger penned a ballad entitled 'The Wild Hunter'. It tells the tragic story of an arrogant hunter who was condemned to eternal damnation for hunting on the Sabbath, in flagrant disregard for warnings from the pious village elders. Back in the DRC, an elderly hunter related this information about how to prepare for a successful hunting outing.

Before going into the forest, we gather wine, eggs, cassava and sometimes meat to leave for the ancestor spirits in a special sacred space in the forest (*etumbelo na mbeka*). These gifts pardon our sins and show respect to the ancestors. A successful hunt is then possible. Without these sacrificial libations and gifts we know the hunt will fail.[37]

On the other hand, hunters believe the hunt will fail if they go into the forest 'impure'. Mary Douglas describes the perceived need for sexual abstinence before hunting;[38] and, according to Frazer, the 'practice of observing strict chastity as a condition of success in hunting and fishing is very common among rude races' because the effects of sexual activity are considered to offend the animals, 'who in consequence will not suffer themselves to be caught'.[39] While the language may strike us as outdated, these beliefs correspond to current accounts:

We don't sleep with our wives the night before the hunt because we have to be clean to receive the blessing of our ancestors. They are the ones that give us good luck and watch over us. Going impure into the forest is a sign of disrespect and will have consequences. And two men who have slept with the same woman cannot hunt together because that would attract ferocious beasts.[40]

Conversely, a world away, among the Inuit, where hunting with harpoons and spears is practised, sexual intercourse is believed to bode well because it symbolically prefigures the killing of an animal. The in-and-out thrusting action during intercourse is seen as a metaphor for the thrust of the hunter's weapon into his prey.[41]

Doing the right thing to cultivate good luck is crucial, but in-depth knowledge of the forest is at least as important. 'It's essential for a hunter to know the forest – which means its signs, sounds, noises, smells, the trees and the animals' habits. There are no miracles for us – to be successful you have to know what you're doing.'[42] Knowing what you're doing also involves skilfully managing prestige to avoid jealousy. The hunter has to be careful not to attract too much attention because jealousy is a very powerful social reality and a cause of social-levelling interventions. Reprisals take the form of witchcraft spells, animosity and accusations of selfishness. The process of putting a too-proud hunter in his place was explicitly described in Richard Lee's study of the !Kung Bushmen of the Kalahari: 'when a young man kills much meat he comes to think of himself as a chief or a big man, and he thinks of the rest of us as his servants or inferiors. We can't accept this ... So we always speak of his meat as worthless. This way we cool his heart and make him gentle.'[43] Success and prestige are desirable traits, but they can be dangerous if not managed carefully, which explains the importance of secrecy. In southern Cameroon, hunters hide their meat behind their huts to keep it secret whereas, conversely, they proudly display their agricultural yields in front.[44] Similarly, Baka Pygmies in the same region are accused by their non-Baka neighbours of concealing their meat to avoid having to share or sell it.[45]

The following narrative reveals how vulnerable hunters are to the social-levelling dynamics that govern interpersonal relations in all walks of life. It is a powerful statement about secrecy as a cultural reality, applied specifically to managing one's identity as a hunter.

> Success as a hunter and secrecy go hand in hand. A key to my success as a hunter is knowing how to keep my mouth shut. The number of animals I've killed and their species determine if we walk back to the village in daylight hours for everyone to see, or in the dark of night. If there is a lot of meat, we hide it and sneak back to the village at night. I've learned not to spark jealousy because my neighbours wouldn't hesitate to cast a spell on me. If I kill an animal that is on the endangered species list, my assistant and I smoke it in the forest; I don't even tell my family what animal it is. I only tell my wife; no one else because I could be betrayed and sent to prison. I never tell anyone when or exactly where I'm going in the forest. If we ever see other hunters, we hide – which is also why we wear trainers and not

boots. Boots are noisy so can scare away animals being stalked and give ourselves away to other hunters. Obviously, I never tell anyone how much money I earn. I'm particularly close-mouthed when it comes to selling feline skins, teeth and claws because of the law. Sorcerers need these things for their ceremonies and rituals. One time I sold a small bottle of panther urine to a white guy for a pile of money. He told me, drug traffickers use it because sniffer dogs don't like the smell.[46]

Secrecy, cunning and stealth are obsessions that extend to all levels of society. In a study of the power of secrecy in Africa, Beryl Bellman shows how it manifests itself in all societies, under different forms.[47] It can be considered as the absence of transparency, controlling the flow of information (who gets to know what?) and blurring everyday situations. Central Africans camouflage their intentions and hide their convictions out of fear that the forces of the occult will somehow interfere. Secrecy was also a resilience strategy used by Africans to hide their intimate feelings, activities and expectations from their European masters. Secrecy, moreover, is a survival mechanism and a powerful cultural reality that has direct implications for bushmeat hunting, although it goes far beyond that realm.

Hunting and providing meat to the family and community are a significant source of prestige in the village. So is having money to buy things and drinks for friends. The hunter who returns to the village with a good quarry commands respect because it shows that the ancestors are smiling on him and he has done what was necessary to cultivate and deserve his good luck. Offering meat to important guests is a requirement of village hospitality that has carried over into the urban setting. The prestige of the hunter – both self-proclaimed and attributed – is mentioned repeatedly. 'Crocodile hunting gives me social status in our village – I've taught my sons to hunt with me. If we catch ten, I sell seven to a trader and keep three to eat at home.'[48] The willingness to confront wild animals is 'indisputable proof of prestige and bravery'.[49] Legends about great hunters are told and retold in villages – somewhat akin to the way many Americans are familiar with the folk legend of Daniel Boone, famous for killing bears. A sign of changing perceptions of prestige is captured in another exchange with Dieudonné Dsholing: 'I'm a schoolteacher during the week and a hunter at the weekend and during holidays. It's prestigious to be a hunter, but not as much as a schoolteacher.'

Hunters' respect for tradition, while engaging in commercial networks, reveals the hybrid – and opportunistic – nature of their attitudes and behaviours. They are both traditional and modern at the same time, similar to Central African religious beliefs. Hunters have embraced Christianity with open arms while remaining stubbornly animistic. The following quote reveals the enduring importance of totems,[50] while reinforcing one of the main messages of this book: wild animals are food, but they are likewise an enduring and powerful cultural reality.

> Unlike in the towns, here in the village, the environment defines who we are. Animals mean a lot more to us than just eating. They fulfil spiritual needs, they are our ancestors. Every family has their own totem. We would never kill the totem animal of our family because it would be a terrible sin and we would have to pay for it. Our chiefs need to have animal symbols to manifest their stature – an elephant or buffalo tail, for example, or a panther skin or tooth.[51]

This next quote from an interview, about totems and beliefs in animal symbolism, tells a story that blurs superstition, irrationality, clear-headed realism and pragmatism.

> Parrots are the totem of our family. We don't eat them because they bring us good luck in the forest. Our neighbours eat them but don't eat panthers because they can protect them from other wild animals by hoisting them up high into the trees out of their reach ... Pregnant women aren't allowed to eat turtles because of the way the head goes in and out of the shell – you wouldn't want the baby to be doing that during delivery, would you? We men give the seed but that doesn't stop

us from eating turtles. Before, women were told by their fathers not to eat animals with a strong smell but they've figured out that that was just a trick to keep the good meat for themselves.

Another example of shifting world views has to do with inter-generational conflicts. This narrative relates specifically to how village youth reject their parents' relations with wildlife and helps contextualise the important connection between youth and unsustainable hunting.

> We never hunted young male animals before, but today our young men hunt whatever they can to get money. Masculinity for my peers meant wives, children and a house. For the young men today it's a phone, travel, fashion, cigarettes and girlfriends. Before, money didn't talk; but oh how that has changed: money shouts now. Kill, kill, kill – youth just don't care. They slaughter for money. They don't think about the future and don't realize that our ancestor spirits can take their revenge a long way down the road – sometimes even after a generation. Revenge is a very slow process – but inescapable. Our boys say we're old-fashioned. They want change.[52]

Such views about the sustainable ways of the past compared with the unsustainable ways of today need to be qualified. People have always had very pragmatic relations with forest resources and, for various good and bad reasons, exploit them as sources of quickly earned cash, thereby engaging in environmentally detrimental practices. Abusive resource exploitation has always existed in the region, flying in the face of the myth of the 'noble savage', dear to the French Enlightenment philosopher Jean-Jacques Rousseau.

Another village elder emphasised how outside influences revolutionise expectations, exacerbating pressure on wildlife: 'Envy leads young men to steal and hunt. When they see someone with a new style of trainers or a brand name backpack, they do whatever they can to get money to have the same. Their desire becomes obsessional.'[53] Unsustainable fishing practices are somewhat similar to unsustainable hunting practices. Increasingly, recourse is being made to fine-mesh mosquito netting or toxic chemicals to poison fish so as to increase catch volumes. Unsustainable hunting and fishing are, for both of these older men, examples of plundering whatever resources are available.

Even though there was no cellphone coverage in Dzeke where I conducted interviews, young men absolutely had to have the latest model of smartphone – both for their own ego and to impress their girlfriends. Hunting and selling game is the only possible way of finding the money to buy one, unless a relative from the city provides it. This helps explain the bitterness expressed by another village elder: 'Our kids are contaminated by whites and their immoral Western values. When you come here and ask me these questions, I feel like my heart is going to break.'[54] Unsustainable wildlife management for him, therefore, is exacerbated by outsiders. The shift in values is clearly a concern for older men: 'We are going through a period of moral and social decadence which has a negative impact on hunting practices. Today, our boys catch baby animals, tie them up and wait for the mother or herd to come looking for them: then they slaughter the whole lot.'[55] Although not referring to hunting specifically, AbdouMaliq Simone has observed this type of problem: 'As the socializing capacity of local institutions declines, so does their capacity to structure productive activities.'[56] Simone's observation has an indirect policy implication: improved natural resource management requires an understanding of social organisation.

Shifts in behaviours and attitudes relating to wildlife are not unlike other types of inter-generational shifts in the region's villages. One example is the gradual disappearance of fruit trees. Village elders who would plant avocado, mango and African bush plum trees around their homes for shade and fruit did so primarily for the benefit of their offspring. These same elders observe that their children don't bother doing so anymore, complaining that the perception of well-being has become an immediate material concern, no longer a priority for future legacy. These shifts are influenced by the pull of the city and the desire to leave village life behind.

Although ostensibly associated primarily with forest environments, the hunter's universe today is also a dominant urban reality, accompanied by a host of social, cultural, economic and political metaphors. Hunting and warfare offer a lens through which to understand power relations.[57] The popular Congolese singer Werrason promoted himself as an urban cultural icon by adopting the epithet 'King of the Forest' (*mopao na nzamba*), while also advocating bonobo conservation on radio and television, and through music. Hunting for diamonds became a major socio-economic enterprise that took off in the DRC in the 1990s.[58] Urban youth hunt for money, women and prestige by transforming the urban bar into a metaphorical forest to be plundered.[59] These examples show that while hunting is anchored in the past, it is also an inescapable pathway to understanding the subtleties of present and future urban life.

Motorbike bushmeat transport

The increased availability of relatively inexpensive Indian and Chinese motorcycles has been a major transportation and social innovation throughout much of Central Africa – tantamount to the mobile phone revolution of the late 1990s. The motorcycle has become a key link in the bushmeat transportation chain used by both hunters and traders – a phenomenon observed in Brazil as well.[60] Easily maintained and cost-efficient, the 125 cc motorbike is ideal for navigating the region's rainforest and has thus become a welcome innovation. This form of transportation has been a significant factor in social change, especially for isolated communities who live in villages far from feeder roads. Poor road infrastructure is one of the major handicaps for getting goods to market. Hauling low-value, high-volume crops (such as cassava) from village to market is a major development challenge in the rainforest and helps account for the persistence of the rural poverty trap. Bushmeat, conversely, is a high-value, low-volume commodity, easily strapped onto the rack of a motorcycle. Although rugged, they are light enough to be placed in a dugout canoe to cross over rivers where there are no bridges. The dilapidated bicycle, heavily laden with a bag of cassava, plastic jug of palm oil, or even a pig or goat, is rapidly becoming a thing of the past. It is now the motorcycle that serves the purpose of getting all sorts of goods to the roads and intermediary markets that are accessible to pick-up trucks or large lorries. In many places, the road itself is the market: people wait, long-sufferingly by the side of the road, for buyers to stop their vehicles and purchase bags of charcoal, produce or bushmeat. That the road has become the market makes law enforcement particularly difficult in areas without a visible presence of staff from wildlife management agencies.

Hunters and traders employ motorcycles to shuttle between village and forest, sometimes using their own, sometimes paying motorcycle taxi drivers. Hunters illegally operating in the Luki Biosphere Reserve (DRC) claim the motorbike relieves them from long walks carrying meat out of the forest.[61] In the Salonga National Park (DRC), getting meat out of the forest is a physically exhausting and costly operation. Commercial hunters have no alternative but to hire porters, who receive 'one monkey for every five they carry out'.[62] The Luki hunters say the motorbikes are efficient in expediting game to markets or directly to clients who may have placed orders by mobile phone. Hunters rely on motorcycles to sell the prestigious expensive species such as buffalo, antelope and boa to their clients in Boma, a one-hour ride from the reserve. Motorcycles, especially when used at night, help to avoid rangers in the reserve, roadblocks and riverboat controls. The motorcycle has even entered the litany of praises to the Lord Almighty: 'God gives us good luck for a successful hunt and the motorbike to transport it to our buyers.'[63]

Many young men in Central Africa dream of having their own motorcycle. It is a symbol of prestige, modernity, liberty, and success par excellence, especially in rural areas. They will consequently do whatever they can to acquire one by hook or by crook. The motorcycle has contributed to improved mobility for goods and people who may have had to use their two legs to get around until recently: in this sense it is a positive change. For the bushmeat trade, however, it has had a negative twofold effect. First, as described above, it has greatly facilitated the marketing of bushmeat; and, second, the desire to have a motorcycle pushes young men to take advantage of whatever economic options may exist. In many rural areas, hunting and trading bushmeat is the only such option. They need bushmeat to buy their motorbikes and they need their motorbikes to sell bushmeat. Before the motorbike was available, the bicycle served the same purpose. This nexus was mentioned in the memoirs of a Belgian colonial agent who described encountering a hunter on a brand-new red bicycle (the encounter took place in 1955). Although bicycles of different colours were available at the store, the hunter chose the red one because, he said, it reminded him of the red blood of the animals that provided him with the money to buy the bike.[64]

The following anecdote is a good example of how the motorcycle contributes to hunting and trade, forging the link between the local village and the illegal global trade in pangolin scales (used in Asian traditional medicine). Pangolins are perceived as being 'anomalous animals endowed with mysterious properties'.[65] A trader in south-eastern Cameroon drives his motorbike through rural villages shouting out *kupke kokolo!*

kupke kokolo! (scales, pangolin!). The villagers, who eat pangolin but previously hadn't much use for the scales, are happy to sell them – and await the arrival of the buyer who passes through their village at regular intervals.[66] This is just one small link in what *National Geographic* reports as being an international criminal network operating between West and Central Africa, on one hand, and China and Vietnam, on the other – the two main recipient countries of the approximately one million pangolins poached between 2010 and 2020.[67]

Conclusion

Using original ethnographic data and a review of the relevant literature, this chapter delves into the life of the Central African hunter, traditional and modern dynamics, and world views. It connects with the important themes of urban commercial networks and law-enforcement problems developed in other chapters. Historical information and, in a few cases, findings from outside Africa were also presented and analysed in order to reveal long-standing and possibly universal patterns. While hunting for family consumption and trade are the two main motivations that push hunters to take up their shotguns, this chapter also reiterates a main theme of the book: while wild animals are food and money, they are also deeply embedded in Central African cultural reality and identity. The issue of identity leads to the next chapter about the culture of consumption.

5

THE CULTURE OF CONSUMPTION

Why eat it?

Why do people eat bushmeat in Central Africa? There are definitely no easy political economy or sociological answers to that question, essentially because there are no single overriding explanations. Depending on the specific setting and the person, the response can be either simple or incredibly complex. Complexity stems from the fact that aspects of these drivers are entangled with different ways of accounting for them.[1] Interpretations can also be subjective because what may be cultural for one bushmeat consumer, for example, may be economic for another. The way people talk about eating bushmeat helps decipher their consumption habits and desires. 'I'm going to devour you like a monkey' can actually be a term of endearment heard in Kinshasa, quite the opposite of the British slang 'I couldn't give a monkey's'. One Congolese researcher reported that during interviews with bushmeat consumers, their faces lit up with joy when talking about their favourite species and their taste.[2] I interviewed a chef in an up-scale restaurant in Ouesso (Republic of Congo) and observed how his face lit up with pride while he explained his recipes for monkey, duiker and red river hog. The chef also mentioned that clients from Brazzaville considered a work trip to Ouesso as a kind of bushmeat gastronomic opportunity. Another researcher told me that when bushmeat is rare, women cooking it tend to sing out of pure joy at the prospect of eating and sharing it.[3] Whether such accounts are true or not is less important than the way those sentiments are interpreted and expressed. They indicate how even talking or thinking about the flesh, skin and fat of bushmeat triggers visceral and emotional reactions. These considerations serve to highlight how deeply embedded the bushmeat diet is in the psyche of its avid consumers.

With widely varying degrees of nuance, caveat and qualification, motivations can be clustered around socio-cultural, economic and nutritional needs, expectations and perceptions. The objective of this chapter is to untangle these compelling motivations, arguing that understanding them is essential in improving wildlife management in a culturally sensitive way. Bushmeat is without a shadow of a doubt a 'total social fact' in Central Africa. As elaborated by the famous French sociologist Marcel Mauss, this concept refers to something that has implications throughout society, primarily in the economic, legal, political and religious spheres.[4] These broad categories need to be deconstructed before they can make sociological sense for improved wildlife management. This deconstruction exercise is one of the objectives of this chapter, which ultimately aims to make the relationships between wild animals and the people who eat them less bewildering. Doing so, incidentally, also reveals something profound about the broader role of nature in people's lives.

Why do people eat bushmeat in Central Africa? This is also one of the most intractable questions facing wildlife conservation practitioners. While conservation experts and other researchers have done a reasonably good job at monitoring the quantities of bushmeat entering urban markets, they have not come up with satisfactory answers about the deeper question of why people trade and eat it. Counting is one thing, but to curb pressure on unsustainable bushmeat consumption, experts need to appreciate the essential drivers of consumption patterns from within the framework of cultural norms. A better understanding of consumer motivations is a prerequisite for the design of culturally sensitive policies aimed at nudging attitude and behaviour change. Like so many other development challenges in Africa, we may know what the problems are, but we just don't know how to solve them. Conservationists are pushing towards diminishing consumption of wild animals – especially in urban settings – but many consumers believe that eating bushmeat, when affordable and available, is, quite simply, normal and desirable. They also feel that they are entitled to do so and perceive messages to the contrary as Western NGO meddling, as one wildlife management expert states: 'Many consumers of wildlife products ... see it as their right to consume and utilize wildlife regardless of environmental consequences and see environmental advocacy against it as an intolerable encroachment on their lifestyle.'[5]

This perception of bushmeat consumption as normal is a serious challenge to sustainable wildlife management because it is difficult to instigate behaviour change for something that is not seen as unhealthy, illogical or fundamentally wrong. Conservation experts have thus far been unsuccessful in formulating any persuasive answers to Central African consumers' questions about why they shouldn't eat bushmeat. Discourses about zoonosis and over-exploitation and unsustainable hunting practices, albeit based on ostensibly solid scientific research, tend to fall on deaf ears. I've heard multiple iterations of the beliefs that 'bushmeat is a gift from God so it will always be there' and 'yes, we know that there are fewer wild animals today than in the past'. These seemingly contradictory beliefs reveal that for hunters and consumers, there is not necessarily a linear connection between cause (hunting) and effect (resource depletion).

How much and how often people eat bushmeat is another difficult question to answer, in part because there are no systematic or comprehensive data sets or surveys – and there is no common methodology. A comprehensive set of cross-city surveys would require quantitative and qualitative data about age, gender, religion, level of education, marital status, occupation, ethnicity and geographical origin. There is, nevertheless, enough evidence to be able to confirm that urban bushmeat consumption is a sustained reality with little likelihood that most social groups will voluntarily reduce it.

Although not perfectly comparable because they are derived from different methodologies, the following figures put consumption in an insightful perspective. In Gabon's capital, Libreville, 27% of participants in a survey reported eating bushmeat at least once per week.[6] In Port-Gentil (Gabon's second-largest city after Libreville) 24% of households consumed bushmeat at least once in the three days prior to being surveyed.[7] As elsewhere throughout the region, preferred species are porcupine and blue duiker.[8] Bushmeat was reported to be 'commonly consumed' in households in half of Kinshasa's 24 districts and was 'the primary source of animal protein ... in seven of the 12 districts surveyed'.[9] But as the Kinshasa diet is largely vegetarian or vegan (by necessity, not by choice) 'the primary source' does not necessarily amount to much. The same study suggested that bushmeat formed '18.79% of the daily diet',[10] although this figure seems rather high in the light of other evidence. Indeed, one qualitative study found that bushmeat was consumed '*par horoscope*', which in idiosyncratic Kinshasa lingo means 'once in a blue moon'.[11] This corresponds to the results of a quantitative survey conducted in Pointe-Noire, Brazzaville and

Kinshasa that concluded that bushmeat is an 'occasional food' or a 'rare treat'.[12] In Bangui, the capital of the Central African Republic, a household consumption survey found that bushmeat was eaten at 19% of daily meals (compared with 54% for beef and 35% for fish).[13] In Brazzaville 88% of households consumed bushmeat but the majority of them 'only on rare occasions' because of cost.[14] In Lubumbashi 86% of residents surveyed confirmed eating bushmeat approximately once per month.[15] A survey carried out in cities in the West African countries of Burkina Faso, Niger, Nigeria and Togo, where bushmeat is more scarce, reported that '12.8% of men and 8.8% of women said they liked bushmeat and ate it regularly' (interpreted as approximately once a week).[16] This same survey found 'that younger men and women were less likely to eat bushmeat compared to older groups'. This is significant because it could be an indicator of broad shifts in food consumption patterns.[17] In terms of volume, rural communities in Cameroon consumed an estimated 20 kg of bushmeat per person a year.[18] While percentages and volumes are important, they tell only part of the story: even though the 17 million Kinshasa residents may consume bushmeat only 'once in a blue moon' that megacity's pressure on wildlife is much greater than that of a much smaller city like Libreville or Bangui where residents eat bushmeat more frequently. The set of figures presented here is admittedly a bit random and disordered, but it does give an idea about consumption levels. The main point is to show that urban residents cling to a sustained desire to eat bushmeat.

Craving for bushmeat continues among Africans living in Europe. Based on a study conducted at the Brussels airport that monitored passengers travelling from West and Central Africa, it was estimated that an average of 3.7 tonnes of bushmeat was illegally brought through the airport each month.[19] A previous study at the Paris Charles de Gaulle airport also identified large quantities of bushmeat coming in from the same countries.[20]

Sandrella Morrison-Lanjouw and colleagues conducted a study of bushmeat consumption among Ghanaians living in the Netherlands. They found that attachment to eating bushmeat there was motivated by very similar reasons that city dwellers in Africa state as motivations for eating bushmeat. Respondents highlighted taste, culture, the fact that it comes from the wild, social connections, and the link with a sense of home.

Socio-cultural and psychological drivers of consumption

An analysis of socio-cultural factors is unavoidable in helping to account for urban bushmeat consumption. Some people say they eat bushmeat because it is part and parcel of being African, because it is the taste of a mother's love, and because it is traditional – meaning something that their parents and grandparents ate back in the village. The desire to eat bushmeat is a gradual enculturation process that starts in childhood with both actual consumption and stories about it.

Personal trajectories relating to a person's age, gender, place of birth, purchasing power, family status, and status within the family also influence food choices and the motivation to eat bushmeat. Youth born and raised in urban areas crave bushmeat less than their village-born parents, but this doesn't mean they won't eat it if the opportunity presents itself and the price is right. These urbanised youths, who are increasingly exposed and attracted to Western ways of life and food consumption trends, may be more inclined to shy away from what for others is perceived as traditionally African. It is not uncommon for urban youth in middle-class families to choose fish or chicken while their parents have bushmeat. Bushmeat is being gradually replaced by fast food, which is emerging as the preferred 'social diet' of urban youths.[21] This is part of an Africa-wide 'nutrition transition' induced by 'socio-economic development, urbanization, and acculturation'.[22]

THE CULTURE OF CONSUMPTION

A similar example of family splintering is presented by youths attending evangelical church services while their parents pray in Catholic or traditional Protestant churches; this once again reveals the social dynamism of the urban landscape. Commercial advertising and the massive consumption of white bread, soft drinks, powdered baby formula and other agro-industrial food imports in urban Africa are part of this trend – persuasively summarised by the revolutionary Burkinabe president Thomas Sankara: 'if you're wondering where imperialism lies, just look in your dish'.[23] The social universe of food is a special place where traditional and modern logics simultaneously resist, persist, invent and adapt.

Other factors that shape personal trajectories are social relationships in the form of family legacy, kinship ties, and identity with an ethnic group or community. Sharing bushmeat can help cement these relationships, especially in urban areas where ethnicity simultaneously coincides with – and competes with – a wide range of other solidarity structures based on, for example, church groups, professional associations, neighbourhood organisations, rotating savings and credit associations, leisure associations (sports and fitness, music and fashion), and the plethora of ad hoc problem-solving NGOs that encompass all the visible and invisible dimensions of society aimed at circulating ideas and fulfilling aspirations.[24] The urban melting pot of Yaoundé offers a good example of bushmeat's social value beyond its nutritional function:

> Connecting with kin, culture, and home through consumption of familiar foods, gains unique significance in urban centres, at the confluence of many different ethnic groups, where one's social identity may be lost without special efforts to reconnect through things and people from home. Clearly, bushmeat consumption in urban areas is as much about food preferences as it is about people and cultural connections because they originate from family and kin ties.[25]

Urban consumers of bushmeat who grew up in village environments are subject to what psychologists term the Proust phenomenon.[26] This refers to memories of taste and smell that stimulate sense organs and emotions. Like the famous 19th-century French writer's fond childhood remembrance of eating a madeleine butter cake, the taste of bushmeat conjures up a host of bygone – and perhaps idealised – memories. Fond memories of bushmeat experiences 'back in the village' – from catching and roasting small rodents and eating them with childhood playmates, to family meals – regularly resurface in interviews with urban bushmeat consumers.

Many people who buy bushmeat in urban markets have some kind of personal or family association with the forest. City dwellers who grew up in the village tend to have mixed feelings about the contrast between the perceived advantages of the city (cash and salaries, school and health care, music and fashion, cold beer and sexual freedom) and the backwardness of the village (strict social rules, witchcraft, struggle for life, non-existent infrastructure, and the absence of hope for a better economic tomorrow). Food memories from the village, however, tend to be positive and characterised by recollections of satiety and family. Bushmeat memories about taste and abundance are well represented in fond discourses about village food consumption, epitomised by the recollection that 'stewed monkey and my mother's bosom go together'.[27] Another person who grew up in the Sankuru forest remembers a pot of stewed meat constantly simmering over three stones: 'as a child I always had meat to nibble on, that pot was never empty'.[28]

The following two anecdotes also reveal the power of memory. In 2020, a woman from eastern Congo described to me with vivid accuracy her experience of eating smoked elephant in 2005 at a friend's home in Butembo. 'I remember the taste of that meat like it was yesterday; it was so delicious I'm salivating now just thinking about it. I even remember the white dish with a blue border I ate it from, with a mountain of fufu.'[29] Second, I had a random encounter with a well-heeled Congolese businessman at the Fischer fish and bushmeat market in Boma, who was buying three smoked cane rats. When I prodded him about his motives for wanting those animals, he explained that he lives in Essex in the UK: 'eating that meat will make me feel reconnected with my country'.[30] The sentiment is often expressed that eating bushmeat is a kind of umbilical cord connecting consumers to their past.

Bushmeat is a frequent centrepiece on the urban table at weekend gatherings with family and friends, and when hosting meals for relatives and other visitors. While it can be more prosaically considered as food that just contributes to the daily fight against hunger, it also satisfies a powerful desire for togetherness. In many households, bushmeat is just as much a thing of feeling and emotion as of taste or sustenance. Serving bushmeat is good etiquette and a means of showing respect, gratitude and acknowledgement. When a Congolese friend's first daughter was born, his Batetela clansmen paid homage by presenting him with a haul of twenty porcupines as a symbolic gesture of respect and celebration.[31] Through 'the allotment of quarry' both bearer and receiver command respect.[32] Bushmeat is 'associated with a desire to please, reward, honour, show appreciation, or obtain favours'.[33] Along the same lines, 'a woman may treat her husband to a special bushmeat meal if she feels guilty and needs to be forgiven for having done something bad like wasting money or having committed adultery'.[34] A woman in Kinshasa will make the effort to prepare bushmeat for her fiancé in the hope of convincing him that she will be a good wife.[35] 'Bushmeat is the family meal par excellence for us, especially when I can get hold of some red river hog. That makes for a real joyous family treat.'[36] Prices peak prior to New Year's Eve and other celebrations. In a routine search, rangers from the Lake Télé Community Reserve in northern

Republic of Congo found crocodile meat and smoked duiker in a nun's car for the prestigious ordination ceremony of a new bishop in Impfondo.[37] Another informant spontaneously claimed, 'If I were at a village feast and had the choice between fish, chicken, goat or red river hog – my choice without thinking for a second would be the hog.'[38] These various examples testify to the social importance of eating and sharing bushmeat.

The value of sharing bushmeat at family gatherings is encapsulated in the declaration 'a party without bushmeat isn't a party'.[39] The absence of bushmeat would be like American Thanksgiving without turkey or Greek Easter without lamb. The UK equivalent is roast dinners, which ranked second place in a 2012 survey about what is best about Britain, just behind the bacon sandwich but ahead of the BBC, Big Ben, Shakespeare, James Bond, the Beatles and the Queen.[40]

Religion is a dominant force throughout Central Africa. Adherence to Christianity in particular can have direct, and sometimes astonishing, influences on people's bushmeat consumption practices. There is no book more widely read in the region than the Bible, particularly by women. A striking example of the link between bushmeat consumption and Christianity comes directly from the New Testament (I Corinthians 10:25): 'Eat whatever is sold in the meat market without raising any question on the ground of conscience.' This is echoed in popular discourse in the belief that 'everything is sanctified by the blood of Jesus so we can eat whatever we want'.[41] 'Everything that lives and moves about will be food for you. Just as I gave you the green plants, I now give you everything' (Genesis 9:3) is another biblical injunction to consume wild animals. The unrelenting Christian evangelical discourse that traditional beliefs and practices are satanical, backward, anti-Christ and governed by witchcraft has contributed to changing attitudes towards bushmeat consumption. In the Salonga National Park, the messages conveyed by evangelical churches, combined with the attitudes of youths who have experienced life in cities and towns, have undermined taboos that helped govern bushmeat consumption over generations.[42] This example is representative of a widespread trend in the region. These shifts are particularly significant because they open the floodgates for new and substantial consumer groups: women and youths.

Women were traditionally limited to certain species of wild animals which they were allowed to eat. Numerous restrictions, as described in Table 5.1, were imposed on them by their male family members. Some restrictions – but far fewer – were also imposed on unmarried, uninitiated men. Table 5.1 doesn't have a section on food restrictions applicable to men because, other than not being allowed to eat their family's totemic animal, there are too few examples to present. One exception, however, is the exhortation for sexually active men not to eat turtle because it is alleged that their penises will droop like the turtle's tail. Hunters even have a double restriction about consuming turtles because the reptile's sluggishness will compromise a hunter's ability to sprint during a pursuit. Table 5.1 is an indication of practices, not a definitive set of restrictions and recommendations, which depend on the beliefs of different clans and families. Food restrictions, *biloko ya ekila* (in Lingala) and *mzio* or *kijila* (in Swahili), translate as forbidden things.[43] The terms conjure up ideas of fear, punishment, evil spells and bad luck. A village chief in the DRC, nudged by a local environmental association, has raised his voice for the protection of giant pangolins. Playing on fear, he announced that anyone who kills a pangolin will be banished from the village and their house will mysteriously burn down.[44] The key message is the threat of witchcraft reprisal.

An early European ethnographic account of these taboos, in this case among the Alulu of what is now the DRC's Ituri

Province, came from one of King Leopold II's military officers during the Congo Free State period. Although accounts such as this one need to be critically examined as discourse influenced by colonial mentality – and, in this case, racist 'civilising mission' propaganda – the specific observation of taboos and the symbolic transfer of food attributes has retained its currency.

> Although women and children are not allowed to eat certain foods, the Alulus always eat together ... Eating the flesh of wild beasts – lion, panther and leopard; the meat of hyenas, jackals, wild pigs, crocodiles, turtles, snakes, cats and monkeys, and all types of birds, are forbidden for the weaker sex and children. The reason is bizarre: they attribute to food substances the property of influencing the instincts, tendencies and mentality of the person who consumes them. They therefore imagine that the ferocity of the leopard, the crudeness of the pig, the deceptiveness of the cat, and the mischief of the monkey can exert an action on the character of the woman by making her unpleasant, even evil. While to men, these same foods would give them warrior virtues, flexibility of mind and body, skill and intelligence.[45]

Table 5.1: Animal taboos in the DRC

Characteristics	Animal	Taboo
Taboos for Women		
Health and body	African genet	Consuming this strong-smelling animal will give women body odour.
	Hyrax; giant pangolin; pangolin	Consuming these animals will turn a woman's skin scaly or rough.
	Python	Consumption causes skin peeling, like the reptile, which sheds its skin.

Characteristics	Animal	Taboo
	Taboos for Pregnant Women	
Childbirth delivery problems	Sitatunga	Sitatunga allegedly lose a lot of blood during delivery so a woman who consumes one is susceptible to haemorrhaging during childbirth.
	Bat	Causes haemorrhaging during childbirth.
	Turtle	The hard skin of the turtle will tighten the uterine neck; and delivery will be as slow as the turtle's gait.
	Water chevrotain (also known as the fanged deer)	Consumption aggravates fatigue during delivery because the animal allegedly always looks tired and sleeps a lot.
Birth defects	Hippopotamus	Consumption causes miscarriages.
	Monkey; squirrel; turtle	Consumption causes sight defects or malformation of the lower limbs. The eyes of new-borns will resemble those of monkeys or squirrels, and their gait will be awkward like that of the turtle.

Characteristics	Animal	Taboo
Undesirable growth and behavioural problems with infants	Python Crocodile	Consumption will cause retarded mobility – the infant will slither instead of crawl.
	African genet	The infant will be as ugly as the genet and will become a thief since the genet is reputed to steal chickens.
Taboos for Unmarried Women and Men		
Luck in finding a marriage partner	Bat	Consumption causes unpleasant body odour, which repels a potential husband or wife.
	Squirrel	The sound of its barking is associated with mockery, so if an unmarried woman eats its meat she will be shunned by potential suitors.
Infidelity	Gambian pouched rat	This animal burrows in multiple dens, so if an unmarried woman eats it, she will have multiple extra-conjugal partners.
Sterility	Blue duiker Red duiker Giant pangolin	Consumption renders unmarried women sterile.

Characteristics	Animal	Taboo
Respiratory problems	Squirrel	The sound of a squirrel's breathing can be like a heavy moaning, so if an unmarried woman eats it, her child will snore or have respiratory problems.

Source: Interviews with Daniel Mpoyi Mpoyi (Kisangani); Krossy Mavakala (Kinshasa); Olivier Igugu (Bukavu); Noël Kabuyaya (Kinshasa).

In rural Central Africa, power is ostensibly controlled by married Bantu men; they are the elders – 'the wise men' – who arbitrate, judge and decide. They claim to dictate how the community should preserve its past, use its resources and organise its future. Women, children and hunter-gatherers have little voice. Female hunter-gatherers are particularly marginalised and vulnerable. These social norms, however, are gradually falling by the wayside in towns and cities to some extent. Urban women are emancipating themselves from these restrictions by different means – a good example of what has been described as 'the plasticity of social phenomena in west and Central Africa'.[46] The multi-ethnic and cosmopolitan nature of many Central African cities allows women to see that other women who eat certain tabooed animals are not stricken with negative repercussions. For example, one informant originally from Kisangani, now living in Kinshasa, whose mother would never eat turtles in deference to a traditional family restriction, testily declared after seeing a pregnant neighbour eat them who subsequently gave birth to a strong healthy baby: 'I tasted turtle flesh, liked it and now eat it when the spirit moves me. I don't need to believe the lies I was told as a child.'[47] Women openly condemn their fathers and ancestors for being greedy and manipulative: 'We know they just wanted to keep the most succulent meats for themselves.'[48] This evolution in food consumption, nevertheless, cannot mask the continuing low social status of women in the region, where discrimination prevails and domestic abuse is often seen as normal and acceptable. Despite this low status, which is the legacy of socially constructed gender roles and discriminatory laws, emancipation from food restrictions is emerging in step with timid economic empowerment. Central African women are important economic actors in both the formal and informal sectors, including the bushmeat commodity chain.

Eating the meat of wild animals, using their body parts and metaphorically associating with them are activities full of mystical power and symbolism. The range of this symbolism is extraordinary and extends from the rather trivial (a man needs to eat meat to be strong) to the remarkably esoteric (to eliminate an enemy, brush their footprints with an aardvark's tail, and the enemy and the prints will both disappear). Infants are given their first baths in water with chimp and gorilla bones to give them strength. 'When a chimp falls from a tree, does it break a leg?'[49] In his acclaimed satire of post-colonial African dictatorships, Ahmadou Kourouma replaces the real identities of Zairian president Mobutu, Ivorian president Houphouët-Boigny and Emperor Jean-Bédel Bokassa of the Central African Empire with their magically symbolic totems – the leopard, the crocodile and the hyena respectively. Wild animal symbolism is paramount in witchcraft beliefs and practices. Evans-Pritchard observed Azande initiation ceremonies that included the following litany: 'Your relatives are animals, your father is an elephant, your father's elder brother is a red pig, your wives are cane-rats, your mother is a bushbuck, your maternal uncles are duikers, your grandfather is a rhinoceros.'[50] In the African Great Lakes region, home to the Virunga volcano range, the Nyanga people traditionally held ceremonies to calm the volcano spirits. In a sacrificial incantation, a young girl to be sacrificed is compared to an antelope: 'a powerful spirit deserves offerings, we give him this young girl who sleeps in her grandfather's arms, as beautiful as a young antelope'.[51]

Although the language is politically insensitive by today's standards, observations about the primal relationship between animals and people made by one of the 20th-century's most influential social anthropologists, Bronisław Malinowski, is still culturally relevant in Central Africa – even though the description was inspired by research in the distant Trobriand Islands. The example points to shared beliefs of people in different parts of the world.

> By their general affinity with man – they move, utter sounds, manifest emotions, have bodies and faces like him – and by their superior powers – the birds fly in the open, the fishes swim under water, reptiles renew their skins and their life can disappear in the earth – by all this, the animal, the immediate link between man and nature, often his superior in strength, agility, and cunning, usually his indispensable quarry, assumes an exceptional place in the savage's view of the world.[52]

African history (and that of other continents) is replete with associations between lions and leopards, on one hand, and royalty and power, on the other. Leopards, according to Jan Vansina, are the 'quintessence of leadership'.[53] Julien Cosyn observed first-hand in the Belgian Congo that the position village elders occupied in the community depended on the number of leopards' teeth that hung around their necks.[54] Even where they have been extirpated, such as in the Central Kongo Province of the DRC, bridewealth gifts still include a cloth with a leopard motif. The cloth in this case has the symbolic value of the real hide. Most languages in Central Africa, moreover, have designated vocabularies for 'animals of leadership'.[55] In 2018 the Zimbabwe Electoral Commission banned the use of the lion and leopard (and other emblematic animals) in electoral campaigning, fearing that the power of the animal's symbolism could be instrumentalised through witchcraft for political gain.[56] The French expression 'Did you have lion for breakfast?' is a familiar question to someone who is exceptionally full of energy. To 'lionise' is an English word meaning to treat someone as an object of great interest or importance. The DRC's national football team is nicknamed the Leopards, Cameroon's the Indomitable Lions, Gabon's the Panthers. Simba (lion) is the name of a popular beer in DRC and other breweries have adopted animal symbolism: Ngok (crocodile) in the Republic of Congo and Tembo (elephant) in the DRC. On a more gruesome note, Emperor Bokassa is known to have fed his enemies to his pet lions and crocodiles kept in his private zoo in Bangui. Leopard-men secret societies – initiated men who are dressed in leopard skins – existed in West and Central Africa. Also known as *aniota*, they were organised warrior forces; and, in the case of the DRC, their 'activities were a way of maintaining local power relations, performing indigenous justice in secret and circumventing colonial government control'.[57]

These examples of animal symbolism provide a useful lens through which contemporary African political and cultural dynamics – and conservation ideology – can be analysed.[58] Zoomorphism (the psychological device of giving animal-like qualities to humans) and anthropomorphism (the attribution of human characteristics to non-human entities, as in Aesop's fables) have both been a part of the human imagination throughout history. In a scathing diatribe about how Europeans and Americans invented 'green colonialism' in Africa, Guillaume Blanc notes how conservationists attached greater importance and affection to wild animals than to Africa's human population.[59] He gives the example of Joy Adamson's famous autobiography, *Born free*, in which her pet lion has a name, Elsa, but the Africans in her narrative are nameless. That example from another epoch is perhaps not a fair representation of today's attitudes because the human factor is increasingly recognised by conservationists. Nevertheless, a somewhat similar story was told to me about gorillas in the DRC's Virunga National Park. 'When a baby gorilla is born, we know its father's and mother's names – and sometimes the names of its grandparents; its weight at birth is carefully recorded. When our babies are born, does anyone really give a damn?'[60] When Ndakasi, the mountain gorilla, famously posed for a selfie with her keeper in the Virunga National Park, the image went viral on social media.[61]

African proverbs draw heavily on the animal kingdom to account for social organisation, power relations and human nature. 'A piece of wood can float in a river for a hundred years but will never turn into a crocodile' or 'Rain beats the leopard's skin but it does not wash out its spots' are proverbs that convey the idea that no matter how hard one tries, it's impossible to change a person's character. 'Frogs can croak as loud as they want but that won't stop an elephant from drinking' is a blunt statement about how the weak can clamour as much as they want without bending the will of those in power. 'Don't bother complaining about the crocodile to the hippopotamus because they both live in the same murky water' is a reminder about the impunity and complicity of the powerful to the detriment of the common people. 'Don't tie up a goat in the vicinity of a leopard' can be interpreted as not tempting the devil or not inviting misfortune. The political battle between ex-DRC president Joseph Kabila and his successor, Félix Tshisekedi, is described in Kinshasa as powerful Kabila, the python, strangling vulnerable Tshisekedi, the antelope. Acting like an elephant is used to describe aggressive or pushy behaviour.

Beliefs such as those presented in Table 5.2 are deep-rooted and held at the 'tribe', clan, family or individual levels. The table presents a quick summary based on a few interviews with

Congolese colleagues. Other studies have gone into great detail about the symbolic use of wild animals. In the countries of Benin, Ghana, Nigeria and Sierra Leone, researchers identified 40 uses of pangolin scales alone, in addition to multiple uses of its other body parts. Traditional healers prescribe the use of scales for ailments ranging from sexually transmitted diseases to mental illness.[62] As these uses and beliefs are culturally and psychologically complex, one can't make tempting generalisations from them. What applies to a village in Gabon isn't relevant to one a short distance away. Beliefs in Cameroon may be incomprehensible to a Congolese. These kinds of beliefs are not endemically African, as comparable beliefs are held in other cultural environments. The meat of the houbara bustard, for example, a shy bird the size of a chicken, is sought after in the Middle East for its supposed aphrodisiac qualities.

Table 5.2: Symbolic importance of wild animals in the DRC

Characteristics	Animal	Usage
Perceived Health Attributes		
Reinforces sexual strength, desire and stamina	Civet, pangolin, grasscutter, Gambian pouched rat	As food recommended for men
	Elephant	Ground ivory mixed with water is considered an aphrodisiac
Assists childbirth	Lion	Rubbing the stomach of pregnant women with the water in which a lion hide was soaked assists delivery

Characteristics	Animal	Usage
Gives physical agility and strength	Blue duiker, baboon, chimpanzee, monkey, frog, Bosman's potto, lion, elephant, red river hog, hippopotamus, hyrax	As food recommended for pregnant women; and for bathing new-borns with their bones
	Lion	By smearing children with its excrement
	Buffalo	By rubbing the hide on the arms of new-borns
Gives children intelligence and agility	Monkey, blue duiker	By eating their brains
	Fish	By eating bones of the head
For skin-healing after burns	Pangolin	By applying powder made from ground scales
	Python	By applying fat
	Snail	By applying powder made from ground shell
For dressing wounds	Chimpanzee	By applying powder made from ground bones to heal wounds
For miscarriages	Pangolin	By inhaling the powder of dried scales to diminish the risk of miscarriage

BUSHMEAT

Characteristics	Animal	Usage
As contraception	Pangolin	Scales tied around a woman's waist serve as a contraceptive
	Turtle	String made from skin serves as a contraceptive
Poison, immunisation and cures	Crocodile	Dust of crocodile brain or pancreas is a lethal poison when added to a person's food
	Hyrax	A concoction made of excrement and water is an antidote for poisoning
	Aardvark	Hunters rub their bodies on the body of a dying aardvark, which secretes a protective smell
	Bees	Honey immunises against poison
Epilepsy	Lion	Rubbing dried excrement on the body cures epilepsy
	Monkey	Washing body with powder from dried bones cures epilepsy
	Turtle	Powder made of burnt shell mixed with water is a cure

THE CULTURE OF CONSUMPTION

Characteristics	Animal	Usage
Gout	Lion	Rubbing dried excrement on the body cures gout
Rheumatism	Lion	Powder made from dried paws is rubbed into painful joints
Whooping cough	Snail	Drinking the slime mixed with salt and water alleviates condition
Polyuria	Bat	Eating the liver offers relief
Cataracts and eyesight problems	Turtle	Sprinkling crushed shell dust in the eye offers a cure
Itching	Python	Rubbing fat on irritated skin relieves itching; fat rubbed on the anus relieves haemorrhoids
Social Regulation,* Magic and Witchcraft		
Magic spells	Turtle	During a trial, a guilty defendant keeps a bit of shell under his tongue or wears a bracelet made of shell so the judge will acquit him. Consuming a concoction of turtle bones makes a person invisible
	Lion	During a trial, a guilty defendant anoints himself with lion urine so as to be seen as powerful

BUSHMEAT

Characteristics	Animal	Usage
Social levelling	Aardvark	Sweeping a person's footprints with the tail will cause death
		Rubbing a person's photo or piece of clothing with an aardvark's tooth will cause death
	Leopard	Liver is administered as poison
	Porcupine	Dried bones or skin are used in ritual ceremonies to emasculate enemies
Invulnerability to snake bites	Python	Snakes can't attack someone who eats python flesh
Talisman against evil spirits	Hyrax	Nailing its skin at the entrance to the home wards off evil spirits
Protection	Leopard	Urine carried in a small flask protects one against other carnivorous animals
	Python	Applying python fat to the body keeps wild animals at bay
Good luck in trade	Gambian pouched rat	Head and tail are used in ritual ceremonies

Characteristics	Animal	Usage
Pronouncement of death and malediction	Owl	If an owl lands on the roof of the house, a family member will die; eating an owl will bring a curse – its eyes are like those of witches
Representations of Power		
Symbols of power	Leopard	Ornamental display of skin and teeth for chiefs
	Cow	Ornamental display of tail
	Parrot	Ornamental display of feathers for chiefs
	Pangolin	Ornamental display of scales for chiefs
	Elephant	Ornamental display of tusks for chiefs

* Domestic animals such as goats, cattle and chickens also serve important social roles in the form of bridewealth and in-kind fines.

Source: Interviews with Daniel Mpoyi Mpoyi (Kisangani); Krossy Mavakala (Kinshasa); Olivier Igugu (Bukavu); Noël Kabuyaya (Kinshasa).

While some of these uses and beliefs may appear far-fetched, there are multiple examples from the field of ethno-ecology that are well founded. They help explain why there is not always a clear cognitive explanation or linkage between consuming the flesh of a wild animal for food and ingesting it for its perceived symbolic appeal. This may have been what Elias Canetti had in mind when he asserted that 'everything that is eaten is the food of power'.[63]

Anthony Rose was an early proponent of the need to tackle wildlife conservation challenges with socio-cultural research, emphasising that 'the complexity of rural African values for wildlife comes from a robust and varied history infused and influenced by myths, rituals, taboos, and totems'.[64] Similar calls were voiced from Brazil and Colombia.[65] While it is often assumed that education and literacy may help influence the advancement of science and Western-style rationality in general – and not only in relation to bushmeat and conservation – anthropological research about witchcraft in Nigeria has disproved that assumption.[66] It showed that witchcraft beliefs remained prevalent even among educated Nigerians. Similarly, the novelist Ahmadou Kourouma mockingly describes the metamorphosis of a man into a whirlwind and back into human form, offering two explanations: one, a mysterious African witchcraft interpretation and, two, the 'childish White man's need for rationality to understand things'.[67] This is a good reminder of the fundamentally hybrid way in which one has to account for people's relationships with wild animals, which combines both rational and non-rational perceptions. What's perfectly logical in one cultural group can be far beyond the comprehension of others.

Conclusion

This chapter provides insight and analysis into the question of why people in Central Africa eat bushmeat. It's a complex question because there is no single or dominant reason. On the contrary, the motivations are a jumble of collective and personal realities, beliefs and emotions such as the power of tradition, taste, availability, cost and lack of alternatives. This chapter has also shown the impact of rapidly evolving socio-cultural and socio-economic dynamics on motivation. Acculturation, induced by – and coinciding with – economic development, growing exposure to Western values, urbanisation, and Christianity and education, dilutes the power of these motivations. While they still persist, they are less and less respected, especially in urban Central Africa. Examining these motivations by means of an anthropological analysis provides a fundamental contribution to understanding people's relations with wild animals and, consequently, rural, urban and international bushmeat consumption.

6

THE BUSHMEAT ECONOMY

Bushmeat is money

Other chapters in this book focus on bushmeat as food for the heart, mind and soul just as much as food for the stomach. This chapter looks at another facet: bushmeat as money. Bushmeat is cash for the hunter, transporter, wholesaler, retailer and restaurateur. It's graft for corrupt park rangers, police posted at checkpoints, and airport staff. 'Bushmeat is a large but largely invisible contributor to the economies of West and Central African countries.'[1] In other words, as the bushmeat trade is informal, often hidden and unreported, it doesn't contribute to national taxable resources. Bushmeat itself is visible all over the landscape; its economic, financial and fiscal value, however, is largely 'invisible'. Bushmeat is big business with a tentacular reach and is also one dimension of the illegal wildlife trade, which is 'a major transnational organised crime, which generates billions of criminal proceeds each year'.[2] International financial crime-prevention agencies are particularly worried about how the illegal wildlife trade (particularly in rhino horn, ivory, pangolin scales and pets) feeds into criminal money-laundering networks. After drugs, wildlife is the black market's most profitable resource.[3]

As there is only scant hard data available, we do not know much about the monetary value of the regional bushmeat trade.[4] It's a murky business of dependent and independent economic relationships with multiple actors and dozens of species with highly variable prices. These characteristics contribute to the data problem. Some local studies do, however, give anecdotal information about earnings per actor along the commodity chain. Because most research is conducted by conservation biologists as opposed to social scientists or economists, our understanding of the value chain is limited. Most of these conservation biologists work and publish in English and tend not to make sufficient use of published and unpublished sources in French, which is another part of the data gap. Besides being exacerbated by deficiencies in across-the-board data collection and reporting in Central Africa, this information gap can also be explained by the fact that scrutiny of the bushmeat economy falls essentially under the purview of international conservation NGOs (and wildlife crime agencies) more so than that of national governments, which ostensibly do not view the issue as a priority or even a problem. Economic, political and military elites are involved in bushmeat trade networks, which also accounts for why governments are reluctant to make the bushmeat economy a visible policy priority. For reasons of identifying sources of taxable revenues, a case could be made that governments should be more interested in formalising the trade to take it out of the realm of the invisible. While such formalisation is a good idea because it could 'contribute to economic growth in countries where there are few other options',[5] implementation challenges and the political implications of doing so make it improbable.

The bushmeat economy has changed considerably over the past few decades as it has adapted to urban dynamics, political considerations, economic opportunities, conservation concerns and consumer preferences. Karl Polanyi's research on embedded versus disembedded economies helps put the subsistence–commercial shift into perspective.[6] Subsistence hunting with all its social, spiritual, nutritional and ecological interactions can be considered as embedded, providing benefits to local populations. Commercial hunting, conversely, being disconnected from these interactions, is disembedded and disproportionately benefits outside traders. Profit margins tend to increase all along the commodity chain from actor to actor, a situation common for other products as well.

Pioneering research into bushmeat value chains carried out in Nigeria in the early 1980s revealed the disproportionate profits earned by traders compared with hunters[7] – an ongoing economic pattern and a reality that is widespread in any market that involves intermediaries. When the population was predominantly rural, bushmeat was mainly a matter of family subsistence. It was consumed primarily in hunters' households – although it was sometimes sold, bartered or gifted. Before money circulated in Central Africa, it even served as a medium of exchange, for example for the payment of bridewealth. The Mongo people of the central Congo Basin have the expression *nyama wae liatsi*, which translates as 'meat is wealth'. Voices from Cameroon echo this relationship: *'la viande c'est l'argent'* (meat is money).[8] These examples from different societies confirm trends and patterns.

The economic downturn in Cameroon in the 1980s was a watershed, as meat and money became synonymous.[9] The devaluation of the CFA franc, the collapse of coffee and cocoa prices on the world market, drops in the salaried employment sectors, and the World Bank's structural adjustment programmes were all factors converging into a suite of regional economic crises. The real and perceived needs associated with well-being, Western consumer values and the seemingly irreversible pull of modernity's fashion and gadgets translated into exploitation of the most readily accessible sources of cash – bushmeat, timber and artisanally extracted minerals. Increased industrial logging also turned meat into money, as supply networks spontaneously emerged around camps which needed to feed their workers. Importing tinned sardines and frozen chicken is an artificial and only partial response to the environmental and social safeguards that logging companies are required to respect.[10] Logging lorries transporting timber to port also transport bushmeat.[11] These sets of problems put tremendous pressure on wildlife populations as bushmeat became increasingly commoditised. These problems also indicate the links between global economic dynamics and the multi-layered intricacies of the bushmeat economy with its bevy of actors.

Open access resources

At the local and macro levels, economic crisis – and particularly unemployment – incites people to fall back on natural resources to earn money. This has negative environmental consequences when resources are 'open access', a political economy term for resources that are perceived by communities as being owned by everyone, through customary inheritance for example, or being controlled by no one. Resources may theoretically be the property of the state but in practice there are often no clear consensual or enforceable systems, rules or regulatory sets of constraints. Access to resources can therefore be appropriated forcefully by well-connected professional commercial networks just as it can be negotiated with local chiefs or elites. The situation described two decades ago still has currency: 'Despite existing legislation, wildlife is almost invariably treated as a *de facto* open access resource and as such there is very little hope for a sustainable bushmeat trade.'[12] The hybrid land-tenure systems in Congo Basin countries, characterised by ambiguous arrangements between state and traditional leaders, are not conducive to diminishing the pressure on open access resources such as bushmeat.

The forest is perceived as a giant pantry (*garde-manger*) and pharmacy. Both terms frequently come up in conversations. Food, fuelwood, building and craft materials, trees for carving dugout canoes, medicinal plants and other resources can be found in the forest. They are free of charge (but of course not free from labour), unlike in towns and cities, where a price is attached to all of these vital resources. As these resources are plundered according to the logic that they belong to no one and to everyone, they become an ill-fated example of what has become known as the 'tragedy of the commons'. Garrett Hardin coined the term in his seminal but controversial article of the same title. 'Ruin is the destination toward which all men rush, each pursuing his own best interest in a society that believes in the freedom of the commons. Freedom in a commons brings ruin to all.'[13] This seems an appropriate summary of the plunder of bushmeat in Central Africa. The following passage about bushmeat as an open access resource is a relevant example that supports Hardin's judgement.

> The extraction timeline of an open access resource like bushmeat in a particular forest can be broken down into three broad time periods. In the first period, one of constant returns, the numbers of hunters are low and wildlife populations relatively high. Each additional hunter who enters the forest is able to kill as much bushmeat as he can without affecting the amount of bushmeat other hunters in the area catch. In the second period, one of diminishing returns, the growing number of hunters begins to reach the limits imposed by the total amount of wildlife. While each additional hunter adds to the total amount of bushmeat caught, other hunters see their individual take decrease with every new hunter. In the third period, one of absolute diminishing returns, too many hunters are chasing a limited number of wildlife.

Animals are being killed off faster than they can reproduce, overhunting is occurring, and each new hunter only adds to this overhunting. Because of this, the total amount of wildlife caught actually decreases with each new hunter who enters the trade.[14]

Although there are other examples – such as artisanal mining – the dynamics of charcoal production and trade are similar to those of the bushmeat trade. The comparison is relevant here because it highlights the broader political economy context, including the perception of open access, the development of trade networks, ease of entry into the sector, and the presence of multiple actors along the commodity chain. Like the bushmeat trade, the charcoal business demonstrates how people seize opportunities in the fend-for-yourself informal economy to adapt to situations when public services are inadequate. Well-organised charcoal networks develop to create the link between producers (often young urban unemployed men), transporters, wholesalers, retailers and consumers. There are therefore a multitude of stages and actors involved in the charcoal commodity chain. Entry costs for producers are low (tools are rudimentary) and no particular technical *savoir faire* is required. The pre-production step consists in negotiating access to a forest with a village chief. Production steps involve felling the trees and cutting them up into the right-size chunks, then stacking and blanketing them with earth before setting them on fire to start carbonisation. The mound of charcoal-covered earth is then uncovered and the charcoal is bagged once it has cooled off. The complicated process of getting it to consumers follows; again, this involves every imaginable type of transporter, intermediary and government parasite. Given economic hard times, micro-retail is common – again, as with bushmeat. As few families have the wherewithal to purchase an entire bag of charcoal, it is micro-retailed in neighbourhood markets in very small quantities – even as little as a single cooking portion. Another link between charcoal and bushmeat is camouflage: traders and transporters conceal bushmeat in bags of charcoal to keep it hidden from park rangers, police or other security agents along the forest-to-market circuit.

Prices, earnings and costs

Another point of comparison is the approximate price increase from hunting or production area to end user. By the time a bag of charcoal produced in DRC's Kongo Central Province reaches the market in Kinshasa 350 kilometres away, the price is multiplied by seven (from 5,000 Congolese francs to at least 35,000). Research conducted in Cameroon's capital, Yaoundé, in 1996–97 revealed price spreads of between one to four for large animals (large duikers and buffalo) and one to eight for small species (porcupines, grasscutters and pangolins).[15] While prices rise significantly from village to large city, they rise only slightly from village to small town, as documented in DRC's Sankuru Province.[16]

Table 6.1 offers a spot-check of these price increases but it is no more than a glimpse of the situation. Major surveys would need to be conducted to calculate the amounts of money actually earned; this would require massive investment in terms of funding and research finesse. Having an idea of profits and costs along the commodity chain is important because, from a policy perspective, it could be helpful in targeting the incentives per category of actor for behaviour change or law-enforcement efforts.

Mbandaka in the DRC is a large city surrounded by forest and is a trade hub for meat coming from its hinterland. As it lies on the Congo River, meat is transported from there by boat to Kinshasa's ports and then dispatched to urban markets. Table 6.1 indicates an incomplete price increment because it does not take into account the prices paid to hunters before reaching the intermediary markets of Mbandaka. It is sufficient to show, nevertheless, the significant price increases along the chain of transactions.

Table 6.1: Approximate prices and price increments from
Mbandaka to Kinshasa market (in Congolese francs*)

Species	Mbandaka price	Kinshasa price (Libongo port)	Kinshasa price, urban market – Simba Zigida	Price increase, Mbandaka–Kinshasa
Monkey (whole, smoked)	10,000	25,000	35,000	3.5
Bush pig (smoked, sold in parts)	100,000	150,000	220,000	2.2
Turtle (live)	8,000	25,000	40,000	5.0
Small duiker (whole, smoked)	10,000	25,000	35,000	3.5
Buffalo (smoked, sold in parts)	220,000	300,000	500,000	2.3
Dwarf crocodile (live)	50,000	85,000	120,000	2.4

*At the time US$1 was worth approximately 2,000 Congolese francs.

Source: Interviews and market inquiries by Noël Kabuyaya, Kinshasa, September 2020.

Even though hunting provides relatively significant earnings to hunters,[17] it is not an economically efficient source of revenue given the investment in time and the risks involved.[18] Among all the actors along the bushmeat commodity chain, hunters are the lowest earners in terms of value added. Findings from Cameroon put local hunters' profit margin at around 22%.[19] This is comparable to value-added shares in the DRC farming produce chain for small-scale farmers.[20] Although the costs for transporters and traders are higher, they earn proportionately more than hunters. As bushmeat reaches towns and cities, the profits for traders increase. 'The revenues of hunters are minimal in this process, while traders – with profits growing as the bushmeat is passed along the supply chain – achieve substantial profit margins.'[21] There is, however, a need to nuance these assumptions because results from some research do not always correspond with the findings of others. The following observation about hunter and trader benefits from Equatorial Guinea is a case in point. 'Trade with hunters in isolated locations maximized trader profits, whereas trade with hunters close to markets maximized hunter profits.'[22] This example again reinforces the assumption that proximity to urban markets is a cost factor and influences profitability. That these examples do not follow the same economic patterns confirms the need to look at every transaction on a case-by-case basis.

Each category of actor outlined in Table 6.2 has widely varying sets of profits, indirect costs and opportunity costs. Opportunity costs are the missed benefits that could have been earned from an option not chosen, which is relevant here once more in the context of policy design for alternative economic activities. The main common denominator between all these actors is economic opportunism, a reality that characterises trade for most other resources all over the globe. Involvement in the bushmeat trade is frequently an activity based 'quite simply on the realm of what's possible'.[23] The observation is significant because it reinforces the interpretation of bushmeat as an open access resource subject to plunder in complacent legal environments. While Table 6.2 provides a reasonably comprehensive list of actors, it's necessary to emphasise the fuzzy boundaries between categories.[24]

Table 6.2: Actors and costs along the bushmeat commodity chain

Actors	Direct costs	Indirect and opportunity costs	Comments
1. Hunters			
1.1 Part–time hunters who eat for subsistence and sell for cash (primarily men but women lay snares in their fields)	Shotguns, cartridges, gunpowder and wire snares Food and camping equipment for prolonged hunting excursions Transportation of bushmeat to villages/roads/rivers	Sharing and gifting (for example, with village chiefs or other people who grant access to the hunting zone) Bribes to park rangers, Environment Ministry officials, police and soldiers to avoid hassles or having meat confiscated	Part–time hunters with mixed-livelihood activities – sometimes referred to as farmer-hunters – hunt in proximity to their fields to capitalise on time spent in the farm–forest mosaic and to keep predators away from their plots. Most part–time village hunters engage in farming (and fishing) activities and, depending on the hunting and agricultural calendars, shift from one activity to the other.

Actors	Direct costs	Indirect and opportunity costs	Comments
1.2 Professional commercial hunters (mostly men operating full-time)	Shotguns, cartridges and gunpowder Hunting permits (an official requirement rarely respected) Firearm maintenance material Food and camping equipment for prolonged hunting excursions Meat or cash paid to porters	'Courtesy' fees paid to village chiefs Gifts or fees for trackers Bribes to park rangers, Environment Ministry officials, police and soldiers to avoid hassles or having meat confiscated	Politically well-connected commercial hunters can avoid some indirect fees, but police and soldiers usually demand either meat or cash (whether or not hunters have their permits) and chiefs expect gifts. Commercial hunting has a negative impact on village nutrition because, instead of consuming meat themselves, hunters prefer selling or trading it, breaking with traditional food consumption patterns.

Actors	Direct costs	Indirect and opportunity costs	Comments
2. Village traders			
2.1. Village traders (mainly men, part-time and full-time)	Purchase of bushmeat or goods to trade for meat	Gifts for facilitation and information	Generally young men, they supply urban-based networks and have good relations with hunters and other people in villages who can facilitate trade.
	Purchase of salt for curing (which is rare because smoking is the primary way of preserving meat)	Bribes to park rangers, Environment Ministry officials, police and soldiers to avoid hassles or having meat confiscated	Village traders facilitate purchase and sale of bushmeat when urban traders go to rural areas.
	Fees paid to artisans who make the wooden splints for splaying carcasses	Spoilage due to deterioration*	Mobile phone communication is crucial for the bushmeat trade and for arranging prices, credit and payment.
			Good relations at the village level also help monitor the whereabouts of rangers and other officials.

Actors	Direct costs	Indirect and opportunity costs	Comments
3. Transporters			
3.1 Porters (men, part–time)	Camping equipment Drugs and alcohol to boost energies (this is physically exhausting labour)	Risks (resulting from accidents or confiscation, for example)	Porters are used by professional commercial hunters to carry meat from the forest to a market or transport node.
3.2 Bicycle porters (men, part–time)	Cost and maintenance of bicycle		Motorcycles are increasingly replacing bicycles, even in rural areas.
3.3 Motorcycle porters (mostly men, part–time)	Cost of motorcycle; petrol and maintenance	Formal and informal road taxes	There has been a rapid increase in the availability of cheap motorcycles made in China and India throughout Central Africa in the past two decades. Motorcycles facilitate the transport of bushmeat to market.

Actors	Direct costs	Indirect and opportunity costs	Comments
3.4 Taxi drivers, private SUV owners, pick-up truck and lorry drivers, boat, railway and aeroplane transporters (mostly men, part–time)	Transport fees Maintenance, repairs and petrol	Bribes to park rangers, Environment Ministry officials, police, soldiers and other authorities to avoid hassles or having meat confiscated Spoilage due to deterioration	Transporting bushmeat by these means is complementary to transporting other goods and people. Rail was previously the major means of transporting bushmeat to Yaoundé,[1] today it is road; boat is the main means into Kinshasa.[2] Bribes can be cash or meat.
4. Wholesalers, retailers and other traders			
4.1 Wholesalers (both men and women, mostly full-time)	Paying hunters and buying their guns and cartridges Extending credit and cash advances	Gifts for political patronage Bribes to park rangers, Environment Ministry officials, police, soldiers	These are trade intermediaries with the relations and financial means to buy and sell in large quantities. They are one of the main interface categories between the forest and urban consumers.

Actors	Direct costs	Indirect and opportunity costs	Comments
	Transport Storage and refrigeration Surveillance to avoid theft Phone credit	and other authorities to avoid hassles or having meat confiscated. Spoilage due to deterioration	There can be large differences in volumes traded depending on where the wholesaler fits along the trade chain. Bribes can be made in cash or meat. The ability to communicate by phone depends on the presence of mobile phone antennae; large tracts of forest are not covered by a provider.
4.2 Retailers (mainly women market sellers, full–time)	Purchase of stock Market taxes Storage Surveillance	Raids by law–enforcement agents Confiscation of stock Bribes to sanitation officials	These market sellers tend to buy in relatively large quantities and sell in small quantities according to their clients' purchasing power. Theirs is a competitive

Actors	Direct costs	Indirect and opportunity costs	Comments
		Spoilage due to deterioration	activity with widely variable profit margins. 52% of Brazzaville market retailers are female,[3] as are 82% in Yaoundé;[4] 75% of Kinshasa retailers are female; 60% of both female and male retailers completed high school.[5]
4.3 Hunters who sell directly in towns (men)	Transportation Lodging Storage fees	Gifts to family members Bribes Spoilage due to deterioration	Hunters sometimes go to town to sell their game directly to avoid fees for intermediaries and to combine with family visits or administrative business.

Actors	Direct costs	Indirect and opportunity costs	Comments
5. Restaurant owners/managers			
5.1 Small informal restaurants (mainly women, full-time)	Purchase of stock Formal taxes Paying staff Rent	Informal taxes paid to avoid hassles Spoilage due to deterioration	Many people who eat bushmeat in Central Africa opt for this category of eatery (as described in the following chapter). Often catering to a faithful clientele and extending credit, they generally have limited seating and rather basic amenities. While some specialise in bushmeat, others serve other national dishes too.
5.2 Expensive formal restaurants (both men and women, full-time)	Purchase of stock Formal taxes Paying staff Rent	Informal taxes to sanitation and other officials Spoilage due to deterioration	Bushmeat can be found on the menus of formal up-scale restaurants along with other choices, some serving luxury species (including endangered species) and prestige parts (such as the head or internal organs).

Actors	Direct costs	Indirect and opportunity costs	Comments
6. Brokers	Purchase of stock Communication costs	Establishing and maintaining relations in villages and towns Spoilage due to deterioration	Workspace can be virtual. Brokers are part of a relatively new category of bushmeat traders; they liaise with buyers and sellers according to specific individual requests and supply opportunities. Bushmeat can be delivered directly to buyers to avoid storage costs as a just-in-time stock management strategy that depends on a well-developed network of suppliers and clients. Brokers can avoid law enforcement and circumvent bans.

Actors	Direct costs	Indirect and opportunity costs	Comments
7. 'Invisible' actors	–	Spoilage due to deterioration	Bushmeat arrives in the urban pot through channels difficult to identify – and even more difficult to quantify. One assessment estimates that 30% to 50% falls in this category, ascribing it to family networks.[6]

* Spoilage is estimated at 10% of operational costs (Gore et al. 2021: 9).

Sources: Author's research and 1. Edderai and Dame 2006: 474; 2. Pembela Ekwamba 2015–16: 40; 3. Mbete et al. 2011: 206; 4. Edderai and Dame 2006: 472; 5. Pembela Ekwamba 2015–16: 22; 6. Fargeot 2004: 35.

A person can be a hunter and trader at the same time, for example, or a woman who runs a bushmeat restaurant may also be a bushmeat retailer or wholesaler.

The complexity of the trade as revealed by Table 6.2 also points to the difficulties in estimating the value of bushmeat throughout the region. Although they have suggested methods to calculate its financial and economic value, Guillaume Lescuyer and Robert Nasi are cautious about their findings: 'Given the complexity, heterogeneity and informality of the bushmeat sector, it is not possible to quantify precisely the benefits of this activity.'[25] One approach they use defines the structure of the commodity chain (a market chain analysis, which looks at the range of activities and actors) and the other, a cost-benefit analysis of hunting and trade (a calculation of the costs an actor needs to incur to receive financial gain).

Supply and demand drivers

Do hunters hunt and provide urban consumers with meat because consumers want it and are willing to pay for it? Or do consumers purchase and eat bushmeat because it is available and affordable? Is urban bushmeat consumption, in other words, supply- or demand-driven? Finding responses to this extremely complex question can contribute to the broader understanding of urban bushmeat consumption and more specifically to the design of conservation policies.[26] The question is important even though hunters will continue to hunt wildlife whether it feeds into commercial networks or not. A balanced position, based upon a complicated set of variables, would be to accept that there is no definitive answer for the cities in Central Africa because they present very different characteristics. Market dynamics are crucial but they cannot explain everything. Urban consumption is not either supply- or demand-driven but both supply- and demand-driven – it's a 'mixed bag', meaning that the drivers are *both* supply and demand.[27] This is not unique to the bushmeat trade because most economic systems of exchange entail dynamic interactions between supply and demand. It would be imprudent to generalise between a city of 1 million inhabitants with mid-level development indicators, such as Libreville, and a city of 17 million poor individuals, like Kinshasa. The time factor is another important variable because supply and demand is dynamic. Today's patterns in Central African cities are different from those of twenty years ago and may be unrecognisable twenty years from now. Table 6.3 gives an indication of today's main drivers influencing supply and demand (but without trying to rank them in order of importance).

Table 6.3: Key variables influencing supply and demand consumption drivers

Purchasing power of a city's residents
Local and national development levels
Transportation and mobility
Employment options
Demographics and population size
Food choices and preferences
Perceptions of modernity and tradition
Access to and availability of alternatives
Proximity and access to hunting zones (such as distance and transportation options)
Legal framework and law enforcement

Source: Author's research synthesis.

The predominant argument that urban consumption is supply-driven is based on the importance to local economies of selling bushmeat, a reality repeated throughout bushmeat literature.[28] In places where cash is hard to come by, bushmeat hunting is perceived as a logical, necessary and legitimate cash-earning activity. Bushmeat hunting and trade form a viable economic option because demand does exist. Hunters continue to supply urban markets even when prices fall in the cities. Legislation, law enforcement, exclusion from protected areas, and environmental education are policy options being tested to try to curb supply, but these efforts seem disconnected from the demand side of the equation. Direct compensation to hunters according to the Payments for Ecosystem Services strategy[29] is another strategy in the making. The (largely unsuccessful) promotion of wealth creation through alternative livelihood projects at the village level has likewise been advocated by national governments, donors and conservation partners as efforts to disrupt supply lines. Some very modest progress has been made in these areas but they are far from the scale needed to have a meaningful impact. Even if some hunters decide to put aside their snares and shotguns, others will replace them.

Conversely, if consumption is demand-driven, then other responses would need to be put in place, such as taxing bushmeat sales or campaigning to encourage urban consumers to shift their food habits. Such responses would involve environmental messaging and social marketing. People's potential receptiveness, however, is largely unknown. One would also need to provide urban consumers with alternative and affordable animal protein sources that they find palatable – again on a massive scale.

Supporting the production of domestic meat (mainly poultry, pork and beef) is a policy strategy that theoretically could contribute to the reduction of bushmeat consumption. Increases in domestic meat production have been sustained in the past two decades (notably in the Republic of Congo), but serious challenges remain. These increases are not keeping up with the demand resulting from demographic growth. Likewise, local production cannot compete in terms of price with cheap, subsidised meat imports from Europe, the US and Brazil – and price strongly influences consumer choices. National budget allocations to the agriculture sector – of which domestic meat production is a part – are extremely low in all the Congo Basin countries. In the DRC for example, the national budget for agriculture is less than 1%. This is an insignificant amount considering that the entire annual budget has been hovering at around US$5 billion over the past decade. The little money that is available in this package is largely spent on salaries in Kinshasa, with minimal trickle-down into the field. The vast majority of state-employed agronomists and veterinarians work in Kinshasa or in the provincial capitals. Despite – or, paradoxically, perhaps because of – the fact that most Congolese are subsistence farmers, the food production sector is far from being a priority for key decision-makers.[30]

Central Africa has an expansive lake and river network which was once teeming with fish but is increasingly depleted owing to overfishing. Fish is a staple which is not only rich in proteins but widely appreciated by people too. Fish farming could, therefore, be a meaningful contribution to food security. It is not a particularly complex enterprise but it does depend upon the right blend of biological, economic and engineering knowledge. Intensive or semi-intensive hatcheries are necessary to produce fry and manage fingerlings – and these require a constant source of electricity. Specialised feed mills need to be maintained because the volume and quality of the fish depend on the quality of feed. Farmers need coaching in how to maintain their ponds and stock, to avoid the degeneration of strains of cultivated species, to get the right balance of fish densities per cubic metre of water, and to understand appropriate drainage techniques. This set of conditions helps explain why fish farming has not developed extensively in Central Africa. The fundamental prerequisites include significant financial investment, training, infrastructure and political will. Production of chicken and pork exists in the region but on a limited scale; the ecology of the Central African rainforest hampers significant development of cattle ranching. Disease-transmitting tsetse flies are a serious barrier to cattle breeding in much of sub-Saharan Africa because they are the biological vectors of trypanosomes which cause animal trypanosomiasis – in addition to human sleeping sickness. Large-scale cattle breeding could diminish reliance on bushmeat consumption but would usher in other devastating ecological imbalances. In South and Central America, livestock production is the predominant driver of deforestation.[31] These challenges help explain why bushmeat hunting and trade continue to flourish.

Farm raising of some game species could also theoretically contribute to satisfying demand. Technically, game breeding is quite possible from a veterinary perspective and has been carried out for some preferred species such as porcupine and cane rat.[32] On the South African veld, entrepreneurs have proved that game farming of, for example, eland, crocodile, zebra and ostrich is technically possible and financially sustainable. The challenges in Central Africa, however, remain complicated. There are no examples of industrial-scale game farming because forest productivity is not the same as savannah productivity, and, as a household economic or subsistence activity, the idea of expending energy to gather fodder for an animal in a pen or, worse, buying food is perceived as burdensome – and, in many cases, absurd. One of the inherent attractions of ingesting the flesh of wild animals is that these animals roam the forest and eat naturally. Consumers crave bushmeat precisely because it is wild – not farmed.[33]

A feasibility study of the socio-economic viability of duck breeding in Kinshasa revealed numerous myths, highlighting the need to combine successful breeding techniques with cultural acceptability.[34] Ducks are perceived as dirty and their eggs unhealthy to eat; women claim they do not like to prepare them because if they talk while plucking them, the feathers will grow back; and if submerged in a pond, they might metamorphose into snakes. Despite these beliefs, our survey also found that most people would not hesitate to eat duck meat if the price was right and if it was cooked in a way that was acceptable. This kind of contradiction exists for other creatures too: snakes are perceived as dangerous and repulsive, but many Central Africans love the taste and texture of their flesh. Efforts to promote small-scale livestock breeding to increase the supply of alternatives to bushmeat are confronted by the complexity of food choices, which force people to pragmatically balance perceptions about taste, quality and beliefs with price.

Price is a complicated variable, raising the question of the extent to which cost determines consumer choices. A key issue in this context is price elasticity, or the degree to which the desire for something changes as its price changes. Better understanding of the costs of hunting and trading, and the sales price of bushmeat, could have useful implications for policy design. Putting pressure on actors along the commodity chain could influence supply costs. Evidence from one area, however, does not necessarily apply elsewhere, showing that the theory and reality are more complicated. Some consumers tend to want things less as they become more expensive, but for some things their desire can stay the same, even with a big price increase. As bushmeat prices rise in the urban market, it could be assumed that bushmeat becomes a luxury food for people with available cash, instead of a more commonplace dietary staple. Geography is a related variable that influences consumer behaviour because

'As the price of bushmeat rises with its movement across the rural to urban gradient, the characteristics of the consumer change as well. Thus, the "poor" person's meat in the country becomes the "rich" person's meat in the city.'[35]

The reasons why bushmeat is eaten are therefore ambiguous and contradictory. Some people consume certain species or parts of wild animals because they are cheaper and available; others say they crave bushmeat because it is rare and expensive – and sometimes because it is associated with prestige or even aspirational spending. Vanity is a relevant factor: some middle-aged men unabashedly say they like to eat bushmeat in public places just to show off their ability to do so. That example corresponds to the attraction of Veblen goods.[36] In economic theory, these are luxury products that increase in demand as their price goes up – like champagne or Ferraris. Part of the demand for them comes from the prestige that the exclusively high price gives to a conspicuous consumer.

In his analysis of food consumption in France, Pierre Bourdieu identified an important distinction in food choice that has clear resonance in Central Africa – the one between the 'taste of liberty' (denoting luxury) and 'the taste of necessity' (the need for sustenance).[37] A rich man in Brazzaville may be motivated to eat a baby chimpanzee as a luxury food – 'the taste of liberty' – while a poor villager in rural Central African Republic will eat a duiker out of necessity. A West African proverb gives some nuance to this distinction: 'If a rich man eats a chameleon it's because it's healthy to do so; if a poor man eats one, it's because he's a glutton.' The proverb is curious because it could make social sense by being read backwards. The taste of necessity was expressed to me by one Congolese informant who lamented, 'We are not free to choose what we eat – we have to eat what's available.'[38] That lament was sparked by a discussion about the increasing scarcity of wildlife, which is sometimes believed to be a sign of the end of the world. It also reinforces one of the main arguments in Carolyn Steel's account of the historical intertwining of the growth of cities and access to food: 'Whether or not we are vegetarians by choice, we are omnivores by nature, and meat, quite simply, is the most privileged food we can eat.' Aside from some religious reasons, she continues, 'most humans who have forgone meat in the past have done so mainly due to lack of opportunity'.[39] The reasons stirring an elderly man in a poor Kinshasa neighbourhood to sit down alone to a dish of smoked porcupine stew with cassava in a makeshift restaurant are likely to be quite different from those of a young affluent woman in Libreville who is sharing a meal of fresh monkey with family and friends. A park ranger, who would presumably be respectful of rules, needled me by pointing out that 'in Europe you embellish your cities with ponds full of ducks. We would sneak to those ponds at night to devour those ducks.'[40]

The cost of bushmeat and its availability are frequently cited as reasons to explain why people buy it or not. In Bangui, Central African Republic, for example, 'urban consumers are sensitive to prices and consequently choose the most affordable meat on the market'.[41] The same study found that bushmeat consumption increased with wealth.[42] Likewise, 'economic factors were important determinants of meat consumption among Gabonese urban households'.[43] That price matters was also found in another Gabon study: 'price and income have significant roles in determining the level of bushmeat, fish, chicken, and beef'.[44] The pattern does not apply only to Central Africa, but has been observed in Central and South America as well.[45]

Conclusion

Twenty years ago John Robinson and Elizabeth Bennett raised a profoundly important question: 'Will alleviating poverty solve the bushmeat crisis?' Their research was pioneering and their response was clairvoyant: 'Experience from Africa and Asia has shown that as wealth increases so does the demand for wildlife; the expanding wildlife markets in towns and cities from Libreville and Brazzaville to Bangkok, Jakarta and Shanghai epitomize this'.[46] Their observation was supported by research carried out in Gabon: 'successful development assistance efforts to alleviate rural poverty may have adverse effects on the conservation of wildlife species most threatened by bushmeat hunting' because 'a small increase in the wealth of poor, rural families may result in a correspondingly large increase in the consumption of wildlife'.[47] Increases in wealth, in addition to accelerating consumption, can also 'extend the scale and efficiency of wildlife harvest'.[48] These pieces of evidence are not entirely convincing, however, because in some cases increases in household budgets can coincide with shifts in food consumption patterns. There is 'strong evidence' from Madagascar that 'poverty is the principal driver of protected species consumption'.[49] This divergence from patterns in Central Africa may be attributed to the low status of bushmeat in Madagascar compared with domestic meat. These contrasting situations highlight the difficulty in identifying causal relationships between wealth and bushmeat consumption. Again, there is no one-size-fits-all answer to these complex issues, which are influenced by a jumble of cultural, economic, social, ecological and political realities.

This chapter on the economic dimensions of bushmeat hunting, trade and consumption reveals a situation of extreme complexity, one characterised by ambiguity, unequal power relations, and seemingly random and even contradictory realities. While it is obvious that bushmeat is an important economic resource to a host of actors in Central Africa, there are big gaps in our understanding. There has been insufficient research carried out into the monetary value of the regional bushmeat trade; there are no clear answers to the supply or demand debate from the village to the regional levels; costs and profits along the bushmeat value chain are unclear; ownership of the resource depends on who is being asked; and there are incongruities between subsistence and prestige motivations for consumption. This chapter has helped clarify these issues, while also serving as a reminder that far more robust research into the bushmeat economy is needed. Improved understanding of these different aspects of the bushmeat economy is indeed necessary, but will not provide complete answers. While we should not underestimate the economic drivers of bushmeat hunting, trade and consumption, we should not overestimate them either. This, again, is one of this book's main arguments, reinforcing my opinion that we need to look at the bushmeat economy through a holistic lens.

7

EATING OUT IN KINSHASA

Urban access to food

To begin to understand the culture and economy of urban bushmeat consumption in Central Africa, we need to examine the broader context of people's attitudes and practices with respect to food in general – how in fact they manage to feed themselves. We also need to take into account the vastly diverging levels of people's purchasing power resulting from a highly stratified class system. Much of the information in this chapter comes from Kinshasa, the region's largest city by far, but patterns and trends there are to be found in many other Central African cities. One study suggests that there are 700 bushmeat 'outlets' (markets, restaurants, butchers, cold storage facilities, and street stalls) per 100,000 inhabitants in the Congolese capital.[1] Assuming there are 17 million inhabitants, this means a total of 24,285 outlets. In Brazzaville estimates are 366 outlets per 100,000 inhabitants.[2] Accumulating reliable data in Africa's large cities is extremely complicated, so these figures need to be considered with a great deal of caution.

The single mother who sells peanuts or doughnuts on street corners at the crack of dawn to make ends meet, and the up-scale VIP caterer for business lunches and official ceremonies, represent the two extremes of changing patterns of food consumption in urban Central Africa. Street food, such as grilled goat, pork, chicken or fish, is a big feature of this trend. Street food and the love of beer also form a large part of urban leisure culture. Although nothing is really cheap for low-income households, food cooked and sold in makeshift street stands can be relatively affordable – sometimes as a treat or to fight off hunger – and provides some nutritional value. Urban street food, however, is often unhealthy and unsafe.

Urbanisation and rapid population growth have led to what is an unmanageable food security problem in urban areas. While eating at home was once an ideal option, doing so today is not always possible or desirable. Distance between place of work and home, transportation costs and traffic jams, and the need to respect regimented work hours help account for evolving eating habits. The official introduction of a mandatory lunch break in Cameroon in 1994 (ending the shorter uninterrupted work schedule) led to a flurry of hundreds of women selling bushmeat snacks to professionals and civil servants who did not have the time or inclination to go home for lunch.[3] Mothers in low-income households are confronted by a terrible problem: whose turn is it to eat today? There isn't always enough food for everyone in the household. This means that some household members eat one day and others the next, a form of segregation that usually follows age and gender distinctions. This isn't surprising in the light of the poor food security rankings of countries in the region. The DRC ranks 103 out of 113 countries surveyed, putting it in the category of countries with serious food insecurity.[4] A low-income family in Kinshasa earns somewhere between

$350 and $500 per month. This is the largest socio-economic category in the Congolese capital. Medium-income families earn between $500 and $1,500. Depending on the family, food is among the four most important items of expenditure along with housing, medical costs and school fees. The place of food in the Congolese household budget corresponds to results from global surveys which indicate that people in poorer countries devote a considerably higher portion of their expenditure to food than those in wealthier countries. US households spend 6.4% of their budgets on food while in Cameroon the figure jumps to 45.6%.[5] Individuals in these poorer families do not have the possibility of consuming the recommended 2,000 calories per day.

Sociologists and economists used to consider a household as a group of individuals who live in a common dwelling and share meals. This characterisation has, however, given way to multiple new and complex nuances. The 'blended family' (a family where at least one parent has children who are not genetically related to the other spouse or partner) has particular significance on the Central African cityscape. While some households in Central African cities consist primarily of nuclear family members, most are increasingly multi-generational and extended, in which nieces and nephews, stepchildren and distant relatives sleep under the same roof. Table 7.1 indicates the size of urban households in some of the region's large cities. A bed or even a foam mattress is a dream for many outside the nuclear unit who end up sleeping on a couch, a mat or a sheet on the floor. But securing a place to sleep for family members is one thing; providing food is something else. As one Congolese colleague from North Kivu mentioned to me, 'family means everything to us, but helping out our relatives is a constant burden'.

Table 7.1: Average household size in large Central African cities

Country	City	Population	Number of household members
Cameroon	Douala	2,768,436	5[1]
	Yaoundé	2,765,568[2]	4
Central African Republic	Bangui	1,145,280[3]	5[4]
Democratic Republic of the Congo	Kinshasa	12,071,463[5]	7[6]
	Lubumbashi	2,096,961	7.5[7]
	Mbuji-Mayi	3,367,582	6
	Goma	1,101,306	5
	Bukavu	1,012,053	4
	Kisangani	1,602,144	5
Equatorial Guinea	Bata	290,712[8]	6[9]
Gabon	Libreville	895,940[10]	7[11]
Republic of Congo	Brazzaville	1,838,348[12]	5[13]

Sources: 1. http://www.ilo.org/surveydata/index.php/catalog/374/ study-description; http://www.statistics-cameroon.org; http://catalog. ihsn.org/index.php/catalog/2256; 2. https://www.populationdata.net/ pays/cameroun/; 3. https://www.populationdata.net/pays/republique-centrafricaine/; 4. https://documents.wfp.org/wfp290682; 5. https://www. populationdata.net/pays/republique-democratiayue-du-congo/; 6. https:// www.idrc.ca/default/files/Mongraphie_Ville_de_Kinshasa; https://www. unicef.org/french/infobycountry/drcongo_statistics.html; 7. https://www. reliefweb.int/report/democratic-republic-congo/informations-sur-la-securité-alimentaire-en-rdc-no-27; 8. https://www.populationdata.net/pays/ guinnee-equatoriale/; 9. http://catalog.ihsn.org/download/GNQ_EEH2006_ Rapport_d_Analyse; 10. https://dgstat.ga/index/php/13-effectif-de-la-population; 11. http://www.bioline.org.br/pdf?ep04025; http://documents. worldbank.org/pubs/pdf; 12. https://countrymeters.info/fr/Congo; 13. The DHS Program, https://www.dhsprogram.com/pubs/pdf; http://www.cnsee. org/index.php?option=com_content&view=section&id=36Itemid=37.

Food scarcity has created new lifestyles and a reconfiguration of institutions of solidarity. People who can afford to eat, and provide food or money to buy it, are perceived as having prestige and status. Traditional interpretations of the ideas of household, rights and duties of household members, household organisation, and household values have evolved significantly, and this has a direct impact on food consumption. Like social stratification, intra-household inequality is also an urban trend – especially when it comes to food. Mothers give priority to their young children, who are usually fed every day despite the challenges that entails – but sons first, daughters after. The Haitian-born anthropologist Suzanne Comhaire-Sylvain conducted research in colonial Léopoldville (today's Kinshasa) in the 1940s, revealing how mothers trained their children to cope with hunger at a young age.[6] Today, adolescents and young adults in Kinshasa have to eat in shifts. Flexitarians before the word existed, these individuals follow a mostly vegetarian or vegan diet, only occasionally eating meat or fish.

Parents have little choice but to drive their older children on to the street to fend for themselves as far as food is concerned. Kinshasa, for René Lemarchand, is a place where 'keeping body and soul together requires treasures of ingenuity'.[7] For boys, in addition to stealing, pandering, brokering, hustling, extorting and pilfering, survival involves the less dubious activities of shining shoes, washing cars, hauling loads and flogging random cheap items on the street. These activities are the entry point to the informal economy which thrives in the cities of Central Africa, where wheeling and dealing is acceptable and normal. Girls wait tables, clean houses and babysit, assist their older sisters in beauty shops, sell drinking water in plastic bags in traffic jams, clean houses, wash dirty laundry and hawk fruit from plastic basins which they carry on their head. They also sell or barter themselves, with obvious consequences in an environment without regular access to – or a culture of – sexual and reproductive health care. The DRC government estimates that 21% of sexually active unmarried women use a modern method of contraception.[8] It is, however, unclear – and unlikely – that they do so consistently.

Children born to single mothers are particularly vulnerable, being low on the list of those who need – or who are perceived as deserving – to be fed. The single mother caring for her child without help and without sympathy is the urban Central African version of the 'Cinderella story – without a happy ending'.[9] There is nothing particularly Congolese or African about this. Elias Canetti, in his reflections on the psychology of eating, elevates this to a universal level: 'The family becomes rigid and hard when it excludes others from its meals; those that must be fed provide a natural pretext for the exclusion of others.'[10] In this fend-for-yourself environment, traditional forms of family and lineage support systems have transformed into poverty solidarity. Urban Central Africans tend to be willing and able to extend psychological support; lack of available money, however, limits solidarity to a pragmatic system of exchange. People expect something concrete in return for rendering a favour – gratitude is appreciated but it is not enough.

Problems related to affordability and access to food are exacerbated by inadequate cooking options. While Table 2.5 indicates the fairly widespread availability of electricity in most Central African cities (aside from low rates in urban DRC and CAR), these figures are deceptive when it comes to cooking. Most low-income and many middle-income households simply do not possess electric stoves. Electricity is used primarily for refrigeration, lighting, watching television, listening to music, and charging cell phones but not necessarily for cooking. The most striking example comes from Bangui where more than 92% of households use wood to cook with,[11] yet, as Table 2.5

shows, 34% of urban households in the country have access to electricity. Preparing food, in other words, is not as easy as turning on an electric or gas stove. Cooking is a time-consuming and labour-intensive activity, which also helps account for the need to choose who will be fed.

Where do people eat bushmeat in the region's urban landscape? Answers vary depending on the city and the country. The options range from the home, cheapish informal restaurants in poorer peripheral neighbourhoods, restaurants that cater to a formal sector clientele in the downtown zones, and expensive exclusive restaurants. An informal restaurant may occupy a space with a few plastic tables and chairs in an outside area, on hard-packed dirt, with no roof and no written menu, and without plumbing. In these places, whether temporary or semi-permanent, the cook or her daughter or niece is likely to serve. Food is served in plastic or metallic dishes. These informal-style restaurants are strategically located near markets, transport hubs, government ministries, schools and hospitals. Others, like stalls that prepare grilled goat meat (*nganda ntamba*), are found in proximity to bars where conversation is difficult because of the blaring music. A formal bushmeat restaurant, on the other hand, will be indoors with more refined furnishings and dishes, a written (and more extensive) menu, and servers. Eating bushmeat in all of these settings is motivated by economic, family, social and cultural factors.

This background about the urban food landscape is necessary to understand the emergence of informal restaurants serving relatively cheap food and the way they contribute to the bushmeat consumer market. Its relevance is supported by other researchers who argue that 'the increase in [bushmeat] demand is accompanied by shifts in human attitudes, values, taboos, and food preferences, all of which make wildlife and forest conservation more difficult to promote in the region'.[12]

Reference to 'shifts in human attitudes' is particularly relevant in Central African cities because they involve, for example, family structures, perceptions of modernity, the meaning of urbanity, and definitions of personal identity.

Informal restaurants – referred to as *aides-mamans* and *maquis* in Cameroon (and elsewhere in West Africa), *malewa* in DRC (derived from the word *kolewa*, or food), *dos tourné* in Gabon, and *ndo ti omba* (literally, 'at auntie's place') in Central African Republic – alleviate the constant hunger of the urban poor. On the days when they do not have food at home, they can eat out if they are lucky enough to have a bit of money to spare. Eating bushmeat in the informal restaurants of the urban landscape in Central Africa has thus become a way of life. These restaurants are also a dynamic contribution to the empowerment of women, who are most often their owners. The informal restaurants run by women contribute to resilience, social prestige and family survival. When they are neighbourhood-based with regular customers, owners allow people to eat on credit. These restaurants also allow people to have something different from the usually monotonous home meal. The relevance of the following ethnographic description of Mama Régine's establishment lies in the fact that there are thousands of such lower-priced restaurants in Central Africa, propelling urban bushmeat consumption. Most people who eat bushmeat in the region opt for such informal restaurants, instead of eating at home.[13]

Mama Régine's bushmeat restaurant

Mama Régine runs Anti-Formol, a *malewa* in the bustling, populous Kinshasa district of N'djili.[14] (*Formol* is the French word for 'formaldehyde'.) It is located on the main boulevard that links the city centre to the city outskirts and the highway past the airport extending out to Bandundu Province. Every square centimetre of land in her neighbourhood is occupied. Ramshackle and makeshift are the words that immediately come to mind to describe the setting. There are private homes, hardware stores, pharmaceutical wholesalers, banks, cash transfer agencies and the inevitable informal traders such as money changers and phone credit sellers sitting under their colourful umbrellas, tyre repairmen, hairdressers, shoe repairmen, and small-scale peddlers of all sorts. They, along with their customers, are Mama Régine's patrons.

She has given her hole-in-the-wall the name Anti-Formol, which in her mind means 100% organic. She says this is important because people believe (sometimes correctly) that bushmeat traders inject formaldehyde into the carcasses of unsmoked animals to preserve them. Defending in no uncertain terms the choice of name, she prides herself on being able to say: 'Everything I serve is natural. Nothing has been frozen and the only reason I have a refrigerator is to keep the beer cold. People come to my place primarily because they know they'll get top quality bushmeat, although they know they can also savour fish and vegetables from my pots. Anti-Formol makes sense to me because I deal in healthy Congolese food – and, believe me, no one has ever come back complaining about a stomach ache from my cuisine.'

Her premises are located between a used tyre merchant and an unlicensed pharmacist who sells medicines under the baking sun. When you enter Mama Régine's world, the first thing you see is large plastic basins full of live fish and turtles. Behind them is a large wooden table upon which sits a row of pots and metal catering trays. When I lifted one of the catering tray lids, the face of a cooked monkey flashed in front of me with an inquisitive look: 'Why am I here?' it seemed to say. There is also a designated shelter for butchering animals into cooking portions. This is near an open-air space where king-size aluminium pots simmer on charcoal stoves with the day's fare.

BUSHMEAT

A visit to the backroom pantry reveals the treasures of her activities – and the daunting challenges facing wildlife conservationists. Large plastic trash bins full of smoked carcasses of antelope, wild boar, porcupine and buffalo sit next to a bask of live dwarf crocodiles, their muzzles and legs tied with vines. 'Sometimes I can get a hold of live pythons too – I keep them in that wooden crate.' Elsewhere in the courtyard, a few languid duikers are confined to a pen. She pays neighbourhood kids a few francs to gather grass to feed them. 'Some clients prefer their duiker cooked fresh – others smoked – so I offer both to keep everyone happy.' In a tone somewhere between boastful and courteous, she claims she is able to procure any kind of fresh or smoked meat. 'You want elephant trunk or hippopotamus liver? No problem, I'll get it for you.' This, however, is not standard fare; they are ingredients for special occasions and prestige offerings for the well-to-do.

Clients wishing to satiate their craving for bushmeat have the choice of sitting in a covered courtyard or inside in the main dining area with about ten plastic tables. For those interested in a more quiet and intimate setting, they can choose the courtyard because the main dining area is subjected to a cacophony of blaring music, a competing television and loud voices. As most clients choose to eat with their hands (especially when their meat is accompanied by *fufu*[15]) and want to wash before and after eating, Mama Régine has improvised a plastic bucket and spigot contraption to compensate for the absence of running water in her compound.

Régine, who holds a degree from a Kinshasa art institute (l'Institut Supérieur des Arts et Métiers), has waitresses and kitchen assistants to help her, but she does most of the cooking herself. While she enjoys everything she cooks, she admits to having a particular fondness for turtles and snails. She prepares meats and fish in a variety of traditionally Central African ways, such as *liboke*. The ingredients, along with hot chilli, garlic, ginger, parsley and fresh tomato, are wrapped in banana leaves and steamed over a smoky fire smouldering in a cut-out oil drum. Unlike numerous cooks throughout Central Africa, Mama Régine refuses to use the widely prevalent Maggi cube and tinned tomato paste, considering them to be unnatural additives and culinary shortcuts. (The Maggi cube, produced by Nestlé and widely marketed throughout Africa, is composed of salt, trans fats and monosodium glutamate.) The only imported ingredients found in her kitchen are bay leaf and nutmeg. Her more discerning customers savour the way she stews smoked meat of monkey, duiker, porcupine, buffalo and crocodile in palm oil (*mosaka ya mbila*) and peanut sauce (*mwamba nguba*). While some customers make a special effort to reach her place from distant parts of the city, her base clientele is local – and she makes an effort to remember who likes what.

One key to her success is the finesse she has in welcoming the urban poor from her neighbourhood who have a few extra banknotes in their pockets and drop by for a dish of meat, while at the same time catering to those who arrive in expensive SUVs (they sometimes pre-order specific dishes). Around one in three of her customers are women. A tyre repairman in patched overalls can be found sitting next to a bigwig sporting a neatly pressed button-down with two expensive cell phones in hand. This image highlights the fact that there are no dominant profiles or stereotypes when it comes to describing who eats bushmeat in Central African cities. Régine's prices reflect this diversity. As with most such restaurants, there is no written menu or chalk board. Although she knows how to read and write, some of her customers do not. Not having anything in writing is also part of Régine's strategy of keeping a low profile vis-à-vis real and self-proclaimed tax collectors, hygiene inspectors and other administrative predators. This also partially explains why most of her business is generated by word of mouth, as is the case with Ghanaian 'chopbars'.[16]

Customers choose their fare by looking into the pots. Most bushmeat dishes accompanied with *fufu* or cassava cost in the vicinity of US$3 (for approximately 150 g of meat). This is equivalent to the price of two beers. There are nevertheless luxury parts of the animal such as the liver which cost twice as much. The meat of rare species – wild boar, buffalo or elephant – is also more expensive than the more frequently consumed duiker or porcupine. When it comes to paying, Régine gives the impression of trusting her customers but discreetly verifies the money to make sure that she has not been short-changed.

Mama Régine is a self-described corpulent *mama ya kilo* (referring to both her weight and worth). Even standing over her pots, she is well dressed, bejewelled and carefully coiffed – with a slight touch of nonchalance added by going barefoot. A divorced mother of six, she grew up in the Kisangani region. Although its biodiversity is in decline, the region was renowned for its forests full of animals and rivers full of fish. 'With us Kele people, bushmeat and fish are staples. Girls from our tribe grow up learning the art of preparing them from their mothers and aunts. We know what we are doing.' According to one of her clients, her bragging is justified. 'If you ever have the good luck to taste her river turtle or crocodile, you'll get why I keep coming back here.' Another man reported: 'I love bushmeat and buy it for my wife to cook for me at home. But when I want a real treat, I come here.'

In contrast to her culinary hubris, Mama Régine acknowledges that her establishment does not come across as fancy. 'The outside appearance isn't a problem for me; the food is what matters. I deliberately maintain a low profile to keep the greedy tax collectors and other administrative parasites at bay. I'm proud of my business but don't want to show off my success.' Mama

Régine is pragmatic in this respect: she knows her regulatory obligations but is well aware of her rights too. To avoid being harassed by administrative agents, she keeps her papers in order. She has a commercial licence, a certificate of hygiene, and a tax registration number. The fact that she has a nicely printed colour sign above her gate proves that she feels confident in the running of her business. Similar signage has been described for Ghanaian bushmeat restaurants: 'some chopbars use painted billboards or facades (adorned with colourful pictures of stews, meat and fish, and even caricatures of the owner) to advertise the name of the chopbar and its most popular dishes'.[17] Régine acknowledges that some people may be put off by appearances, but that doesn't keep lots of well-to-do connoisseurs away. 'Come by Sunday morning and you'll see expensive SUVs parked out front.' From Yaoundé to Kinshasa and from Brazzaville to Bangui, middle-aged men have adopted a Sunday-morning health walk. Their routine includes eating a bowl of meat stew after their exercise. The SUVs alluded to by Régine are what they drive. Some of the more well-to-do who love Régine's cooking but shy away from her décor take away their orders and have their food either at home or in their favourite beer-drinking hang-out.

Mama Régine has worked out a successful strategy to obtain bushmeat. Key in this are her family network, opportunistic business relations and a keen sense of doing business. As with other people interviewed in this research, her cell phone works magic. Family in Kisangani serve as relays for meat coming from the Tshopo Province; she also relies on a network of go-betweens in the cities of Mbandaka, Boende, Gemena and Mushie and the town of Oshwe, which lies just outside the southern area of the Salonga National Park. 'I'm lucky to have brothers-in-law who are boatmen. They ply the rivers to Equateur, Tshopo, Mai-Ndombe and the Kasai. I get lots of my fresh and smoked meat from them.' Payment takes the form of barter: her brothers-in-law transport loads of used clothing to trade for the meat. An astute businesswoman, she makes money at both ends of the exchange: used clothing costs less in Kinshasa than it does in the hinterland and meat is cheaper there than in Kinshasa. Régina also has a network of brokers who send her meat by air from Gemena, Mbandaka and Inongo in exchange for payment through increasingly available smartphone money-transfer providers such as M-Pesa, Tigo Cash and Airtel Money. 'I've worked hard to make sure my supply lines are reliable.' She has indeed clearly spread her nets wide. Régine's reliance on a broad network of suppliers seems to run counter to research that indicates that 'lower-priced restaurants had smaller networks and were more dependent on local markets for their bushmeat sourcing'.[18] Again, this indicates the complexity of the problem and underlines the need to be extremely nuanced when discussing the bushmeat trade.

Mama Régine says that she has chosen her work deliberately and is pleased with her success. 'I don't see any reason to worry about the future. My business is flourishing and I'm even thinking about opening up another Anti-Formol in a fancier part of town, catering to people with deep pockets. There are plenty of people out there willing to pay good money for a well-prepared 100% organic bushmeat meal.' While she has other plans for her sons (one of whom is a lawyer in Bandundu), she is grooming her daughters to step into the business. 'The money is decent. I own my own house and was able to buy a SUV with my profits.' When asked about wildlife depletion, the conservation discourse and sustainability, Régine took to the defensive. 'I'm a businesswoman and bushmeat is my livelihood. Everyone has the right to earn a living, no?' It is precisely that kind of attitude that makes wildlife managers' ambitions of reducing bushmeat consumption in Central African cities such an overwhelming challenge.

8

BUSHMEAT AND ZOONOSIS

Introduction

Zoonotic diseases are public health issues directly and indirectly related to human interactions with domestic and wild animals. While some have insignificant impacts on human health, others – such as HIV – are deadly. Rich and poor people in developed and developing countries are affected. However, 'a number of zoonotic diseases disproportionately affect poor and marginalized populations'.[1] Zoonosis therefore needs to be studied by considering socio-economic class structures because not everyone has equal access to information about risk, healthcare services and money for prevention or treatment.

When I discussed the idea of this book with colleagues in late 2018, indicating that I would dedicate a chapter to zoonotic diseases, one well-informed journalist quipped that the idea was interesting, but as no one knows what zoonosis means, I'd need to come up with a different chapter title. The Covid-19 pandemic hit with a bang a few months later. After more than 6.5 million Covid-19-related deaths, zoonosis has entered the popular vernacular and is consequently on the list of the top 9% of searched words on the Merriam-Webster Dictionary website.[2] Covid-19 sparked public awareness about zoonotic diseases and contributed to new interest in an already ongoing scientific debate about emerging infectious diseases. At the centre of the debates are issues such as where they come from, how to cope with them, victim demographics (e.g. poverty), and the global health context.[3] This chapter touches only superficially on the medical dimensions of these debates. Instead, its main objective – in the spirit of political ecology – is to show that the interconnections between history, culture, ecology and globalisation can help us understand zoonotic trends and, perhaps, from a policy perspective, shed some light on human populations' future relationships with zoonotic diseases. Political ecology is relevant in this framework because it is an approach that politicises these connections. In addition to a short section on the drivers of spillovers, I analyse the connections between bushmeat and beliefs about risk and disease, sanitation and conspiracy theories. This is relevant because – again from a policy perspective – popular perspectives about diseases are crucial when designing public health responses to disease outbreaks.

This chapter's main argument is that zoonotic diseases are just as much about culture, socio-economic factors and global change dynamics as they are about medical and biological science. Cultural (mis)understanding of risk is a thread running through the following pages. I fully adhere to the analysis of social and behavioural risks of emerging viral threats expressed by Karen Saylors and colleagues: 'By understanding the culturally-specific context and meaning of behaviours driving disease transmission, response efforts can react faster and design more culturally appropriate interventions that are acceptable to the populations being affected. In addition, contributions from social scientists can help to identify rumours, fears, and misinformation that may be amplifying risks for transmission.'[4] This chapter also respects the appeal made by Charlotte Milbank and Bhaskar Vira that emphasises 'the need for more nuanced approaches to protect an increasingly globalised and interconnected world from the potential risks of zoonotic spillover while not stigmatising the consumption practices and livelihoods of communities that rely upon wild resources'.[5] These authors clearly had bushmeat in mind when formulating their views.

Individual and collective world views and, consequently, behaviour patterns help us grasp zoonotic trends, which is why I have included, as much as possible, popular voices in the following pages. At the end of the chapter I present a brief description of hygiene and sanitation challenges in Kinshasa, since it helps put into perspective people's daily struggles to stay healthy. All of these issues are interconnected, which is why they need to be approached in a holistic way. After a section on the drivers and consequences of zoonotic spillovers and then a discussion of bans on bushmeat sales, this chapter looks at three big zoonotic diseases: SARS-CoV-2, the human immunodeficiency virus (HIV) and Ebola. Each of these diseases merits a distinct chapter of its own, but I've chosen to address them here together to succinctly emphasise a key argument: bushmeat hunting, trade and consumption are major public health risk factors. Other zoonotic diseases such as monkeypox could have been looked at here too because it is a good example of a disease that has begun to extend beyond its African niche and could contribute to the debate about vaccination because the smallpox vaccine protects against monkeypox.[6]

Zoonotic spillover

Humans contract innumerable diseases from animals. Of all emerging infectious diseases 75% are zoonotic,[7] and the majority of them originate in wildlife.[8] SARS (associated with bats and civet cats), MERS (transmitted to humans from camels in the Middle East), swine flu, bird flu, salmonella, mad cow disease, rabies, Lyme disease, bubonic plague (which resulted in an estimated 50 million deaths in Europe in the 14th century),[9] and the 1918 influenza pandemic (which also wiped out an estimated 50 million lives,[10] far more than the number of World War I civilian and military casualties) are just a few examples of zoonotic diseases that have wreaked havoc on humanity over time. They can be transmitted through interactions with living or dead animals, animal waste or animal products, depending on the virus, bacterium or parasite. Another risk is pathogen transmission to domestic animals from wildlife.[11] It seems that the risk of disease transmission is particularly high when handling and butchering fresh carcasses. Hunters in Central Africa are thus particularly vulnerable. Once meat is smoked or cooked, the risk diminishes.

Population growth and human-induced deforestation, agricultural intensification, biodiversity loss and environmental degradation contribute to the emergence of new viruses and diseases. The problem of these anthropogenic land-use changes leading to disease spillover is alarming from a global public health perspective because even where people do not eat bushmeat, it does not mean they won't be affected by an emerging zoonotic disease. 'Land use change ... creates a chain reaction of ecological, socio-economic, human behavioral, and regional fauna impacts that are believed to be linked to how infectious diseases emerge.'[12] Cases of HIV and Ebola emerged in Central Africa and spread rapidly throughout the world, provoking dire human, social and economic consequences. David Quammen's *Spillover: Animal infections and the new pandemic* provides an excellent analysis of these problems.[13] Well before Covid-19, he clairvoyantly wrote that zoonotic spillovers 'involve events beyond the ordinary, and the scope of their consequences can be extraordinary too'.[14] Specifically on Covid-19, he's since written: 'We invade tropical forests and other wild landscapes, which harbour so many species of animals and plants – and within those creatures, so many unknown viruses. We cut the trees; we kill the animals or cage them and send them to markets. We disrupt ecosystems, and we shake viruses loose from their natural hosts. When that happens, they need a new host. Often, we are it.'[15]

This emerging understanding of the human–wildlife proximity problem has also been explicitly expressed by Christine Johnson and colleagues: 'Exploitation of wildlife through hunting and trade facilitates close contact between wildlife and humans, and our findings provide further evidence that exploitation, as well as anthropogenic activities that have caused losses in wildlife habitat quality, have increased opportunities for animal–human interactions and facilitated zoonotic disease transmission.'[16] These opinions lend support to the stance that the more we threaten the environment, the more the environment threatens us. This latter point is central to this chapter in particular and to the entire book in general. Although ambitious from a public policy standpoint, this dialectical relationship is the underlying motivation for developing and implementing the One Health approach, which has 'the goal of achieving optimal health outcomes recognizing the interconnection between people, animals, plants, and their shared environment'.[17] The Covid-19 pandemic could be a boost for One Health approach funding and policy implementation.

The accelerating rate of zoonotic infectious diseases – from occasional outbreaks to full-blown pandemics – is in some way a result of the ostensibly sacrosanct right to development, along with its corollaries of road-building, dam construction, large-scale agro-industry, timber harvesting, land clearing for cattle ranching, industrial and artisanal mining, and urbanisation.

This human encroachment into animal habitat, however, comes with a high public health cost as it is a major driver of zoonotic emergence. Many – probably most – large-scale development projects in Africa are designed and implemented without adequate consideration of public health risks and implications. This is why, according to Rebecca Hardin and Philippe Auzel, 'these models of unrestricted expansion need to be reconsidered'.[18] While it is hard to imagine that zoonotic risk will incite African governments and their international partners to halt development strategies and resource extraction, it is equally hard to imagine them pursuing potentially devastating development patterns unabated. While development experts have a pretty good idea of what they should be doing, nudging policy changes on a meaningful scale to work towards an integrated development approach is something they have not been able to accomplish.

The Covid-19 pandemic also indicates that political interest at a global level is sparked only once severe economic consequences are felt. Certain disease programmes, such as measles vaccination, were put on hold because resources were redirected to the Covid-19 pandemic, revealing a lack of concerted global preparedness and an inability to respond to simultaneous public health crises – or to prioritise relevant humanitarian funding.

Bans and behaviour change

International calls for banning or controlling bushmeat sales abounded as the Covid-19 pandemic developed, along with a general plea for caution, given the then prevailing uncertainty about Covid-19's origins. In April 2020 a broad coalition of more than 200 conservation organisations wrote an open letter to the head of the World Health Organization imploring him to advise governments around the globe to rethink their relationships with animals and their place in nature more broadly. They called for a permanent ban on the sale of live wildlife in markets and a curb on other forms of trade in wildlife.[19] The coalition also asked the WHO to exclude the use of wildlife – even from captive-bred animals – in its endorsement of traditional medicine. This would necessitate a reversal of policy because in 2019 the WHO officially recognised the use of animal body parts in traditional Chinese medicine by adding it to its usually well-respected International Classification of Diseases. This recognition sparked concern because it was seen as a way of legitimising illegal hunting. Chinese traditional medicine is an acknowledged driver of the illegal trade in such emblematic body parts as rhino horn, tiger teeth and bones, and pangolin scales, even though the perceived effect of these substances is not based on scientific evidence.[20] China reportedly removed pangolins from its list of traditional remedies, apparently in the wake of the outcry.[21] Another coalition – Prevent Pandemics – also took advantage of Covid-19 'to ensure that never again does high-risk wildlife trade lead to a global pandemic', by publishing an online petition. Its objective was to snowball support to shut down high-risk wildlife markets, with a priority focus on those in high-density urban areas; to urgently scale up efforts to combat wildlife trafficking and halt trade of high-risk taxa; and to strengthen efforts to reduce consumer demand for high-risk wildlife products.[22]

While these policy recommendations thought up in Europe and the US may make some sense for wildlife conservation – and perhaps the prevention of further human health crises – they are only a very timid first step in dealing with the phenomenon in Africa. Concrete, realistic implementation measures ranging from awareness campaigns to law enforcement and investment in health infrastructure would require colossal efforts at social engineering in developing countries, most of which suffer from inadequate governmental and institutional capacities. The fact that only a small fraction of people in sub-Saharan Africa have been vaccinated against Covid-19 is an indication of the challenge. Less than 1% of DRC's population is vaccinated against Covid-19.[23] In the DRC, and in other African countries, the low level of vaccination is due to vaccine reluctance and not necessarily to inadequate access to vaccines.[24] Initiatives to establish bans on the bushmeat trade are also controversial because they could negatively impact on hunter-gatherers, for whom 'consuming and also selling wild meat remains the backbone of their ways of life and food security'.[25] The decline in bushmeat consumption has been explicitly linked to health problems among hunter-gatherers by nutritional anthropologists.[26]

Can recommendations to ban the trade in bushmeat work? Are they holistically informed? I argue that they are not, even though they have stimulated a lot of policy debate. Tamara Giles-Vernick, a medical anthropologist, explains why she thinks they will not work: 'Our research in equatorial Africa reveals that efforts to suppress wild meat trades and consumption ... simply drive those activities underground.'[27] Similarly, James McNamara and colleagues consider that 'in the West and Central Africa context, the immediate banning of the wild meat trade during the Covid-19 outbreak is likely to have only a short term and limited impact on demand and associated hunting pressure'.[28] Bans, according to another team of researchers, 'fail to account for the complexity, uncertainty and plurality of values associated with wildlife trade, with non-compliance and the emergence of illicit markets potentially undermining such approaches'.[29] A related perception of Covid-19 shared by Central Africans is that it did not emerge from 'their' meat, which might explain their relative unwillingness to comply. 'People are endlessly creative about finding ways to circumvent these restrictions, and during epidemics, even more so.'[30] In July 2020 a bushmeat market seller in Lagos, Nigeria, reported that he was selling around 20 carcasses a day, down from 100 before the pandemic hit.[31] The decrease may be related to law enforcement or to consumers voluntarily reducing their risks of contagion. Another explanation, however, is that the trade went underground: people bypassed the market by relying on relations with hunters and traders or even bought online or through social media channels, a situation that happened in China when the Huanan Seafood Wholesale Market shut down. The *New York Times* reported that 'On Taobao, a popular Chinese online shopping platform, all manner of live wildlife can be had'.[32] Analysis of Facebook groups in Brazil and Indonesia also revealed a flurry of online wildlife sales during the first Covid-19 lockdown.[33] Indeed, hidden markets emerge or mutate as traditional ones are shut down by government. In the aftermath of Covid-19 and the subsequent international surge in cases of monkeypox, the Nigerian government established another ban on the sale of bushmeat despite the fact that there is no evidence of any linkages between monkeypox and bushmeat handling or consumption.[34]

Another problem with these relatively unenforceable recommendations is existential. Deciding between earning money and refusing work due to a potential health risk is a difficult choice for a bushmeat trader and the population at large. Hunting and trapping are the source of most of the bushmeat people consume. Stumbling across dead carcasses in the forest – even in serious degrees of decomposition – is another source. A study in the DRC led by the US Centers for Disease Control and Prevention found: 'In remote areas where access to income and nutrition are scarce, finding dead animals is often considered a gift rather than a source of zoonotic infection.'[35] 'Gift' is the word that matters here, because it recalls the oft-repeated expression that wildlife is a gift of God.

People tend to modify their behaviours when it makes sense to them – not because of orders from the government or international actors, whose messages moreover are not always conveyed in culturally sensitive language. There is nothing idiosyncratically African in these attitudes. Across the Atlantic, an anti-Covid-19 lockdown protester in the American state of Pennsylvania voiced what could be interpreted as a widespread opinion: 'I'm gonna do what I got to do to feed my family ... If it means I got to risk my health then so be it.'[36] Overnight, the citizens of rich developed nations faced death, restrictions around funeral ceremonies, lockdown, mandatory mask-wearing, anxiety and social distancing due to measures taken for them by government without their being given a choice. This led to protests against anti-democratic measures and the militarisation of health policies, which were never questioned before when these policies were imposed in other countries, such as those in West Africa during Ebola outbreaks. As the world was scrambling to deal with Covid-19, Ebola continued to ravage eastern DRC largely unnoticed by global health institutions, and China reported cases of the even deadlier bubonic plague not far from its border with Russia. Despite evidence that consumption of infected marmot meat is a known transmission route of plague, Russian shepherds, who traditionally hunt marmots and eat the meat, persisted in doing so in flagrant disregard for a government ban.[37]

Covid-19

The debate around the origins of Covid-19 is riddled with uncertainty, distrust, controversy and ideology. Perhaps Covid-19 originated in bats and spilled over into humans, possibly through an intermediary animal at a bushmeat market in Wuhan, China. Perhaps it was created in a laboratory and leaked out. The Office of the United States Director of National Intelligence reported that an animal-to-human transmission and a lab leak were both plausible hypotheses but admitted that there was not adequate information allowing for a definitive conclusion.[38] The Chinese government dismissed the lab leak theory, accusing the US of politicising the debate. Thanks to ongoing scientific research, however, there is new evidence that Covid-19 did in fact originate from an animal–human spillover in Wuhan.[39]

The emergence of Covid-19 followed in the wake of the massive culling in 2018 of China's pig population due to an outbreak of African swine fever. Pork is an important source of animal protein in Chinese diets. The culling disrupted pork supplies and increased the potential for human–virus contact as people sought alternative domestic and wild meats.[40] While it is impossible to confirm a causal relationship, the coincidence is another reason to exercise extreme caution, as the culling could have indirectly facilitated animal-to-human spillover.

Dr David Nabarro from the World Health Organization, who was appointed the UN Special Envoy on Covid-19, explicitly stated that the bushmeat crisis is part of the wider public health environment, and urged governments 'to be respectful of how viruses from the animal kingdom are rife'.[41] That is another main take-away point of this chapter. The following passage is interesting because it is informed by scientific analysis but concludes with a note of humility: 'The critical steps that led a South-East Asian bat virus to start a pandemic could have happened inside or outside of China – whether in wild-animal markets or farms, or in traders or hunters. The virus may have jumped directly from bats into people, or come via an intermediate species. The story is waiting to be told.'[42]

Epidemiologists distinguish between the disease, Covid-19, and the agent causing the disease, which in this case is a coronavirus named SARS-CoV-2. The outbreak was a harsh reminder that the 20th century's unfaltering quest to constantly increase and facilitate the mobility of goods and people has its drawbacks. Border closures and confinement forced people to recalculate the costs of mobility – and to rethink their lifestyles and expectations. All sorts of action groups, lobbies and political organisations seized upon the pandemic to promote their agendas. The outbreak became a timely opportunity for wildlife conservationists, emboldening them to push for a ban on wildlife trade. The political aphorism 'never waste a good crisis', attributed to Winston Churchill, is perfectly appropriate here. Animal rights groups such as PETA (People for the Ethical Treatment of Animals), also driven by ideology, used the Covid-19 frenzy to deploy new media energies in their fight against animal production for the fur trade.[43] The first reverse spillover event happened in mink farms: people infected by SARS-CoV-2 passed it on to the minks, who in turn passed it back to humans. This again indicates the need to carefully monitor human–wildlife proximity.

The socio-economic context of Covid-19 in Africa has – in addition to all the other forms of havoc – created a devastating policy paradox in countries that generate revenues from ecotourism. With border closures, travel bans, flight cancellations and national parks shutting down, ecotourism revenues dwindled. Approximately 70 million ecotourists visited Africa annually before Covid-19, the majority of them for wildlife experiences. With no money to pay rangers, the parks went unprotected. This security vacuum gives free rein to poachers, which leads to the slaughter of more wildlife. Rangers may take up poaching themselves to feed their families. The security vacuum also raises questions about established conservation funding models: it has taken years to gradually shift from a government- or donor-funded approach towards self-sufficient ecotourism revenue generation for nature conservation. The Covid-19 shock has revealed the fragility of the approach.

As was the case the world over, popular discourses and perceptions of Covid-19 in Kinshasa were full of contradictions, inconsistencies and surprises. Rumours and conspiracy theories abounded. While some people practised social distancing as best they could in an environment which makes doing so extremely difficult, others continued to gather in groups and shake hands or cheek-kiss to greet. The wearing of masks caught on slowly. Ironically, once contamination risk and recommendations to wear masks diminished, some people thought mask-wearing was cool. A young woman in Brazzaville told me that she liked to wear a mask 'because that way people will think I just got back from Paris'.[44] Socio-economic and education status played a significant role in the acceptance of or reluctance to adopt social distancing measures. There was some acknowledgement that recommendations to avoid eating bushmeat during the crisis were well founded; people said, however, they would revert to their bushmeat eating habits once the crisis passed. A widespread sentiment also emerged that the disease didn't really exist and, if it did, it was invented by the American CIA to strategically decimate the populations of China and Africa (an opinion also voiced to explain the origins of HIV). It was similarly suggested that the virus was invented by greedy pharmaceutical companies to sell cures. Discriminatory prejudices also flourished: 'the Coronavirus is a punishment from God to the LGBT community'.[45] Prayer, of course, was declared to be both prevention and remedy. Perhaps Pope Francis offered inspiration to believers confronted by Covid-19 by praying in a church which houses a wooden crucifix that devotees say helped to end a plague outbreak in Rome in 1522.[46]

Congolese are avid consumers of traditional and social media – as well as rumours. Covid-19 surprised people everywhere with rumours, not only in Africa. A video in Spanish that recommended gargling with salt water to prevent infection had more than seven million views, and false news associating Covid-19 with 5G technology was widely circulated.[47] Belarus president Alexander Lukashenko suggested combating the virus with hard work, the sauna and vodka.[48] Donald Trump encouraged his senior health experts to consider bleach injections into the human body to fight Covid-19.[49] President Magufuli of Tanzania (who may have died from Covid-19) 'was one of Africa's most prominent coronavirus sceptics, and called for prayers and herbal-infused steam therapy to counter the virus'.[50] These far-fetched examples serve, again, to emphasise that there is nothing idiosyncratically Congolese or African in the perceptions and responses to Covid-19.

When Jean-Jacques Muyembe, the head of the DRC's taskforce against the pandemic, publicly declared (while sitting next to the United States ambassador Mike Hammer) that the country would be willing to participate in testing the soon-to-be-developed experimental vaccine, there were vociferous accusations that the government was selling its people as guinea pigs for laboratory experiments. Public outcry forced Muyembe to retract the offer.[51] These sorts of conspiracy theories need to be understood in the context of terrible foreign meddling in the Congo. The hypocrisy of King Leopold's 'civilising mission', the brutality of Belgian paternalism during colonial rule, post-independence Cold War politics which led to the murder of Patrice Lumumba and the installation of a 32-year-long dictatorship, and the war of aggression spearheaded by Rwanda and Uganda during the brief presidency of Laurent-Désiré Kabila prior to his assassination, all give people legitimate reasons to be sceptical. These tragic events and the need to be mistrustful to survive are embedded in Congolese collective memory.

Another reason for collective scepticism and distrust relates to high-level corruption during another epidemic. In March 2020, when Covid-19 was on everyone's mind, Oly Ilunga, a former health minister, was convicted of embezzling more than $400,000 from Congo's Ebola response funds. In 2018 and 2019,

Ebola killed more than 2,200 people.[52] In July 2020 the health minister Eteni Longondo was accused of being part of a mafia-style network involved in embezzling Covid-19 funds from the government and its international aid partners.[53] Corruption and mismanagement of international medical assistance – whether it be for vaccination campaigns, Ebola, measles or AIDS – are endemic. The Congo Research Group reported that only $6 million of the $363 million Covid-19 funding extended by the International Monetary Fund in 2020 was publicly accounted for.[54] Distrust led derisive Congolese to nickname the 'Corona' virus *'kuluna'* (thief). Expatriate whites were, moreover, nicknamed 'Corona' by Kinshasa street kids, replacing the usual *'mundele'* (whitey) because Congo's first cases came from Europe.

This discussion of conspiracy theories and distrust in public authorities may at first glance seem to be disconnected from the links between Covid-19 and bushmeat. It does serve, however, to show that the weight of history and popular beliefs need to be harmonised with public policy campaigns for prevention or behaviour change. This harmonisation was absent in the DRC during the different phases of the Covid-19 pandemic.[55]

HIV

The origins of the different strains of HIV – the pathogen responsible for acquired immunodeficiency syndrome (AIDS) – are unclear. Despite years of research, the origins of HIV are still subject to debate, primarily in the fields of virology and epidemiology but increasingly among medical anthropologists and social scientists as well. One strain of simian immunodeficiency viruses (SIV) from south-eastern Cameroon was identified in chimpanzees, and another from West Africa was identified in sooty mangabey monkeys. Although there is no perfect explanation of when it spilled over from animal to human, or how that spillover happened, there is consensus that there was zoonotic transmission.

While there are still gaps in the understanding of the precise origins of HIV, the culturally insensitive myth that 'AIDS came from some guy fucking a monkey' has been dismissed. The theory that HIV was invented by the CIA in a secret government laboratory has also been put into question. Another explanation, promoted in a controversial book called *The river: A journey to the source of HIV and AIDS* by Edward Hooper, has not stood up to scientific findings. He based his arguments on extensive research of an experimental oral polio vaccine campaign headquartered in Stanleyville (today's Kisangani in the DRC) which used chimpanzee tissues to produce vaccines locally.[56] These chimpanzees, he argues, were infected with SIV. A colonial vaccination campaign from 1957 to 1960 reached more than 900,000 individuals in the Belgian Congo, Burundi and Rwanda.[57]

The 'cut hunter hypothesis' is the more widely accepted explanation of how SIV spilled over to humans.[58] According to this scenario, a hunter cut himself while butchering an SIV-infected monkey or chimpanzee and was contaminated by this blood-to-blood interaction. This type of accident with an animal-to-human transmission is not difficult to imagine on the part of the hunter – but certainly is rather rare. Conversely, once in the human population, human-to-human transmission thrived. Social dynamics such as rapid urbanisation, poor health delivery systems (including the widespread use of unsterilised needles), and population mobility for work and trade created ideal conditions for the propagation of sexually transmitted diseases, and consequently facilitated the spread of HIV. While Kinshasa was ground zero for the HIV crisis, the virus's spread to other continents was only a matter of time.

In the early 1980s when AIDS first appeared as a public health problem, people blindly believed that only certain social groups were at risk. The media coined the expression 'the four-Hs': haemophiliacs (who received contaminated blood transfusions), homosexual men, and heroin users, who reported higher incidences of the disease. The fourth category were Haitians or people of Haitian origin. In 1960, when Congo gained independence from Belgium, there was a dire lack of trained civil servants, engineers, doctors and schoolteachers. Indeed, Belgium did a very poor job at preparing the country for independence in terms of capacity-building. (Without insinuating that this influenced the spread of AIDS, it is a good example of how seemingly unrelated historical realities cascaded into the development of the AIDS crisis.)[59] Congo needed to recruit skilled workers, which became an undertaking carried out by the United Nations in the Congo under the leadership of the UN secretary general Dag Hammarskjöld during the immediate post-independence chaos in the early 1960s. Haiti was a logical source for such recruits: Haitians spoke French, had the requisite skills, and adhered to black nationalist values. As these Haitian workers gradually returned home, they brought the virus with them.[60] Homosexual sex tourism to Haiti and migration to Miami were subsequently decisive factors in the spread of HIV.

Ebola

First observed in 1976 in the DRC near the Congo River, the Ebola virus disease (EVD) is a rare but deadly disease affecting humans and non-human primates such as monkeys, gorillas and chimpanzees. 'All Ebola outbreaks start from a spillover event from wildlife.'[61] More than 2,200 people died of Ebola in eastern DRC between mid-2018 and mid-2020, when the outbreak was officially declared over. The worst outbreak hit Guinea, Liberia and Sierra Leone in West Africa from 2013 to 2016, killing 11,300 people. Without being certain, scientists believe that bats are the most likely reservoir host. According to the US Centers for Disease Control and Prevention, 'viral and epidemiologic data suggest that Ebola virus existed long before these recorded outbreaks occurred. Factors like population growth, encroachment into forested areas, and direct interaction with wildlife (such as bushmeat consumption) may have contributed to the spread of the Ebola virus.'[62] Bats are nevertheless sold in many West and Central African markets for food. Truth is sometimes stranger than fiction: incredible as it may seem, the exact letter-for-letter anagram in French for *chauve-souris* (bat) is *souche à virus* (virus strain)![63]

One report from Kisangani found the central market full of freshly splayed bats despite an ongoing Ebola outbreak in neighbouring Equateur Province. Buyers and sellers described the meat as delicious. Some people said they knew about the connection and respected public health warnings. Others said they did not know about it. One man said he was informed about the risk but didn't care: 'I've been eating bats since I was a kid and am not about to stop. I can't be afraid of a disease when hunger is knocking at my door.'[64] Family habits, tradition, cultural attachment and purchasing power can therefore easily override a health risk. During another Ebola outbreak, this time in Congo's Orientale Province, an unexplained influx of abnormally large bats arrived in the village of Mongbwalu, home to an Ashanti Gold Kilo mining site. Despite explicit public health warnings not to eat them, the population took up their slingshots en masse. In this mining camp where other fresh meat costs up to ten times the price of a bat (50 US cents), the influx was described by one miner as a demonstration of 'Divine Providence'.[65] The belief that animals in the forest are a gift of God is something that is frequently heard.

Divine Providence or other forms of supernatural beliefs are absolutely fundamental in this context because people's attitudes to health are governed by hybrid world views. People believe that human existence is embedded in a cosmology where individual needs and desires depend on social, natural and spiritual forces. The following passage about perceptions of health (and, indirectly, health risks) concerns Kinshasa, but the analysis could well apply elsewhere in rural and urban Central Africa. It helps explain why people feel compelled to consider the supernatural causes of health problems. 'Faced with bad luck, misfortune or disease, even when they understand that the problem might be brought about by a microbe or an accident, people want to know more: why something happened to them, why now, and whose fault it is (who cast the spell). The mechanistic Western logic emphasizing how things are brought about is hardly satisfying.'[66] In more concrete terms, this means that someone may know that if they eat or handle a contaminated animal, they may suffer the consequences. But because they may believe that life trajectories are predetermined, they will run the risk because sickness or death is perceived as the will of the supernatural.

There are various accounts providing evidence of these world views. During the height of the 2014–16 Ebola crisis in Côte d'Ivoire, the government imposed a strict ban on the hunting, selling and consumption of bushmeat. Despite the risk of up to five years in prison for being caught in the act, people still ate their favourite dishes and devised codes when placing orders in restaurants. If a client asked for 'yesterday's meat' or 'Deborah' (which sounds much like 'Ebola') the server knew exactly what was expected.[67] Bushmeat traders in Mbandaka (DRC) during an Ebola outbreak in 2018 demonstrated the same scepticism, clearly declaring they did not perceive themselves as vulnerable to any particular occupational risk.[68] Rumour-mongering, fear and mistrust were also obstacles to response teams during the 2018 Ebola outbreak in the North Kivu and Ituri provinces of the DRC: there was a contradictory sentiment that Ebola didn't exist, and, if it did, it was a disease created by President Joseph Kabila to exterminate the Nande people, who were opposed to his reign.[69] Another problem with international Ebola response strategies was reported by Jason Stearns in an analysis of how donors and the World Health Organization partnered with Congolese men with guns to protect aid workers, resulting in a strategy that backfired. This partnership 'created perverse incentives: although the combatants had reason to refrain from attacking aid workers, they also had an interest in prolonging the epidemic so they could keep profiting from it ... some militiamen and members of the government security forces stoked violence and instability so that the disease would continue to spread and the international aid agencies would continue to pay them.'[70]

These situations of flagrant disregard – or misunderstanding – contrast with findings from a 2015 household study carried out during the Ebola crisis in Liberia which pointed towards 'an overall decrease in bushmeat consumption'. The study qualified this decrease by indicating that 'the consumption of bushmeat in wealthier households decreased less than in poorer households'. Both the price of bushmeat and the perception of health risk contributed to the decrease. Despite the crisis, 'people's preference for specific bushmeat species remained the same'.[71] In the spring of 2020 during the Covid-19 pandemic, the situation in Libreville was somewhat similar, with one bushmeat market woman being quoted as saying: 'we've been eating pangolins for years; don't bring your diseases here'.[72] These diverging responses to risk – and perceptions of risk – once again highlight the complex relationships people have with bushmeat. Thais Morcatty and colleagues have reached a similar conclusion concerning personal trajectories: 'It is important to recognize that the degree to which people can fully comprehend a risk is based on their own lived experiences. It is possible that if the majority of the traders and consumers have not experienced a known event of direct contamination from contact with animals, they may not perceive a risk.[73] The power of desire, emotion, taste, tradition and supernatural beliefs seems to outweigh the logic of scientific knowledge, empirical evidence and the rule of law.

Although not related to bushmeat, the following example also highlights the gap between science and popular belief. Several health-care providers working in a Kikwit (DRC) hospital died during an Ebola outbreak in 1995.[74] The outbreak took place at a time when artisanal diamond digging was a significant economic activity along the Angolan–Zairian border.[75] According to rumour, two friends unearthed a huge diamond. To conceal it from potential thieves, one of the two agreed to swallow it for safekeeping. But the diamond did not come out as expected and the man fell seriously ill. It was then that they sought medical assistance in the Kikwit hospital. The man died and the diamond was not returned to the dead man's partner. Outraged, he cast a spell on the doctor and the hospital. Retribution took the form of a terrible haemorrhagic fever.

Sanitation and hygiene

This section builds on the arguments made above about how socio-economic factors and culture influence people's relations with disease. Although it does not explicitly focus on the human–wildlife nexus, it contributes to the debate about perceptions of risk, which should be a priority in addressing public health policies about zoonotic diseases.

Wild and domestic animals – be they live, smoked, freshly killed or dying – are sold by the road and in rural and urban markets. They are traded at river landings and ports all along the vast river network in Central Africa. A common scene in the Congo Basin is a paddler in a dugout canoe hoping to buy or sell fish or meat by scrambling to reach a wooden boat, barge or makeshift raft of logs carrying traders and travellers from upriver. The sights, sounds and smells in all these settings are astonishing, revealing an unsettling disregard of basic sanitation and hygiene. The omnipresent flies hovering on and around the meat and surrounding filth (market waste, animal excrement, rotting produce and mosquito-filled puddles of stagnant water) do not seem to really bother anyone. They are the visible tips of the disease iceberg – but the germs, bacteria and viruses remain hidden from the naked eye. From a public health perspective it is difficult to campaign for behaviour change with regard to invisible infectious diseases when very poor people cannot respect even basic sanitation recommendations. Inadequate public service provision, lack of funding, chaotic management and practically non-existent awareness about basic hygiene are some of the factors that translate into an overwhelming disregard for biosafety. Although problematic because of its narrow focus on the single factor of illiteracy, research in Brazzaville's bushmeat markets found that the functional illiteracy of market women and 'irrational behaviour' were causes of food poisoning.[76]

Transactions in these places are mostly informal and unregulated. Earning a few francs seems to be more important than worrying about hygiene. If public health or environment representatives are present at an urban market, they would most likely be more interested in collecting an informal tax or bribe than in making sure that the official health and sanitation norms – for which they don't have the means to control – are respected. Sanitation challenges in general, and those concerning the bushmeat trade in particular, are quite simply staggering. As government authorities hardly place hygiene high on the urban management agenda, people have learned to fend for themselves at the individual, family and community levels to deal with these issues.

BUSHMEAT AND ZOONOSIS

Kinshasa, Africa's third-largest city, produces approximately 90,000 tonnes of waste daily, of which only 20,000 tonnes are collected, according to the Kinshasa Sanitation Authority.[77] Based on the questionable assumption that the city's residents would demonstrate responsible civic behaviour, the Kinshasa municipality launched a citizen-based sanitation campaign – *Kin Bopeto* – to clean up the city in October 2019. Inspired by President Mobutu's community *salongo* clean-up efforts, after only a few months it became apparent that the campaign was flawed, especially in the poor, densely populated districts. It was difficult to get people to invest individual effort for collective benefits. Even minor changes were difficult to sustain, and achieving the right balance between awareness and sanctions had not been adequately thought through. There was also an overwhelming lack of institutional and social enabling conditions for such collective action to make sense. 'Why should we bother cleaning the neighbourhood if everything we pile up is just going to be dumped into the rivers and street gutters?' asked one resident. 'The next big rain will wash it all back up.'[78] Some researchers have used solid waste mismanagement as a litmus test to document state failure: their findings indicate that the primary victims are the urban poor.[79] While the Kinshasa challenges – along with those of other Congolese cities – may be more daunting than those in other cities in the region, even somewhat better-managed cities like Libreville or Yaoundé are also confronted with similar problems.

African urban markets are microcosms from which much can be learned about people, their food habits and sense of community, as well as their municipality's economy and political culture. When foreign anthropologists descend on a new research site, the marketplace is usually one of their first stops. The following description of a Kinshasa market helps put sanitation and hygiene challenges in the broader perspective of people's struggle to stay healthy despite serious obstacles. Although the links between these challenges and zoonotic diseases may not be direct, looking at them through the lens of social organisation is a relevant public policy priority.

Congolese president Laurent-Désiré Kabila inaugurated the Marché de la Liberté in 2004. Located in Masina – one of Kinshasa's most densely populated districts – it has become a suffocating, rat-infested labyrinth where buyers elbow their way through the different sections while carrying their bundles. This bustling market has just about everything a Kinshasa household has use for. Vendors offer manufactured items such as tinned foods (tomato paste, sardines and corned beef), soaps, skin-lightening creams, scents and other types of cosmetics. There are market sections with new and used clothes, building, plumbing and electrical hardware, fruit and vegetables, salted, smoked and fresh fish, and cooking charcoal. Electronic gadgets imported from Dubai are jumbled together with cheap plastic buckets and aluminium kitchen utensils. The acrid smell emanating from the mounds of cassava leaves mingles with the smell of smoked fish. The adage attributed to Rudyard Kipling, 'The first condition of understanding a foreign country is to smell it',[80] definitely has resonance here. Overflowing basins of cassava flour, providing the staple for most Kinshasa tables, lie next to piles of corn and wheat flour. As there are far more items for sale than space on the market's cement stands, a good part of the food and produce is sold from tarpaulins stretched out on the ground. While there is an increasing number of modern supermarkets in the wealthier districts, as in some of the richer cities in the region, this kind of shopping experience is the daily experience of the vast majority of the region's urban residents – particularly women.

The sounds of cattle, goats, sheep, pigs and chickens converge in a deafening cacophony to greet buyers in the market's Pavilion 20. No one seems to mind either the sound or the smell. This is the place where meat is butchered by machete-wielding men – approximately twenty of them – and displayed on cement slabs: heads, shoulders and legs lie next to the internal organs, which command a higher price. The cuts of fresh meat are sold with skin and fur attached, so buyers can identify the species. Smaller-sized mammals such as porcupine, gazelle, hare, rodents or pangolin are sold whole. Trying in vain to keep insects at a distance, vendors brandish improvised fly-swatters made from sticks and plastic scraps. Market management may appear chaotic, but sellers seem to have a precise understanding of each square centimetre of space they are entitled to. Selling bushmeat is not illegal if it is not on the endangered species list. Scant attention is paid to the legal exclusions, however, unless there is reason to worry about getting caught and consequently having to pay a fine or having the meat confiscated.

Many of the live wild animals for sale are the young of mothers who were shot or trapped. Others are caught in hunting nets. Every seller has their own supply network, but the origins are fairly similar. Professional hunters using 12-gauge shotguns are the main suppliers but Congolese soldiers are also known to be involved in the trade. Cellphone coverage in the forest and phone banking make transactions easy: placing orders, making payment, and tracking the location of the meat.

Pavilion 18 of the market specialises in the sale of live fish from large plastic basins, and reptiles. There are sea and river turtles, monitor lizards, and different sorts of crocodiles whose snouts are firmly tied shut with vines, and their legs anchored to a dead tree branch, also with forest vines. In contrast to the meat section, women vendors predominate. When business winds down in the evening, unsold meat and fish from both these sections are transferred to the market's cold storage units. Smoked meat is sold here and there at the market without a designated section. It can usually be found in the spices section but also at some illogical spots – for example, in the used clothing aisles. Smoked meat has multiple buyers: mainly housewives and small restaurant owners. Another category of buyers consists of the young men who buy pieces which they break up and sell in small snack-size portions in the city's thousands of bars. 'Older men who grew up in the village love these smoked meat treats with their beer.'[81]

Conclusion

This chapter has described the wide range of connections between bushmeat hunting, trade and consumption and the harmful consequences for human health. Eating bushmeat is perceived as healthy and desirable, as other chapters of this book have argued, but this chapter shows that doing so comes with exorbitantly high public health costs. Covid-19 is the timeliest and urgent reminder of how humans, animals and the environment are all part of a fragile balance, but one put under severe pressure in recent decades by human activity. While people in Central Africa have varying degrees of understanding of these linkages, they do not always consider them as issues they have to act on or see them as personal priorities. Malaria, for example, is a far greater family health problem than Covid-19. Like Ebola in the 1970s and HIV/AIDS in the 1980s, Covid-19 is a phenomenon that is in the process of defining a generation. Over the past century, rapid population growth, climate change, urbanisation, deplorable natural resource governance, poverty and dystopian political choices have laid the groundwork for our enduring zoonotic tragedy. While science – in the form of vaccines – can help, more sustainable solutions can best be found by a better understanding of and greater respect for the nexus between humans, wildlife and the environment.

9

LEGALITY, LEGITIMACY AND ENFORCEMENT

The legal framework

This final chapter looks into the logic and efficacy of legal frameworks in environments where hunting, trading and eating wild animals are ordinary, normal and desirable activities for many people. It argues that the current legal frameworks in the countries of the Congo Basin are ill-suited to the sustainable management of wildlife. Laws are unable to significantly curb illegal hunting and, consequently, the supply of bushmeat to urban markets. Laws – and the criminal justice system relating to wildlife hunting and trade – do not correspond to cultural, social, economic, political and institutional reality. More often than not, legal frameworks are the conceptual products of international institutions and organisations that work on behalf of national bodies. Some countries, such as Cameroon and Guinea, have outsourced their wildlife law enforcement to organisations like LAGA (the Last Great Ape Organization) and EAGLE (Eco-Activists for Governance and Law Enforcement).[1] African Parks, through a public–private partnership arrangement, has been mandated to enforce wildlife management in the Chinko Nature Reserve in CAR. In most cases, laws are colonial hangovers that have not been revised to take into account the ecological, political, cultural and enforcement realities in which they need to operate today. The systems that are responsible for enforcing laws and adjudicating violations of the law are also inadequate. For a good many individuals involved in the bushmeat economy, laws are perceived as unfair, arbitrary, illegitimate and irrational.

The legal frameworks applying to hunting and trade, as well as spatially administered forms of zoning (when and where exactly one can or cannot hunt), are riddled with ambiguity. These frameworks are liminal creations characterised by powerlessness and uncertainty. Regulations are poorly defined and impossible to legitimately implement because they are based on contradictory and evolving instruments that are struggling to keep up with dynamic logics and priorities. In places where options to earn hard cash are limited, it makes sense to engage in hunting and trading bushmeat. Passively resistant, rural and urban people alike consider the exploitation of natural resources – bushmeat and other forest products too – as both a legitimate right and a necessity for survival.

Hunters have raised these kinds of questions with me during conversations: 'Who do the NGOs think they are to tell me not to hunt?' 'Are they going to pay my kids' school fees?' 'Are they going to send my mother-in-law to town to see a doctor?' Variations on these kinds of questions, which point to the clash between real basic needs and regulatory failures, are common and perfectly understandable. The absence of reliable work opportunities in the cash economy is a real problem – there are quite simply not many options to earn hard cash to pay for essential services and goods, or even basic commodities such as soap and salt or kerosene for lanterns. A plastic bucket can be a household's prized possession in some villages. Observations such as this from Equatorial Guinea are omnipresent in conversations and the corpus of bushmeat literature: 'Men hunt for income because there are few other livelihood options.'[2]

The legal frameworks that theoretically govern wildlife management throughout most of Africa today have curious European historical origins. The inheritance of laws regarding wildlife is far from unique from a colonial and post-colonial perspective. The entire African nation-state system and issues of sovereignty were based on European models – and failed because of their externally imposed foundations.[3] Patricia Van Schuylenbergh traces current wildlife laws in the DRC to European aristocratic prerogatives in the Middle Ages, whereby the nobility appropriated wildlife and natural space to the detriment of the peasantry.[4] The situation lingered and European states gradually codified hunting rules and regulations, linking hunting to land rights. During the colonial period these rules – like many other European norms – were surrealistically transposed to Africa. European rules about which species could be hunted, seasonality and hunting space, perceived as illogical by African hunters, were superimposed on traditional norms. Following independence, African governments hardly swayed from the European vision. As already discussed in Chapter 3, this legacy was kept in place by the continued presence of Europeans in wildlife management positions and by the dominant role international wildlife organisations were able to carve out for themselves. This is a situation increasingly associated with white saviourism in Africa.[5] White saviourism refers to the assumptions of some white people that they can help solve the problems of black people, indigenous people and people of colour. As a consequence, restrictive legal frameworks relating to hunting, and the bushmeat crisis discourse, tend to be perceived as Western meddling by some Africans who stubbornly adhere to bushmeat culture and economy. Variations on the theme that people have the right or even the duty to transform animals into food often came up in my research conversations.

One overwhelming flaw in the legal framework is its lack of legitimacy – and there is a world of difference between legality and legitimacy. Legality is what the law says. It can be embodied, for example, in an official document such as a hunting permit or an authorisation to carry a gun. An activity can be rendered legal or illegal from one minute to the next by the stroke of a pen, by decree or fiat. Legitimacy, conversely, is what is perceived by people as being empathetic, fair, just, ethical and moral. It is a long-negotiated process based on heritage, beliefs, family values, tradition – and, of course, opportunity. Different people have very different views of what is and isn't legitimate. An American dentist legally shot and killed Cecil, a famous Zimbabwean male lion; public outcry, however, put under great scrutiny the legitimacy of that slaying.[6]

Laws can distort interpretations of individual or collective rights – which is exactly the case when it comes to hunting and trading wild animals in Central Africa. This legality–legitimacy dichotomy has been decried by scholars since the onset of what was to emerge as the bushmeat crisis. Van Schuylenbergh describes how this culturally insensitive dichotomy emerged in the early years of Belgian colonialism, also highlighting the inherently racist attitudes that came to be codified. According to the self-serving logic, European hunters killed respectfully, unlike Congolese hunters whose techniques were considered by Europeans to be 'rudimentary, cruel and primitive'.[7] Louisa Lombard's work in the Central African Republic lends further evidence to the absence of legitimacy: 'A thicket of state laws continues to prohibit much of everyday life in the hunting zone, particularly regarding hunting itself, and significantly affecting wild acquisition and privilege. The laws are spectacularly out of tune with the realities of people's lives and the capacities of public authority in such a remote and infrastructure-poor space.'[8] Elsewhere she says succinctly that these laws 'have little purchase'.[9] The following narrative from the Ntokou-Pikounda National Park in the Republic of Congo captures this dichotomy. Although it relates to a fishing infraction and not hunting, the situations are quite similar. 'I was arrested, handcuffed and dragged in front of a judge for fishing where I always fished, where my father always fished and where my grandfather fished. Whose land is this? Who was here first?' The man was given a suspended sentence.[10] This is a telling example of how, in the words of Mark Axelrod and colleagues, 'conservation governance may sometimes result in unintended consequences that disadvantage groups of stakeholders'.[11]

Another dichotomy is of a semantic nature. What's the difference between a hunter and a poacher, or between a trader and a trafficker? These labels have distinct connotations and again need to be considered as a legality or legitimacy issue. The erstwhile village subsistence hunter – with rights and prestige – became a poacher, an outlaw, when far-fetched legal and bureaucratic norms were drawn up in a distant city. In the legal landscape, a bona fide hunter, however, is someone who respects which species can be killed, when and where, and has paid cash for a licence and a permit to own a gun.

There is a trend in bushmeat literature to call traders traffickers. Bushmeat traders, retailers or wholesalers are increasingly rebaptised as traffickers by conservation organisations, akin to drug traffickers, sex traffickers or people traffickers. TRAFFIC, moreover, is the name of an established lobbying organisation founded by the International Union for Conservation of Nature and the World Wide Fund for Nature with the mission of ensuring 'that trade in wild plants and animals is not a threat to the conservation of nature'.[12] I was only half surprised when a Congolese hunter told me that his quarry of bushmeat was *butin* (which translates from French as loot, spoils or plunder), implying his acknowledgement that his activities were in some way illicit. This analysis shows that legal frameworks criminalise individuals who break rules. The more laws there are, the more laws there are that can be broken. The consequence is exaggerated criminalisation applied to the bushmeat economy. This criminalisation is also caused by blanket laws that prohibit all types of hunting, without respecting or acknowledging differences in hunting patterns and objectives.

Despite actions taken by governments in the region to codify the hunting and trading of wild animals (or at least pay lip service to doing so), they also recognise de facto legal pluralism. This refers to situations where the laws of the state and the conventions and norms of customary authority intermingle. This hybrid system of resource governance makes for a very difficult wildlife management situation because rules, loyalties, ownership rights and privileges are a muddle where negotiation trumps the written laws that many stakeholders, even state authorities, do not always understand – let alone master. The gap between knowledge of laws and attitudes to them is a related handicap. State agents may have a slightly more detailed understanding of what the laws say than ordinary people, but they do not necessarily observe the spirit of the law. Deep in the forest, there is a widespread sentiment that government is far away and, as such, disconnected from people's needs. In the words of a community development worker in the Okapi Wildlife Reserve in the DRC, 'what may be criminal according to the law isn't necessarily criminal in the eyes of villagers'.[13]

This discussion about the legality–legitimacy dichotomy is very much a debate about serious denial problems. Feelings of denial, refusal and rejection were frequently expressed by my interviewees in villages and city offices while discussing the rules and regulations relating to bushmeat. Villagers refuse to curtail their survival activities as dictated by the law, denying that there is a wildlife sustainability problem. State agents and rangers haven't really demonstrated great commitment to their official mandates. Conservationists seem to be trapped in crisis mode, where they feel the need to act at all costs, hoping that serendipity will somehow provide a solution. In the battle between appropriation and acceptance, on the one side, and denial, on the other, denial is winning.

Enforcement challenges

It is admittedly quite challenging for law-enforcement agents (as well as hunters and traders) to navigate the legal landscape to establish what is legal and illegal. Some cases are clear but others are ambiguous. It is illegal to hunt and sell any of the great apes, but it can be legal to trap and sell a cane rat. Some duiker species are protected, others not. When a chimpanzee is butchered and smoked, it is hard for a non-expert to distinguish it from a legally hunted monkey. The lack of clarity and shared understanding of rules also ushers in possibilities of abuse by rangers and agents at roadblocks who may hassle traders and transporters for bribes. How many carcasses can be owned and transported? Which species? During which season? If traders are ignorant of their rights, they can fall prey to unscrupulous men in uniforms. This example serves to show the need to distinguish between claims that laws are not legitimate and the practices of actors who distort them. Another legal ambiguity emerges from the multi-level web of laws, decrees and agreements: national laws on the books may be inconsistent with or in contradiction to the laws of provinces or departments.

The legal framework governing land and forest resources in the Republic of Congo is a good example of the legality–legitimacy dichotomy, and also highlights the difficulty in making legal pluralism work. During the colonial period, customary authority – authority based on the power and legitimacy of tradition – had the right to control land use, including hunting and fishing practices. In the various iterations of land laws since independence, the state has taken ownership of the majority of forest lands; this has ushered in opportunities for all Congolese to exploit resources, within the confines of the law. State ownership is a legacy of the Marxist-Leninist phase of Congolese history (from 1969 to 1991) during which time the Brazzaville government received support from the Soviet Union. The current land laws emasculated the power of traditional authority by rescinding their rights to decide who can hunt on their lands and under what conditions. This is detrimental to sustainable hunting objectives because it opens the floodgates for urban commercial hunters, foreign poachers and other outsiders, such as those from neighbouring areas. This situation has led Germain Mavah and colleagues to call for institutional reforms which give back resource rights to local communities for them to manage according to traditional norms and practices.[14] Across the river, the DRC also has a legally plural land-use system. The 1966 Bakajika Law was designed to ensure state control of the land and resources but did not abrogate pre-existing customary land rights. Throughout much of the vast territory, notably the forest zones, the state is largely absent, leaving land management to traditional authorities.

A second overwhelming flaw in the legal framework is the difficulty of enforcing it, at two main levels. The first is denial, or lack of will to enforce; the second is absence of capacity. The figures in Table 9.1 come from an independent monitoring company that ranks the economic and political performances of 192 countries. The higher the number, the weaker the performance. These rankings indicate that countries in the Congo Basin have a conspicuously poor record in respecting the rule of law. Their rule of law ranking 'captures perceptions of the extent to which agents have confidence in and abide by the rules of society, and in particular the quality of contract enforcement, property rights, the police, and the courts'.[15] Table 9.1 is presented here to place the difficulties in enforcing wildlife laws in a broader law-enforcement context.

Table 9.1: Rule of law ranking (2022)

Country	Rank
Cameroon	170/192
Central African Republic	186/192
Democratic Republic of the Congo	188/192
Equatorial Guinea	180/192
Gabon	144/192
Republic of Congo	172/192

Source: https://www.theglobaleconomy.com/rankings/wb_ruleoflaw/.

The lack of will to enforce wildlife laws is rampant. Meredith Gore and colleagues confirm this analysis: 'Many possible causes or forms of illicit trade are not enforcement priorities; the effects of illicit trade are often underappreciated or unseen by the very people who are best placed to respond.'[16] Conservation authorities who are mandated to curb the hunting, trade and consumption of bushmeat do not always take their roles seriously. The lack of will to enforce wildlife laws is exacerbated by the fact that these authorities are often underpaid, and so feel the need to supplement their incomes by taking bribes, confiscating meat, and participating in trading networks. They therefore take advantage of their positions of authority to participate in the legal and illegal bushmeat economy. For John MacKinnon and colleagues, 'the lack of leadership from politicians on wildlife conservation' is one of the main drivers of wildlife depletion.[17] Another problem relates to political sensitivities. Forestry department officials in the northern Republic of Congo complained that they were under pressure from elected officials to be lenient with poachers and traders, even with repeat offenders.[18] The need to keep the peace between people and officials was the stated reason; the unstated reason was that bushmeat just isn't worth exacerbating tensions in an environment where people are already frustrated by the absence of state service provision. 'The guy had a pangolin [an endangered species], what's the big deal?' summarises the problem.[19]

Even when wildlife crime suspects are apprehended, they are rarely brought to court – except for a handful of high-profile cases usually resulting from elephant poaching. The Sangha Department public prosecutor (in northern Republic of Congo) emphasised the need to 'humanise wildlife laws', 'turn a blind eye to maintain social peace', and 'respect tradition'.[20] He told me that in 2020/21, 10% to 20% of all cases heard by his court related to wildlife crime but there were only a very limited number of convictions. He specifically indicated that someone in possession of a *permit de petite chasse* who was found with a species that would require a *permit de grande chasse* would be dealt with leniently by his office. He also emphasised that for him and his colleagues in the court system, wildlife crime is a relatively new concept. 'Ten years ago, no one would be bothered for selling a chimpanzee. Today, such a trader would definitely be brought to trial.' That evolution represents a slight glimmer of hope for conservation efforts because it shows that awareness campaigns are being heeded, at least by some people. Along those same lines, a restaurant chef in Ouesso, Republic of Congo, said that he would never agree to serve a protected species for fear of losing his job.[21]

Denying that there is a bushmeat crisis, or acting in a way that minimises the problem, is not uncommon among urban elites. An up-scale restaurant in Kinshasa that caters to the local elite offered baby chimpanzee on its New Year's Eve menu.[22] Instagram influencers videoed themselves eating pangolin in a restaurant in Libreville, sharing the gastronomic experience with their followers.[23] Even committed conservationists feel the responsibility to serve bushmeat to respected guests, which reveals a certain schizophrenia between personal convictions about wildlife conservation and the mix of pressure and pleasure in doing so. A former head of the Congolese Institute for Nature Conservation – the agency par excellence that should be serving as a conservation paragon – excused himself from a meeting we were attending together in Kinshasa. He told me that he was having an important guest for dinner. Half-jokingly, I asked if bushmeat was on the menu. His response was: 'I can't help it. I'm not proud, but yes. My wife is preparing a leg of red river hog in palm oil sauce. I'll be serving wine. I owe this man respect.'[24]

The following news item may seem anecdotal, even trivial, but it does say something about enforcement challenges, baggage control, and perceptions about 'what's the problem?' In 2010 a small propeller plane crashed in DRC killing all passengers except one, who survived to tell the story. A passenger had smuggled a live crocodile on board in a sports bag. It escaped by gnawing through the bag, causing passengers to suddenly scramble towards the front of the plane, throwing it off balance. The incident raises the question about bushmeat, or in this case a live animal, being transported by plane. The crocodile also survived the crash but was hacked to death at the accident site.[25]

From research carried out in Gabon and Cameroon, David Wilkie and colleagues note that: 'The daily and highly visible lack of law enforcement by government agents is developing within the polity a pervasive culture of disrespect for the law as wildlife law-breakers are rarely caught and even less often penalized.'[26] This disrespect was expressed to me by a scofflaw state agent in the Lake Télé Community Reserve. His justification was frustration with the state's inability to cover basic health and education services: 'poorly paid state agents like myself have to accept that their situation does not allow them to be governed by their conscience. We turn a blind eye to the trade of protected species at roadblocks. Conscientious behaviour may return the day when the state does its job properly.'[27] One researcher relayed to me the confession of an environment ministry agent in Kisangani: 'When I apprehend a poacher with an animal on the endangered species list, I say hallelujah.' That means that he will be able to seize the meat for his own consumption or sale, or command a bribe.[28] In a similar vein, park rangers, who are drilled, trained and sensitised about the value of their wildlife protection responsibilities, are notorious hunters and consumers of bushmeat when on patrols, which can last for weeks in isolated forests. One quipped to me: 'Who would eat tinned sardines when surrounded by a troop of monkeys?'[29] Another ranger, this one coyishly more conscientious, admitted: 'When our patrol finds a duiker caught in a snare, it would be sinful not to eat it and just leave it to rot.'[30] The ideas in the preceding paragraphs can be summarised as tolerance as a result of indifference versus tolerance for personal benefit, and both forms of tolerance exist at all levels of the legislation and enforcement hierarchy.

The recruitment of park rangers and support staff in protected areas is another challenge related to motivation to enforce the rules and regulations. Workers, be they local hires or staff from other areas, may seek employment in conservation because they are committed to the conservation cause, but many of them do so because it is a job, money, an opportunity – not a passion. Just as the difference between a hunter and a poacher is ambiguous, so is the difference between a ranger and a bushmeat hunter or trader. Even when they are decently paid by either an environmental NGO or a national conservation agency or environment ministry, earnings tend to be insufficient to make ends meet. One logistics expert working in the Okapi Wildlife Reserve complained to me that after he sent money to his wife in Kisangani, he didn't have anything left for the month to live on: 'I had to borrow money from a friend to buy a tube of toothpaste.'[31] While earnings may be limited, real and perceived needs are constantly increasing. This translates into taking advantage of knowledge, proximity, and opportunity for involvement in the bushmeat business.

The national-level legal frameworks concerning the hunting and trading of bushmeat are quite different from the international efforts aimed at combating the killing of high-profile, high-value endangered species or trophies (such as ivory or rhinoceros horn), for which the mobilisation of diplomatic and political resources is impressive. The United Nations Office on Drugs and Crime has a designated Global Programme for Combating Wildlife and Forest Crime.[32] The International Consortium on Combating Wildlife Crime is a collaborative effort of inter-governmental organisations that, among other objectives, coordinates support to national wildlife law-enforcement agencies.[33] Its members include the Convention on International Trade in Endangered Species of Wild Fauna and Flora, Interpol, the United Nations Office on Drugs and Crime, the World Bank and the World Customs Organization. Conservation priorities help explain the motivation for this mobilisation. Another explanation is the international wildlife trade's contribution to 'transnational organised crime, which generates billions of criminal proceeds each year'.[34] International financial-crime prevention agencies are particularly worried about how the illegal wildlife trade feeds into criminal money-laundering networks, terrorist associations and armed groups. This reality is the subject of Rachel Love Nuwer's book *Poached: Inside the dark world of wildlife trafficking*.[35] This reality also helps explain the trend towards paramilitary and security responses relying on enhanced law enforcement and sophisticated surveillance technologies. Of course, not all hunting for money is 'transnational organised crime', which is one of the problems of the discourse expressed by wildlife organisations and conservation criminologists. This trend has led Rosaleen Duffy to argue that 'such responses do not tackle the social, political and economic complexities that fundamentally drive and sustain' the international wildlife trade.[36]

Structural challenges

Rural Central Africa is undeniably under-industrialised, isolated and suffering from lack of infrastructure. By highlighting these structural challenges, this section helps account for the need to hunt to earn cash, while again humanising the rationale behind people's strategic choices. Getting meat (or other forest resources) to the city, main road or port can be an adventurous trek. Private sector investment – and, consequently, salaried work – is rare. Subsistence farming is the primary occupation in these countries (albeit to a lesser extent in Gabon) where informal activities dominate. Table 9.2, based on the World Bank's annual survey Ease of Doing Business, is a good indicator of how difficult it is to find salaried work in an environment that can be interpreted as hostile to investment. Indeed, for Central Africa, it would make more sense to call the survey Difficulty in Doing Business. All Central African countries rank low. Formal sector work, moreover, such as in industrial logging concessions, creates additional conservation challenges because bushmeat is harvested in the concession to feed workers or to sell (as previously discussed in Chapter 2).

Another intractable problem is the persistence of poor public service provision.[37] States in the region are notoriously corrupt (see Table 9.3), inefficient, and predatory. Particularly in the DRC but in other Congo Basin countries as well, civil servants,

Table 9.2: Ease of doing business (2019)

Country	Rank
Cameroon	166/190
Central African Republic	183/190
Democratic Republic of the Congo	184/190
Equatorial Guinea	177/190
Gabon	169/190
Republic of Congo	180/190

Source: http://www.doingbusiness.org/content/dam/doingBusiness/media/Fact-Sheets/DB19/FactSheet_DoingBusiness2019_SSA_Eng.pdf.

the security forces, and other categories of state agents – whether they be in an urban ministerial office or in a remote rural setting – lack operating budgets, technical skill sets, and motivation to respect their mandates. Men in uniform hassle the population, who are often unaware of their rights;[38] office workers abandon their desks to tend to their peri-urban fields or work at other side jobs.

The relative absence of the state in many areas of the vast Congo Basin is a problem related to poor public service provision.[39] Huge tracts of land throughout the region remain beyond the effective reach of any form of state authority. CAR is the most striking example of a state as an absentee landlord: 'significant portions of the country's territory remain outside state control and are ungoverned', according to the US State Department.[40] It is a quintessential stateless space, according to Louisa Lombard, who uses hunting and raiding as a political metaphor there.[41] The observation made by Thomas Bierschenk and Jean-Pierre Olivier de Sardan over twenty years ago that 'the state stops twelve kilometres from Bangui' still has currency.[42] Similarly, the quest by the DRC state to take and maintain control over its vast territory is an ongoing security, administrative and political challenge. The political culture of impunity is a consequence of corruption, which exacerbates the difficulty in ensuring law enforcement when faced with all kinds of violence, human rights violations and wildlife crime. People have to fend for themselves when governments do not provide services. Hunting is a logical option in the fend-for-yourself economy of weak states. The following quote provides a vivid example. 'Before, the state paid the salaries of five teachers in our village. Today it pays just one. So we parents have to make up the difference. How are we supposed to do that if we don't hunt?'[43]

Table 9.3: Corruption index (2018) (0 = highly corrupt, 100 = least corrupt).

Country	Score	Rank
Cameroon	25/100	152/180
Central African Republic	26/100	149/180
Democratic Republic of the Congo	20/100	161/180
Equatorial Guinea	16/100	172/180
Gabon	31/100	124/180
Republic of Congo	19/100	165/180

Source: https://www.transparency.org/cpi2018.

Even in protected areas, there is growing awareness on the part of wildlife conservation experts that their ambitions are unlikely to curb subsistence hunting because of its long-standing ordinary everydayness. Unlike city dwellers, who may have a wider choice of food options, rural populations depend on bushmeat and other forest foods for their daily needs.[44] The focus of conservation experts has, therefore, shifted. Current objectives aim to reduce the professionalisation of hunting by well-organised commercial networks that emerge to feed urban markets, and to design behaviour change strategies while offering protein alternatives. One decade ago, a synthesis of 12 studies carried out in Central Africa indicated that more than half of all bushmeat hunted was sold.[45] This rate has most likely increased since then, given urban demographic shifts and more aggressive commercialisation dynamics. More and improved roads facilitate the transportation of meat from villages to towns and cities.

From community development to behaviour change campaigns

Environmental NGOs, along with a broad range of stakeholders from the donor community, academia and government, have made some conceptual progress in trying to deal with the problems of enforcing wildlife laws. Community development is an example of such progress because it seeks to promote the well-being of local populations while at the same time striving to sustainably manage wildlife. The underpinnings of community development include a rights-based approach to natural resource management, social and political empowerment, and the promotion of economic opportunities for wealth creation. The sustainable livelihood approach is one way of trying to tackle community development challenges by adopting a strategy that considers five key types of capital: human, social, natural, physical and financial. Gender equity and the rights of hunter-gatherers are also key priorities to address in community development strategies. Community development sounds sensible in theory, but implementing it in the countries of the Congo Basin is extremely difficult and there are very few examples of success – at least of the scale that would be needed to make a contribution to the well-being of communities.

There have been high hopes of contributing to community development and reducing hunting through the setting up of alternative livelihood strategies. Conservation partners, frequently in and around protected areas, have toyed with initiatives such as small livestock husbandry, agricultural extension, shade-grown cacao, fish farming, honey production and crafts. Projects have tried to get bushmeat sellers to shift from selling bushmeat to making soap, sewing, carpentry or hairdressing. But these alternative livelihood schemes are often poorly designed and are of too small a scale to have sustainable or real impact. Moreover, there is no evidence that they would displace unsustainable forest use such as hunting; at best they would supplement income from such activities. A woman may stop selling bushmeat herself to start a sewing business but would not abandon her bushmeat table – she would most likely groom her niece or daughter to take over her business, while maintaining a role in managing the process. Consequently, alternative economic activities become complementary.

Many alternative livelihood activities suffer from misguided design, inadequate technical assistance, and poor follow-through. Some of these initiatives utterly fail to analyse costs and benefits and calculate expected return on investment: economic considerations, in other words, tend to be overlooked. Beneficiaries of free money schemes lack the motivation to sustain alternative activities if they do not believe they could work. Getting high-volume, low-value commodities to a market or intermediary road is a serious disincentive. After having analysed 20 alternative livelihood projects in Cameroon, Juliet Wright concluded that 'the key assumptions underlying alternative livelihood projects, relating to the notions of substitution and the homogeneous spatially-bound community, are flawed. The diversified nature of livelihoods, and evidence of the limited uptake of most of the alternative livelihood projects examined, would suggest that the introduced livelihood activities did not replace behaviours such as hunting as hoped.'[46]

The shortcomings in enforcement, community development efforts and alternative livelihood strategies have led to the creation of behaviour change strategies. Sometimes referred to as demand-reduction interventions, behaviour change tries to tackle the problem of unsustainable bushmeat consumption at the demand level, not the supply level, which is the main thrust of regulation and enforcement approaches. These behaviour change campaigns seek to instigate voluntary change among target audiences. While different organisations use different tools in their behaviour change strategies, these can be roughly summarised in the following five steps: behaviour identification, audience segmentation, behaviour modelling, marketing framework development, and campaign development and implementation.[47] I'm frequently struck by the apparent naivety of Europeans and Americans when discussing behaviour change policy design around bushmeat consumption. It seems to me that the designers of these ambitious social engineering policies spend far too little time engaging with the rural poor and with the ordinary Central African city dweller.

Behaviour campaigns in developed economies with reasonably democratic governance structures – for example, relating to recycling, veganism, anti-smoking, or not drinking and driving – are very slow in finding uptake. But they do contribute to attitude and behaviour change, especially when consumers have opportunities to choose. Nudging bushmeat consumers away from bushmeat in Central Africa, on the other hand, is only in the nascent phases, in large part for the reasons discussed in previous chapters about cultural attachment, lack of alternatives, and the power of tradition. These challenges have led Diogo Verissimo and Anita Wan to conclude: 'Given how difficult it is to influence human behaviour, particularly in a complex context, such as wildlife trade, conservationists can only succeed if they can benefit from the incremental learning that comes with a more transparent and rigorous evaluation of demand-reduction interventions.' That opinion, which provides a faint glimmer of optimism, is echoed by Helen Agu and Meredith Gore: 'Ultimately, the global illegal wildlife trade will only likely be solved by a variety of methods: a combination of regulations, enforcement, market solutions, or demand reduction campaigns.'[48] It would be tempting to want to believe that this is possible, but the assessment, at least in the Central African political economy landscape described above, seems to be far more aspirational than realistically operational from a policy perspective.

CONCLUSION

GAME OVER?

The future availability of bushmeat for rural and urban populations in Central Africa is uncertain and, if current trends continue, unlikely. Deforestation, urbanisation, demographic pressure and unsustainable wildlife exploitation are interconnected dynamics that have indisputable negative impacts throughout the natural environment. These dynamics give credence to fears about an emerging sixth mass extinction, caused by human activity, unlike previous extinctions, which were provoked by natural phenomena.

Species loss or extinction and ecosystem collapse can be added to the themes of earth-threatening dangers of the eco-horror art genre – human fears about the natural world – that emerged in the 1980s. There are indeed many examples of reality catching up with fiction. But are the prophetic dystopian cries of alarm really relevant to an analysis of the bushmeat crisis? Without seeking to take an aspirational or ideological stance on the optimism–pessimism spectrum, the preceding chapters have presented a balanced fact-based analysis, emphasising real threats while also hinting at some timidly innovative wildlife management strategies. My conclusion, based on available evidence, is that these strategies will be too little, too late. Cultural attachment to bushmeat, and its economic and dietary importance, make the bushmeat crisis difficult to resolve. That is a concluding reminder of the book's threefold central narrative: bushmeat is culturally and economically important, wildlife is under severe pressure, and management strategies are largely ineffective.

These chapters argued that policies matter, although within limits, and sometimes with unpredictable and undesired consequences. Policies may mitigate pressures on wildlife in some isolated cases but not on the scale that the challenges would require. As long as the cultural appetite for bushmeat remains strong, supply chains will respond. Actions taken today, based on ostensibly sound scientific and governance understanding, will shape our relations with the environment in the future. Today's 'sound understanding', nevertheless, may well shift as unexpected political or ecological realities take form. Climate change is a real threat. It is difficult to predict how cultural norms, social institutions, political economy dynamics and the 'human factor' – individual and collective world views that influence attitudes and behaviours – will influence bushmeat consumption in the future. Trying to accommodate the human factor with wildlife management and conservation therefore remains a delicate exercise characterised by powerlessness, uncertainty and, frequently, disappointment. While this book has presented multiple logics in people's relations with wildlife, it has also emphasised the randomness of these relations, which confound management initiatives. Community development programmes in and around national parks are, as a case in point, intractable quagmires.

The extreme complexity of trying to reconcile human development priorities with biodiversity conservation creates situations where we think we know what to do, but in fact we do not. Policies are in many instances based on unverified hypotheses, ideology and aspirations. Inculcating the values of conservation today for the benefit of future generations in poor villagers who live in the fend-for-yourself economy is an example of a seemingly logical argument that frequently falls on deaf ears. From a policy perspective, nevertheless, the need to change today instead of adapting tomorrow makes sense. There is no shared interpretation of the concept of benefit. Benefit is a mix of money, prestige, power and social relations. A man in the northern Republic of Congo's Lake Télé Community Reserve gave me his opinion about elephant conservation for his descendants: 'I've heard that dinosaurs once roamed the earth but I never saw one – and that doesn't bother me. When my grandchildren or great-grandchildren are told elephant roamed these areas a long time ago, perhaps they will say the same thing.'[1] Environmental messaging in rich developed countries seems to have modified this type of attitude, but in the Central African landscape it is not surprising – and it is enduring because of immediate pragmatic needs. This example leads to another problem, which is that of perceptions of the future. Making sacrifices in the present for future benefits can be a difficult choice for the rural and urban poor.

The time of no or little bushmeat has already come in some places and is worth looking into from the perspective of resilience. Hunters in the Luki Biosphere Reserve in the DRC increasingly complain of the shortage of wildlife.[2] They are consequently laying down their shotguns to make charcoal, to become motorcycle taxi drivers, barbers, brick-makers or woodworkers. Former women bushmeat sellers claim they can earn better money today by sewing. Other examples of resilience include beekeeping for honey production, improvements in agro-forestry practices, backyard breeding of poultry, pigs and goats, and changing food consumption patterns. Protein-rich caterpillars, for example, were rarely eaten in the region in the 1970s but they are increasingly consumed today.[3] While these resilience strategies can be seen as having the capacity to cope with resource scarcity, they are also fragile and unsustainable. Caterpillars will eventually suffer the same destiny as bushmeat owing to forest degradation and habitat loss, and charcoal makers will find it increasingly difficult to find trees to convert to charcoal.

Conservation experts, policy-makers and academics will need to carefully monitor some of the opportunities and trends mentioned in previous chapters. While we know that high-income countries brand themselves as having the greenest economies in the world, private-sector green economic entrepreneurship may also have some – albeit limited – potential in Central Africa. Avenues for wealth creation outside the bushmeat economy could include new forms of adventure tourism, or investment in relatively high-value commodities such as essential oils, chia seeds, coffee and cacao. These avenues, however, could also lead to the trap of natural resource bricolage where policies and actions are not positively impactful or, worse, cause perverse side effects.[4]

As global political economy priorities shift, public bilateral and multilateral funding may become less available, and billionaire philanthropy is unpredictable. While the hunt for solutions goes on, so does the hunting of wild animals. Try, fail, and try again is a humble but inefficient conservation management approach. It is, however, the approach that best characterises wildlife management today. Particularly if the problems are exacerbated by factors that lie well beyond the intervention capacity of national governments and their international partners, the implications for the survival of wildlife in Central Africa do not look promising.

NOTES

PREFACE

1. https://www.etymonline.com/word/meat. In this and some subsequent notes, internet and online sources (as distinct from published articles, chapters and books) are given in URL form and are not included in the Bibliography at the end of the book. Such URL references were last checked on 15 October 2022. Hurst is not responsible for the availability and contents of external websites.

1. MEAT FOR SOME, WILDLIFE FOR OTHERS

1. Gallagher 2008: 6.
2. Interview with Mama Séphora, Ouesso, Republic of Congo, 6 October 2021.
3. Nasi et al. 2008: 6.
4. Bowen-Jones et al. 2003: 391.
5. Lingala is a Bantu language spoken throughout the north-western part of the Democratic Republic of the Congo and a large part of the Republic of Congo. It is also spoken, to a lesser extent, in some areas of Angola and the Central African Republic.
6. Boyeldieu 2008.
7. de Garine and Pagezy 1990: 43.
8. Douglas 1963: 45.
9. Cusack 2000: 221.
10. https://www.quotedb.com/quotes/3764.

11. https://www.bbc.com/news/world-latin-america-62721020.
12. Alabi et al. 2009.
13. Wilkie and Carpenter 1999: 930.
14. Fa et al. 2002: 235.
15. Nasi et al. 2011.
16. Coad et al. 2019: 26.
17. Cornelis et al. 2017: 4.
18. Nasi et al. 2011: 359.
19. https://www.theworldcounts.com/challenges/consumption/foods-and-beverages/world-consumption-of-meat.
20. Milner-Gulland et al. 2003: 351.
21. Janson 1967: 18–19.
22. Gallagher 2008: 63.
23. https://www.equaltimes.org/will-the-coronavirus-stop-the#.XtqZGC4zbIV.
24. Fa et al. 2014.
25. Nasi et al. 2008: 7.
26. Barnes et al. 1997.
27. https://www.ifaw.org/united-states.
28. https://www.humanesociety.org/.
29. Daley 2013; De Waal 2015.
30. https://www.instagram.com/p/B8rWKFnnQ5c/?utm_source=ig_embed.
31. https://www.campfirezimbabwe.org/content/about.
32. https://resourceafrica.net/open-letter-celebrity-campaigns-undermine-successful-conservation-and-human-rights/.
33. Convention on Biological Diversity 2017: 2.
34. Lescuyer and Nasi 2016: 93.
35. Milner-Gulland and Resit Akçakaya 2001: 686.
36. Ripple et al. 2016: 2.
37. Wilkie and Lee 2004.
38. Maisels et al. 2001: 324. This assessment was confirmed elsewhere in Cameroon by Linder and Oates 2011.
39. Coad et al. 2013: 270.
40. Bouché et al. 2009: 6.
41. Kümpel et al. 2015: 244.

42. Vermeulen and Lanata 2006: 5.
43. Van Schuylenbergh 2006: 177–9.
44. Ripple et al. 2016; https://www.iucnredlist.org/.
45. de Merode et al. 2004: 578.
46. Mendelson et al. 2003: 78.
47. Powell et al. 2011; van Vliet et al. 2014.
48. Hladik et al. 1990; Froment et al. 1996; van Vliet and Nasi 2017; Dieudonné 2016; de Merode et al. 2004; and Fargeot et al. 2017 are just a few of the numerous relevant references.
49. Brashares et al. 2014: 376.
50. Sirén and Machoa 2008.
51. Milner-Gulland et al. 2003: 352.
52. Dounias and Froment 2011: 300.
53. Interview with Mr Tanduvibila, Kifudi village, Luki Biosphere Reserve, DRC, 5 December 2020.
54. Inogwabini 2014.
55. Harms 1987: 108.
56. Personal communication, Professor Jean-Claude Micha, University of Namur, Belgium, 20 September 2022.
57. Interview with Francine Luhusu, Luki Biosphere Reserve, DRC, 18 March 2015.
58. Interview with Casimir Mpetshi, Kinshasa, 21 November 2020.

2. A SHRINKING FOREST HABITAT

1. https://www.sciencedaily.com/releases/2021/02/210204101640.htm.
2. https://pfbc-cbfp.org/home.html.
3. Ibid.
4. Eba'a Atyi et al. 2009: 122.
5. Billand 2012: 66.
6. Dargie et al. 2017.
7. https://congo.wcs.org/Wild-Places/Lac-T%C3%A9l%C3%A9-Community-Reserve.aspx.
8. https://www.un.org/sustainabledevelopment/blog/2019/05/nature-decline-unprecedented-report/.
9. https://www.globalforestwatch.org/dashboards/global.
10. Geist and Lambin 2002.

11. Tyukavina et al. 2018.
12. Interview with Casimir Mpetshi, Kinshasa, 21 November 2020.
13. Redford 1992.
14. Ernst et al. 2013.
15. Shapiro 2012: 9.
16. https://www.weforum.org/agenda/2020/09/the-world-population-in-2100-by-country/#:-:text=By%202100%2C%20the%20global%20population,%2C%20Nigeria%20and%20China%2C%20respectively.
17. Guyer 1995.
18. https://sites.ontariotechu.ca/sustainabilitytoday/urban-and-energy-systems/Worlds-largest-cities/population-projections/city-population-2050.php.
19. https://www.borntoengineer.com/infographic-what-are-the-worlds-biggest-cities-going-to-be-in-2100.
20. https://forebears.io/dr-congo/forenames.
21. For a nuanced analysis of this question, see Bulte and Horan 2002.
22. Trefon 2011.
23. Interview with Brice Bionguet, Dzeke, Republic of Congo, 30 January 2019.
24. Heath 2010.
25. https://en.wikipedia.org/wiki/List_of_cities_in_Africa_by_population.
26. Steel 2008: 10.
27. Geschiere and Nyamnjoh 1998.
28. Maffi 2005: 602.
29. Vansina 1990: 255.
30. Hoffman et al. 2003.
31. Bahuchet et al. 2001: 51.
32. Russell et al. 2011.
33. Trefon 2016.
34. Poulsen et al. 2009; Wilkie et al. 2008.
35. Interview with Vincent Istace CIB, Pokola, Republic of Congo 7 October 2021 and Congolaise Industrielle des Bois 2012, unpublished company rules and regulation document.
36. Dubiez et al. 2017.

37. https://www.itto.int/.
38. Interview with a forest concession manager whom, for reasons of confidentiality, I do not identify by name, Republic of Congo, 7 October 2021.
39. Spira et al. 2019: 141.
40. https://ipisresearch.be/story-map-of-asm-sites-in-the-drc/.
41. World Bank 2008: 7.
42. Interview with the park's head warden, 25 August 2021.
43. Hintjens 2006.
44. Matthysen et al. 2019: 7.
45. Verbrugge and Geenen 2019.
46. Van Boekstael and Vlassenroot 2012.
47. Trefon 2011.
48. Marijnen 2018.

3. CONSERVATION, DEVELOPMENT AND WILDLIFE

1. Interview with Solomon Mampeta, Kisangani, DRC, 7 July 2019.
2. Büscher and Whande 2007: 39.
3. Rodary 2008: 84.
4. Büscher and Whande 2007: 22.
5. Haider et al. 2018: 319.
6. Comaroff and Comaroff 1993: xiii.
7. https://www.weforum.org/agenda/2018/10/can-we-balance-conservation-and-development-science-says-yes/.
8. Nelson 2003: 67.
9. USAID 2017: 73.
10. For a detailed study of fortress conservation, see Brockington et al. 2008.
11. https://www.swm-programme.info/homepage.
12. Adams and McShane 1996.
13. http://www.environmentandsociety.org/arcadia/internationalism-heart-africa-albert-national-park-virunga-national-park.
14. Cronon 1996: 13.
15. McDonald 2001: 192.
16. Blanc 2020.

17. https://extinctionrebellion.de/aktionen/kampagnen/nature-needs-justice/racist-and-colonial-roots-nature-conservation-and-its-neo-colonial-present/.
18. Vansina 1990: 39–46.
19. https://wwf.panda.org/knowledge_hub/history/.
20. Lombard 2020: 6.
21. https://www.survivalinternational.org/about/parks-and-peoples.
22. Interview with the chief of the Iliko village, October 2019.
23. https://www.sixdegreesnews.org/archives/29331/leaked-report-us-halts-funding-to-wwf-wcs-and-other-conservation-ngos-over-abuses.
24. https://wrm.org.uy/articles-from-the-wrm-bulletin/section1/wwf-in-the-drcs-salonga-national-park-torture-murder-and-gang-rape/.
25. https://www.fws.gov/press-release/2021-04/us-government-launches-human-rights-and-conservation-curriculum-central.
26. Ford et al. 2020: 2.
27. https://virunga.org/about/.
28. https://www.cambridge.org/core/journals/oryx/article/periurban-conservation-in-the-mondah-forest-of-libreville-gabon-red-list-assessments-of-endemic-plant-species-and-avoiding-protected-area-downsizing/2F9535A82831E7845D33738CADE33364/core-reader.
29. https://pulitzercenter.org/reporting/central-african-republic-fight-chinko#:-:text=Chinko%20was%20founded%20in%20 2014,project%20a%20chance%20to%20succeed.
30. Symes et al. 2016: 657.
31. https://www.survivalinternational.org/news/12475.
32. Wauchope et al. 2022.
33. https://www.nationalparkrescue.org/about/.
34. Mogomotsi and Madigele 2017: 54.
35. Duffy et al. 2019.
36. https://www.survivalinternational.org/news/12475.
37. Bennett et al. 2019.
38. Ingram 2020: 122.
39. Coquery-Vidrovitch 2011.
40. Büscher and Whande 2007: 26.
41. Rodary 2008.

42. Shandra et al. 2008: 16.

43. International Union for Conservation of Nature and Natural Resources et al. 1980.

44. Büscher and Whande 2007: 29–32.

45. World Commission on Environment and Development 1987.

46. https://pdf.usaid.gov/pdf_docs/pa00jrv1.pdf.

47. Vermeulen and Karsenty 2017.

48. Clay 2016; Reed et al. 2015.

49. Wieland 2008: 2.

50. Nelson and Chomitz 2011: 2.

51. Johnson 1992: 15.

52. World Commission on Environment and Development 1987: 12.

53. Ludwig and Macnaghten 2020.

54. https://www.iucn.org/commissions/world-commission-protected-areas/our-work/transboundary-conservation.

55. https://www.internationalconservation.org/united-states/icc/public-private-partnerships-essential-to-combat-wildlife-trafficking-in-africa.

56. Scholte et al. 2018: 8.

57. Nana 2021.

4.   HUNTING IN TRANSITION

1. https://www.thinkafrica.fi/until-the-lion-learns-to-write-every-story-will-glorify-the-hunter/.

2. Interview with anonymous hunter, Luki Biosphere Reserve, DRC, 26 October 2022.

3. Solly 2002–3: 146.

4. Cogels 2002: 238.

5. Interview with Dieudonné Dsholinga, Dzeke, Republic of Congo, 28 January 2019.

6. Lescuyer and Nasi 2016: 2.

7. Hunter-gatherers were previously referred to as 'Pygmies' but the term is now considered to be pejorative, so is rarely used today in academic literature.

8. Padilla-Iglesias et al. 2022.

9. Fa et al. 2022: 261.

10. https://www.un.org/en/chronicle/article/illegal-commercial-bushmeat-trade-central-and-west-africa.
11. Bahuchet 2014; Riddell 2011.
12. Bahuchet 1985.
13. Bowen-Jones et al. 2003: 395.
14. For a detailed discussion of hunting methods, see Fa et al. 2022, especially Chapter 3.
15. Vansina 1990: 92.
16. MacGaffey 1970: 173–4.
17. MacGaffey 1970: 173.
18. Bahuchet et al. 1990.
19. Trefon and Defo 1999.
20. Beuve-Mery 2014–15: 48.
21. Beuve-Mery 2014–15: 49.
22. Interview with Casimir Mpetshi, Kinshasa, RDC, 14 December 2020.
23. Vermeulen 2000: 120.
24. Vansina 1990: 90–1.
25. Kambala Luadia Tshikengela 2018: 143.
26. Noss 1995.
27. Interview with Charles Mumbere, Zongo, DRC, 16 October 2022.
28. Interview with Dieudonné Dsholinga, Dzeke, Republic of Congo, 28 January 2019.
29. Ibid.
30. Frazer 1957: 24.
31. Dounias 2016.
32. Coad 2006: 279.
33. Interview with Chief Rodrigue, Epena, Republic of Congo, 5 February 2019.
34. Interview with Mr Calvin, Dzeke, Republic of Congo, 26 January 2019.
35. Evans-Pritchard 1976: 54.
36. White 2004: 185.
37. Interview with Mr Jean Gaston, Kisangani, DRC, 28 March 2019.
38. Douglas 1963: 207.
39. Frazer 1957: 288.
40. Interview with Dieudonné Dsholing, Dzeke, Republic of Congo, 28 January 2019.

41. Laugrand and Oosten 2015: 356.
42. Interview with Dieudonné Dsholing, Dzeke, Republic of Congo, 28 January 2019.
43. Lee 1969: 24.
44. Trefon and de Maret 1999: 565.
45. Ibid.
46. Interview with Dieudonné Dsholing, Dzeke, Republic of Congo, 28 January 2019.
47. Bellman 1981.
48. Interview with Mr Seraphin Mokomole, Dzeke, Republic of Congo, 26 January 2019.
49. Dieudonné 2016: 178.
50. There are many studies about totems in Africa; see, for example, Mandillah and Ekosse 2018.
51. Interview with Brice Bionguet, Impfondo, Republic of Congo, 6 February 2019.
52. Interview with Mr Calvin, Dzeke, Republic of Congo, 26 January 2019.
53. Interview with Mr Bola Madzoke, Dzeke, Republic of Congo, 26 January 2019.
54. Interview with Mr Ignace Enongama, Dzeke, Republic of Congo, 27 January 2019.
55. Interview with Mr Seraphin Mokomole, Dzeke, Republic of Congo, 26 January 2019.
56. Simone 2004: 180.
57. Lombard 2020.
58. De Boeck 2001.
59. De Boeck and Plissart 2004: 44.
60. Souto et al. 2019.
61. Khonde 2020.
62. La Cerva 2015: 57.
63. Khonde 2020: 71.
64. Cosyn 2020: 32.
65. Vansina 1990: 74.
66. Email communication, Romain Duda and Dan Ingram, 7 May 2020.

67. https://www.nationalgeographic.com/animals/2020/02/pangolin-scale-trade-shipments-growing/.

5. THE CULTURE OF CONSUMPTION

1. Wilkie and Carpenter 1999: 940.
2. Igugu Murula 2019: 23
3. Interview with Ernestine Lonpi Tipi, Luki Biosphere Reserve, DRC, 5 December 2020.
4. Mauss 1966.
5. Felbab-Brown 2017: 11.
6. Schenck et al. 2006: 437.
7. Bachand et al. 2015: 147.
8. Bachand et al. 2015: 438; Edderai and Houben 2002.
9. Hickey 2008: 5.
10. Hickey 2008: 7.
11. Kinshasa research notes, Matumpu Jérémie, May 2019.
12. Wright 2018: 17.
13. Fargeot et al. 2017: 32.
14. Mbete et al. 2011: 191 and 196.
15. Tshikung et al. 2019: 82.
16. Luiselli et al. 2018: 731.
17. Luiselli et al. 2018: 733.
18. Lescuyer and Nasi 2016: 7.
19. Chaber et al. 2018: 3.
20. Chaber et al. 2010: 319.
21. Luiselli et al. 2017: 53.
22. Vorster et al. 2011: 429.
23. Barrot 1994: 26; also http://www1.rfi.fr/actufr/articles/094/article_57741.asp.
24. Trefon 2002.
25. Randolph 2016: 122–3.
26. https://www.psychologytoday.com/us/blog/sensoria/201604/proustian-memory-was-it-really-madeleine-tea-cake.
27. Interview with Shango Mutambwe, Brussels, 23 September 2020.
28. Interview with Papa Didi, Luki Biosphere Reserve, 23 October 2022.

29. Interview with Ivonne Kahambu, Luki Biosphere Reserve, DRC, 3 December 2020.

30. Interview with Joshua Ozi, Boma, DRC, 12 December 2020.

31. Ibid.

32. Lombard 2020: 28.

33. Chausson et al. 2019: 185.

34. Interview with Noël Kabuyaya, Kinshasa, 25 September 2019.

35. Interview with Divan Malekani, Kinshasa, 26 November 2021.

36. Interview with Brice Bionguet, Impfondo, Republic of Congo, 6 February 2019.

37. Email communication, Ben Evans, 3 April 2020.

38. Interview with Mr Ignace Enongama, Dzeke, Republic of Congo, 27 January 2019.

39. Interview with Olivier Igugu, Kisangani, DRC, 7 July 2019.

40. https://www.swnsdigital.com/2012/02/bacon-butty-best-of-british/.

41. Email communication, Charles Mpoyi, 25 April 2020.

42. Kambala Luadia Tshikengela 2018: 148.

43. https://www.africamuseum.be/fr/research/discover/human_sciences/culture_society/blr/results_main?Francais=interdit.

44. https://synergieruraleactionpaysanne.blogspot.com/.

45. Demuenynck 1908: 33–4.

46. Rose 2001: 64.

47. Interview with Kim Neris, Kinshasa, DRC, 15 November 2018.

48. Ibid.

49. Interview with Brice Bionguet, Impfondo, Republic of Congo, 6 February 2019.

50. Evans-Pritchard 1976: 92.

51. Bolle 1958: 21.

52. Malinowski 1955: 45.

53. Vansina 1990: 74.

54. Cosyn 2020: 62.

55. Vansina 1990: 318.

56. https://www.bbc.com/news/world-africa-54554978.

57. Van Bockhaven 2009: 79.

58. McCall 1973–74.

59. Blanc 2020.

60. Interview with Eric Kyungu, Goma, DRC, 28 February 2020.
61. https://text.npr.org/1044333402.
62. Soewu et al. 2020: 245.
63. Canetti 1960: 219.
64. Rose 2001: 65.
65. Morsello et al. 2015.
66. Bastian 1993.
67. Kourouma 1998: 93.

6. THE BUSHMEAT ECONOMY

1. Bowen-Jones et al. 2003: 390.
2. Financial Action Task Force 2020: 5.
3. South and Wyatt 2011: 540.
4. Valimahamed et al. (2017) have attempted to quantify hunting costs and benefits in the Republic of Congo and the DRC.
5. Davies 2002: 587.
6. Polanyi 1944.
7. Martin 1983; Anadu et al. 1988.
8. Dieudonné 2016: 147.
9. Bahuchet and Ioveva 1999: 539–40.
10. Trefon 2006.
11. Poulsen 2009.
12. Bowen-Jones et al. 2003: 399.
13. Hardin 1968: 1244.
14. Gallagher 2008: 62.
15. Bahuchet and Ioveva 1999: 543.
16. Beuve-Mery 2014–15: 50–2.
17. Mendelson et al. 2003: 74.
18. Valimahamed et al. 2017: 16.
19. Lescuyer and Nasi 2016: 6.
20. Email communication, Baudouin Michel, 3 July 2020.
21. Caspary 2001: 14.
22. McNamara et al. 2015: 1447–8.
23. Bahuchet and Ioveva 1999: 550.
24. See Gore et al. 2021 for a stakeholder typology of actors in illegal wildlife trade.

25. Lescuyer and Nasi 2016: 3.
26. Work by David Wilkie and colleagues is particularly relevant: Wilkie et al. 2005; Wilkie and Lee 2004; Wilkie and Godoy 2001; Wilkie and Godoy 2000; Wilkie and Carpenter 1999.
27. McNamara 2013: 154.
28. Fa et al. 2019; Lescuyer and Nasi 2016; Bowen-Jones et al. 2003; and Wilkie and Carpenter 1999.
29. For a brief summary of Payments for Ecosystem Services see: https://www.face.eu/sites/default/files/documents/english/payments_for_ecosystem_services_final_en_0.pdf.
30. Trefon 2016: 51–2.
31. http://www.fao.org/3/a-a0262e.pdf.
32. Jori et al. 1998.
33. Chausson et al. 2019: 182.
34. Kabuyaya and Trefon 2007.
35. Brashares et al. 2011: 13934.
36. Coad et al. 2019: 118.
37. Bourdieu 1984.
38. Interview with Mr Calvin, Dzeke, Republic of Congo, 26 January 2019.
39. Steel 2008: 9.
40. Interview with Christlia Nguidzi, Lake Télé Community Reserve, Republic of Congo, 15 August 2018.
41. Fargeot et al. 2017: 40.
42. Fargeot et al. 2017: 38.
43. Bachand et al. 2015: 156.
44. Schenck et al. 2006: 453.
45. Wilkie and Godoy 2001.
46. Robinson and Bennett 2002: 332.
47. Wilkie et al. 2005: 273.
48. Brashares et al. 2011: 13931.
49. Merson et al. 2019: 3685.

7. EATING OUT IN KINSHASA

1. Fa et al. 2019: 6.
2. Ibid.
3. Bahuchet and Ioveva-Baillon 1998: 179.

4. https://impact.economist.com/sustainability/project/food-security-index/Country.
5. https://www.weforum.org/agenda/2016/12/this-map-shows-how-much-each-country-spends-on-food/.
6. Comhaire-Sylvain 1950: 52.
7. Lemarchand 2002: 395.
8. Ministère du Plan et Suivi de la Mise en œuvre de la Révolution de la Modernité et al. 2014: 5.
9. De Herdt 2004: 116.
10. Canetti 1960: 222.
11. Schure et al. 2013: 4.
12. Bakarr et al. 2001: 7.
13. Fa et al. 2019: 9.
14. Noël Kabuyaya helped with this story by helping me interview Mama Régine and her clients in January 2019.
15. *Fufu* is a widely consumed dish in Central Africa. It is a pasty dough made from boiled and ground cassava or plantain sometimes mixed with corn flour.
16. Mendelson et al. 2003: 82.
17. Ibid.
18. http://www.illegalwildlifetrade.net/2018/11/22/urban-bushmeat-trade-the-restaurants-recipe/4_trading-ideas_restaurant_header/.

8. BUSHMEAT AND ZOONOSIS

1. Fa et al. 2022: 255.
2. https://www.merriam-webster.com/dictionary/zoonosis.
3. Fa et al. 2022 give a comprehensive summary of these issues in Chapter 7.
4. Saylors et al. 2021.
5. Milbank and Vira 2022: 445.
6. https://www.cdc.gov/poxvirus/monkeypox/clinicians/smallpox-vaccine.html.
7. See https://www.livescience.com/21426-global-zoonoses-diseases-hotspots.html.
8. Jones et al. 2008.
9. https://www.who.int/en/news-room/fact-sheets/detail/plague.

10. https://www.cdc.gov/flu/pandemic-resources/1918-pandemic-h1n1. html.
11. Dell et al. 2020.
12. Saylors et al. 2021.
13. Quammen 2012.
14. Ibid.: 83.
15. https://www.nytimes.com/2020/01/28/opinion/coronavirus-china. html. Similar arguments are made by Bloomfield et al. 2020.
16. Johnson et al. 2020.
17. https://www.cdc.gov/onehealth/basics/index.html.
18. Hardin and Auzel 2001: 87.
19. https://lioncoalition.org/2020/04/04/open-letter-to-world-health-organization/.
20. https://news.mongabay.com/2019/05/conservation-groups-concerned-as-who-recognizes-traditional-chinese-medicine/.
21. https://www.bbc.com/news/science-environment-52981804.
22. https://preventpandemics.org/.
23. https://www.gavi.org/vaccineswork/combatting-covid-19-vaccine-hesitancy-through-community-mobilisers-democratic.
24. Barrall 2022.
25. Fa et al. 2022: 255.
26. de Garine and Hladik 1990: 93.
27. http://somatosphere.net/forumpost/wild-meat-markets/.
28. McNamara et al. 2020.
29. Booth et al. 2021.
30. http://somatosphere.net/forumpost/wild-meat-markets/.
31. https://www.bbc.com/news/live/world-africa-47639452?ns_mchannel=social&ns_source=twitter&ns_campaign=bbc_live&ns_linkname=5ef2e6370b6cac0667aec245%26Wildlife%20markets%20still%20open%20in%20Nigeria%20despite%20Covid-19%262020-06-24T06%3A17%3A39.536Z&ns_fee=0&pinned_post_locator=urn:asset:926e8824-93da-408c-83d3-fd2b6af0dfae&pinned_post_asset_id=5ef2e6370b6cac0667aec245&pinned_post_type=share.
32. https://www.nytimes.com/2020/01/25/world/asia/china-markets-coronavirus-sars.html.

33. Morcatty et al. 2020.
34. https://www.bbc.com/news/world-africa-61676841.
35. Monroe et al. 2015: 736.
36. https://www.bbc.com/news/world-us-canada-52371977.
37. https://www.bbc.com/news/world-europe-53319765.
38. https://www.bbc.com/news/world-us-canada-59100114.
39. https://www.bbc.com/news/science-environment-62307383.
40. https://www.theguardian.com/environment/2021/mar/10/deadly-pig-disease-could-have-led-to-covid-spillover-to-humans-analysis-suggests.
41. https://www.independent.co.uk/news/world/asia/coronavirus-china-cases-deaths-who-wet-market-wuhan-a9462286.html.
42. https://www.economist.com/science-and-technology/2020/07/22/the-hunt-for-the-origins-of-sars-cov-2-will-look-beyond-china?fsrc=newsletter&utm_campaign=the-economist-today&utm_medium=newsletter&utm_source=salesforce-marketing-cloud&utm_term=2020-07-22&utm_content=article-link-2.
43. https://www.peta.org/.
44. Interview with Omega, Brazzaville, Republic of Congo, 12 September 2022.
45. https://www.bbc.co.uk/news/in-pictures-52632394.
46. https://edition.cnn.com/2020/03/16/europe/pope-francis-prayer-coronavirus-plague-crucifix-intl/index.html.
47. https://www.bbc.com/news/52216330.
48. https://www.bbc.com/news/world-europe-53637365.
49. https://www.bbc.com/news/world-us-canada-52407177.
50. https://www.bbc.com/news/world-africa-56437852.
51. https://www.lalibre.be/international/afrique/coronavirus-la-rdc-candidate-pour-tester-le-vaccin-au-grand-dam-de-certains-congolais-qui-ne-veulent-pas-servir-de-cobayes-5e881b99d8ad581631b00636.
52. https://www.20minutes.fr/monde/2605319-20190916-ebola-ex-ministre-congolais-detourne-fonds-destines-lutte-contre-epidemie.
53. https://www.reuters.com/article/us-health-coronavirus-congo-corruption/congo-virus-funds-embezzled-by-mafia-network-says-deputy-minister-idUSKBN249225.

54. https://www.bbc.com/news/world-africa-58834108.
55. Mavakala 2021.
56. Hooper 2000.
57. For a detailed review of the different spillover theories, see Schneider 2021.
58. Moore 2004; Timberg and Halperin 2012.
59. Gondola and Lauro 2021.
60. Timberg and Halperin 2012; Jackson 2014; see also https://www.nationalgeographic.com/news/2014/10/141002-hiv-virus-spread-africa-health/.
61. Gryseels et al. 2020: 2209.
62. https://www.cdc.gov/vhf/ebola/history/summaries.html.
63. I thank Christophe Pavret de La Rochefordière for calling this to my attention.
64. https://www.radiookapi.net/2018/06/25/actualite/societe/le-marche-de-kisangani-inonde-de-chauve-souris-un-des-reservoirs-debola.
65. https://www.radiookapi.net/actualite/2014/08/25/province-orientale-mongbwalu-envahi-par-des-chauves-souris-reservoir-debola.
66. Persyn and Ladrière 2004: 74.
67. https://www.lemonde.fr/afrique/article/2020/03/24/covid-19-la-viande-de-brousse-toujours-consommee-en-cote-d-ivoire-malgre-l-interdiction_6034236_3212.html?utm_medium=Social&utm_source=Facebook&fbclid=IwAR3yYkQadB9eqO3Zjfce0wJLAi1WbrppGDvJWLN6-1bvm8DNngZYeJIfi80#Echobox=1585050350.
68. Lucas et al. 2020.
69. Morisho et al. 2020.
70. Stearns 2022.
71. Ordaz-Ne'meth et al. 2017.
72. https://www.lefigaro.fr/international/coronavirus-au-gabon-les-pangolins-retires-des-marches-a-viande-20200318.
73. Morcatty et al. 2020.
74. Hall et al. 2008.
75. De Boeck 2001.
76. Nganga et al. 2013: 4458.

77. Amounts from November 2018; see https://www.afrik21.africa/en/drc-authorities-launch-operation-kin-bopeto-kinshasa-clean/.
78. Email communication, Rita Bisimwa, 4 April 2020.
79. Nzalalemba et al. 2016.
80. Anonymous interview, Kinshasa, 15 March 2022.
81. Ibid.

9. LEGALITY, LEGITIMACY AND ENFORCEMENT

1. https://www.eagle-enforcement.org/guinea/; https://www.laga-enforcement.org/en/laga-family.
2. Kümpel 2006: 2.
3. Bachmann and Olonisakin 2020.
4. Van Schuylenbergh 2009: 27.
5. https://www.theatlantic.com/international/archive/2012/03/the-white-savior-industrial-complex/254843/.
6. https://www.bbc.co.uk/newsround/34502903.
7. Van Schuylenbergh 2009: 30.
8. Lombard 2020: 118.
9. Lombard 2020: 29.
10. The narrative was relayed in an interview with Igor Boris Ossete, Public Prosecutor, Ouesso, Republic of Congo, 5 October 2021.
11. Axelrod et al. 2017: 69.
12. https://www.traffic.org/.
13. Interview with Idriss Ayaya, Epulu, Okapi Wildlife Reserve, DRC, 25 January 2021.
14. Mavah et al. 2021.
15. https://www.theglobaleconomy.com/rankings/wb_ruleoflaw/.
16. Gore et al. 2021: 10.
17. MacKinnon et al. 2016: 45.
18. Interview with Joseph Nzassi, Ouesso, Republic of Congo, 14 October 2021.
19. Ibid.
20. Interview with Igor Boris Ossete, Public Prosecutor, Ouesso, Republic of Congo, 5 October 2021.
21. Interview with Christian Mbuku, restaurant chef, Ouesso, Republic of Congo, 5 October 2021.

22. https://www.7sur7.cd/2019/12/20/rdc-le-proprietaire-de-lhotel-beatrice-risque-10-ans-de-prison-pour-avoir-servi-du-bebe.

23. https://africageographic.com/stories/video-instagram-influencer-eats-pangolin-gabon-calls-armadillo/.

24. Interview with Johnny M (pseudonym), Kinshasa, DRC, 21 November 2020.

25. https://abcnews.go.com/Travel/plane-crashes-crocodile-escapes-panic/story?id=11947027; https://www.jeuneafrique.com/194572/societe/les-vraies-raisons-du-crash-de-bandundu/.

26. Wilkie et al. 2006: 336.

27. Anonymous interview, Epena, Republic of the Congo, 5 February 2019.

28. Interview with Olivier Igugu, Kisangani, DRC, 7 July 2019.

29. Interview with an anonymous ranger, Epulu, Okapi Wildlife Reserve, DRC, 26 February 2021.

30. Interview with an anonymous ranger, Lake Télé Community Reserve, Republic of Congo, 15 August 2018.

31. Anonymous interview, Epulu, Okapi Wildlife Reserve, DRC, 25 January 2021.

32. https://www.unodc.org/unodc/en/wildlife-and-forest-crime/global-programme.html.

33. https://cites.org/eng/prog/iccwc_new.php.

34. Financial Action Task Force 2020: 5.

35. Nuwer 2018.

36. https://www.atree.org/Rosaleen_Duffy_02032020.

37. Trefon 2010; 2009.

38. Rackley 2006.

39. Herbst 2000.

40. https://www.state.gov/r/pa/ei/bgn/4007.htm.

41. Lombard 2020.

42. Bierschenk and Olivier de Sardan 1997: 441.

43. Interview with Mr Rodrigue, Epena, Republic of Congo, 5 February 2019.

44. Fargeot et al. 2017: 40.

45. Coad 2007: 278.

46. Wright 2021: 203.

47. Burgess 2016: 66.
48. Agu and Gore 2020: 10.

CONCLUSION

1. Interview with Chief Rodrigue, Epena, Republic of Congo, 5 February 2019.
2. Information from a field trip to the Luki Biosphere Reserve with graduate students from ERAIFT, March 2022.
3. https://lejournaldelafrique.com/rdc-comment-les-atteintes-a-la-biodiversite-affectent-les-habitudes-alimentaires/.
4. Cleaver 2012.

BIBLIOGRAPHY

Adams, J. S. and T. O. McShane (1996) *The myth of wild Africa: Conservation without illusion*. Berkeley: University of California Press.

Adamson, J. (1960) *Born free*. New York: Pantheon Books.

Agu, H. U. and M. Gore (2020) 'Women in wildlife trafficking in Africa: A synthesis of literature'. *Global Ecology and Conservation* 23 (September).

Alabi, T., S. Patiny, F. Verheggen, F. Francis and É. Haubruge (2009) 'Origine et évolution du cannibalisme dans les populations animales: Pourquoi manger son semblable?' *Biotechnologie, Agronomie, Société et Environnement* 13: 409–25.

Anadu, P. A., P. O. Elamah and J. F. Oates (1988) 'The bushmeat trade in southwestern Nigeria: A case study'. *Human Ecology* 16: 199–208.

Axelrod, M. A., A. Flowers, K. Groff and J. Novak Colwell (2017) 'Governance for conservation risks and crime', in M. L. Gore (ed.) *Conservation criminology*. New York: John Wiley & Sons.

Bachand, N., J. Arsenault and A. Ravel (2015) 'Urban household meat consumption patterns in Gabon, Central Africa, with a focus on bushmeat'. *Human Dimensions of Wildlife* 20(2): 147–58.

Bachmann, O. and F. Olonisakin (2020) 'Revisiting governance: Extended statehood in Africa and beyond'. *Leadership and Developing Societies* 5(1): 1–11.

Bahuchet, S. (1985) *Les Pygmées Aka et la forêt centrafricaine*. Paris: SELAF.

Bahuchet, S. (2014) 'Cultural diversity of African Pygmies', in B. S. Hewlett (ed.) *Hunter-gatherers of the Congo Basin: Cultures, histories and biology of African Pygmies*. New Brunswick: Transaction Publishers.

Bahuchet, S. and K. Ioveva-Baillon (1998) 'Le rôle de la restauration de rue dans l'approvisionnement des villes en viande de brousse: Le cas de Yaoundé (Cameroun)', in D. Bley, J. Champaud, P. Baudot, B. Brun, H. Pagezy and N. Vernazza-Licht (eds.) *Villes du sud et développement*. Châteauneuf de Grasse: Editions de Bergier.

Bahuchet, S. and K. Ioveva (1999) 'De la forêt au marché: Le commerce de gibier au sud Cameroun', in S. Bahuchet, D. Bley, H. Pagezy and N. Vernazza-Licht (eds.) *L'homme et la forêt tropicale*. Châteauneuf de Grasse: Editions de Bergier.

Bahuchet, S., C. M. Hladik, A. Hladik and E. Dounias (1990) 'Agricultural strategies as complementary activities to hunting and fishing', in C. M. Hladik, I. de Garine and S. Bahuchet (eds.) *Food and nutrition in the tropical rain forest*. Paris: UNESCO.

Bahuchet, S., F. Grenand, P. Grenand and P. de Maret (2001) *Tropical forests, human forests: An overview*. Brussels: APFT–Université Libre de Bruxelles.

Bakarr, M. I., G. A. B. da Fonseca, R. A. Mittermeier, A. B. Rylands and K. W. Painemilla (eds.) (2001) *Hunting and bushmeat utilization in the African rain forest: Perspectives toward a blueprint for conservation action*. Washington, DC: Conservation International.

Barnes, R. F. W., K. Beardsley, F. Michelmore, K. L. Barnes, P. T. Alers and A. Blom (1997) 'Estimating forest elephant numbers with dung counts and a geographic information system'. *Journal of Wildlife Management* 61(4): 1384–93.

Barrall, A. L., N. A. Hoff, D. M. Nkamba, K. Musene, N. Ida, A. Bratcher et al. (2022) 'Hesitancy to receive the novel coronavirus vaccine and potential influences on vaccination among a cohort of healthcare workers in the Democratic Republic of the Congo'. *Vaccine* 40(34): 4998–5009.

Barrot, P. (1994) 'Les platitudes culinaires de ma femme ...', in P. Barrot (ed.) *L'Afrique, côté cuisines: Regards africains sur l'alimentation*. Paris: Syros.

Bastian, M. L. (1993) '"Bloodhounds who have no friends": Witchcraft, locality, and the popular press in Nigeria', in J. Comaroff and

BIBLIOGRAPHY

J. L. Comaroff (eds.) *Modernity and its malcontents: Ritual and power in Africa*. Chicago, IL: University of Chicago Press.

Bellman, B. L. (1981) 'The paradox of secrecy'. *Human Studies* 4(1): 1–24.

Bennett, N. J., J. Blythe, A. M. Cisneros-Montemayor, G. G. Singh and U. R. Sumaila (2019) 'Just transformations to sustainability'. *Sustainability* 11(14): 3881.

Beuve-Mery, J. (2014–15) 'Enquête socio-économique dans les Territoires de Lodja – Lomela – Kole, Province du Sankuru, RDC contribuant à la formulation d'un projet de promotion des activités génératrices de revenu dans la zone d'influence du Parc de la Salonga'. Unpublished Master's thesis, Gembloux Agro-Bio Tech, University of Liège.

Bierschenk, T. and J.-P. Olivier de Sardan (1997) 'Local powers and a distant state in rural Central African Republic'. *Journal of Modern African Studies* 35(3): 441–68.

Billand, A. (2012) 'Biodiversity in central African forests: An overview of knowledge, main challenges and conservation measures', in C. de Wasseige, P. de Marcken, N. Bayol, F. Hiol, P. Mayaux, B. Desclée, R. Nasi, A. Billand, P. Defourny and R. Eba'a Atyi (eds.) *The forests of the Congo Basin: State of the forest 2010*. Luxembourg: European Union.

Blanc, G. (2020) *L'invention du colonialisme vert: Pour en finir avec le mythe de l'Éden africain*. Paris: Flammarion.

Bloomfield, L. S. P., T. L. McIntosh and E. F. Lambin (2020) 'Habitat fragmentation, livelihood behaviors, and contact between people and nonhuman primates in Africa'. *Landscape Ecology* 35: 985–1000.

Bolle, J. (1958) *Les seigneurs de la forêt*. Brussels: Fondation Internationale Scientifique.

Booth, H., M. Arias, S. Brittain, D. W. S. Challender, M. Khanyari, T. Kuiper et al. (2021) 'Saving lives, protecting livelihoods, and safeguarding nature: Risk-based wildlife trade policy for sustainable development outcomes post-COVID-19'. *Frontiers in Ecology and Evolution* 9 (February).

Bouché, P., P.-C. Renaud, P. Lejeune, C. Vermeulen, J.-M. Froment, A. Bangara et al. (2009) 'Has the final countdown to wildlife extinction in northern Central African Republic begun?' *African Journal of Ecology* 48(4): 1–10.

BIBLIOGRAPHY

Bourdieu, P. (1984) *Distinction: A social critique of the judgement of taste.* Cambridge, MA: Harvard University Press.

Bowen-Jones, E., D. Brown and E. J. Z. Robinson (2003) 'Economic commodity or environmental crisis? An interdisciplinary approach to analysing the bushmeat trade in Central and West Africa'. *Area* 35(4): 390–402.

Boyeldieu, P. (2008) 'From semantic change to polysemy: The cases of "meat/animal" and "drink"', in M. Vanhove (ed.) *From polysemy to semantic change: Towards a typology of lexical semantic associations.* Amsterdam: John Benjamins Publishing Company.

Brashares, J. S., C. D. Golden, K. Z. Weinbaum, C. B. Barrett and G. V. Okello (2011) 'Economic and geographic drivers of wildlife consumption in rural Africa'. *Proceedings of the National Academy of Sciences* 108(34): 13931–6.

Brashares, J. S., B. Abrahms, K. J. Fiorella, C. D. Golden, C. E. Hojnowski, R. A. Marsh et al. (2014) 'Wildlife decline and social conflict'. *Science* 345: 376–8.

Brockington, D., R. Duffy, and J. Igoe (2008) *Nature unbound: Conservation, capitalism and the future of protected areas.* London: Earthscan.

Bryceson, D. F. (2002) 'Multiplex livelihoods in rural Africa: Recasting the terms and conditions of gainful employment'. *Journal of Modern African Studies* 40(1): 1–28.

Bulte, E. H. and R. D. Horan (2002) 'Does human population growth increase wildlife harvesting? An economic assessment'. *Journal of Wildlife Management* 66(3): 574–80.

Burgess, G. (2016) 'Powers of persuasion? Conservation, communications, behavioural change and reducing demand for illegal wildlife products'. *TRAFFIC Bulletin* 28(2): 65–73.

Büscher, B. and W. Whande (2007) 'Whims of the winds of time? Emerging trends in biodiversity conservation and protected area management'. *Conservation and Society* 5(1): 22–43.

Canetti, E. (1960) *Crowds and power.* New York: Noonday Press.

Caspary, H.-U. (2001) 'Regional dynamics of hunting and bushmeat utilization in West Africa: An overview', in M. I. Bakarr, G. A. B. da Fonseca, R. A. Mittermeier, A. B. Rylands and K. W. Painemilla (eds.) (2001) *Hunting and bushmeat utilization in the African rain forest:*

BIBLIOGRAPHY

Perspectives toward a blueprint for conservation action. Washington, DC: Conservation International.

Chaber, A.-L., S. Allebone-Webb, Y. Lignereux, A. A. Cunningham and J. Marcus Rowcliffe (2010) 'The scale of illegal meat importation from Africa to Europe via Paris: Illegal intercontinental meat trade'. *Conservation Letters* 3: 317–21.

Chaber, A.-L., P. Gaubert, H. Green, M. Garigliany, V. Renault, V. Busoni et al. (2018) 'Report on the illegal importation of meat, including bushmeat, seized at Zaventem airport, 2017/2018'. Brussels: Belgian Federal Public Service Health, Food Chain Safety and Environment.

Chausson, A. M., J. M. Rowcliffe, L. Escouflaire, M. Wieland and J. H. Wright (2019) 'Understanding the sociocultural drivers of urban bushmeat consumption for behavior change interventions in Pointe-Noire, Republic of Congo'. *Human Ecology* 47: 179–91.

Clay, N. (2016) 'Producing hybrid forests in the Congo Basin: A political ecology of the landscape approach to conservation'. *Geoforum* 76: 130–41.

Cleaver, F. (2012) *Development through bricolage: Rethinking institutions for natural resource management.* London: Routledge.

Coad, L. (2007) 'Bushmeat hunting in Gabon: Socio-economics and hunter behaviour'. Unpublished PhD thesis, University of Cambridge.

Coad, L., J. Schleicher, E. J. Milner-Gulland, T. R. Matthews, M. Starkey, A. Manica et al. (2013) 'Social and ecological change over a decade in a village hunting system, central Gabon'. *Conservation Biology* 27(2): 270–80.

Coad, L., J. E. Fa, K. Abernethy, N. van Vliet, C. Santamaria, D. Wilkie et al. (2019) 'Towards a sustainable, participatory and inclusive wild meat sector'. Center for International Forestry Research (CIFOR).

Cogels, S. (2002) 'Les Ntumu du Cameroun forestier, une société de non-spécialistes: Système de production, stratégies d'acquisition des ressources et enjeux du changement'. Unpublished PhD thesis, Université Libre de Bruxelles.

Comaroff, J. and J. L. Comaroff (1993) *Modernity and its malcontents: Ritual and power in postcolonial Africa.* Chicago, IL: University of Chicago Press.

BIBLIOGRAPHY

Comhaire-Sylvain, S. (1950) *Food and leisure among the African youth of Léopoldville (Belgian Congo)*. Rondebosch: University of Cape Town.

Convention on Biological Diversity (2017) 'Sustainable wildlife management: Guidance for a sustainable wild meat sector'. Note by the Executive Secretary, twenty-first meeting, Montreal, Canada, 11–14 December 2017. https://www.cbd.int/doc/c/5e38/77fa/1b93ca796395 94edfee41a73/sbstta-21-03-en.pdf.

Coquery-Vidrovitch, C. (2011) 'Colonisation, racisme et roman national en France'. *Canadian Journal of African Studies / Revue Canadienne des Études Africaines* 45(1): 17–44.

Cornelis, D., N. van Vliet, J.-C. Nguinguiri and S. Le Bel (2017) 'Gestion communautaire de la chasse en Afrique centrale: À la reconquête d'une souveraineté confisquée', in N. van Vliet, J.-C. Nguinguiri, D. Cornelis and S. Le Bel (eds.) *Communautés locales et utilisation durable de la faune en Afrique centrale*. Libreville/Bogor/Montpellier: FAO/CIFOR/CIRAD.

Cosyn, J. (2020) *Mémoires d'un broussard: Avec la 'territoriale' dans les profondeurs de la forêt congolaise*. Kraainem (Belgium): Dynamedia.

Cronon, W. (1996) 'The trouble with wilderness, or, getting back to the wrong nature'. *Environmental History* 1(1): 7–28.

Cusack, I. (2000) 'African cuisines: Recipes for nation-building?' *Journal of African Cultural Studies* 13(2): 207–25.

Daley, P. (2013) 'Rescuing African bodies: Celebrities, consumerism and neoliberal humanitarianism'. *Review of African Political Economy* 40(137): 375–93.

Dargie, G. C., S. L. Lewis, I. T. Lawson, E. T. Mitchard, S. E. Page, Y. E. Bocko and S. A. Ifo (2017) 'Age, extent and carbon storage of the central Congo Basin peatland complex'. *Nature* 542: 86–90.

Davies, G. (2002) 'Bushmeat and international development'. *Conservation Biology* 16(3): 587–9.

De Boeck, F. (2001) 'Garimpeiro worlds: Digging, dying and "hunting" for diamonds in Angola'. *Review of African Political Economy* 28(90): 548–62.

De Boeck, F. and M.-F. Plissart (2004) *Kinshasa: Tales of the invisible city*. Brussels: Ludion.

BIBLIOGRAPHY

de Garine, I. and C. M. Hladik (1990) 'Les conceptions nutritionnelles: Interdits, prescriptions et perception des aliments', in C. M. Hladik, S. Bahuchet and I. de Garine (eds.) *Food and nutrition in the African rain forest*. Paris: UNESCO.

de Garine, I. and H. Pagezy (1990) 'Seasonal hunger or "craving for meat"', in C. M. Hladik, S. Bahuchet and I. de Garine (eds.) *Food and nutrition in the African rain forest*. Paris: UNESCO.

De Herdt, T. (2004) 'Hidden families, single mothers and *cibalabala*: Economic regress and changing household composition in Kinshasa', in T. Trefon (ed.) *Re-inventing order in the Congo: How people respond to state failure in Kinshasa*. London: Zed Books.

Dell, B. M., M. J. Souza and A. S. Willcox (2020) 'Attitudes, practices, and zoonoses awareness of community members involved in the bushmeat trade near Murchison Falls National Park, northern Uganda'. *PLOS One* 15(9): e0239599.

de Merode, E., K. Homeward and G. Cowlishaw (2004) 'The value of bushmeat and other wild foods to rural households living in extreme poverty in Democratic Republic of Congo'. *Biological Conservation* 118: 573–81.

Demuenynck, A. (1908) *Au pays de Mahagi, région du Lac Albert et du Haut-Nil et les pygmées du Haut-Ituri*. Brussels: Société Royale Belge de Géographie.

De Waal, A. (2015) *Advocacy in conflict: Critical perspectives on transnational activism*. London: Zed Books.

Dieudonné, M. (2016) 'La viande des uns, la faune des autres: Analyse anthropologique de la conservation de la faune dans trois villages Badjoué de la zone forestière de l'Est-Cameroun'. Unpublished PhD thesis, University of Liège.

Douglas, M. (1963) *The Lele of the Kasai*. London: Routledge.

Dounias, E. (2016) 'From subsistence to commercial hunting: Technical shift in cynegetic practices among southern Cameroon forest dwellers during the 20th century'. *Ecology and Society* 21(1): 23.

Dounias, E. and A. Froment (2011) 'From foraging to farming among present-day forest hunter-gatherers: Consequences on diet and health'. *International Forestry Review* 13(3): 294–304.

BIBLIOGRAPHY

Dubiez, E., A. Karsenty and H. Dessard (2017) 'Gestion de la faune dans les concessions forestières en Afrique centrale', in N. van Vliet, J. C. Nguinguiri, D. Cornelis and S. Le Bel (eds.) *Communautés locales et utilisation durable de la faune en Afrique centrale*. Libreville/Bogor/Montpellier: FAO/CIFOR/CIRAD.

Duffy, R., F. Massé, E. Smidt, E. Marijnen, B. Büscher, J. Verweijen et al. (2019) 'Why we must question the militarisation of conservation'. *Biological Conservation* 232: 66–73.

Eba'a Atyi, R. and N. Bayol with S. Malele Mbala, J. Tunguni, P. Mwamba Kyungu and F. Yata (2009) 'The forests of the Democratic Republic of Congo in 2008', in C. de Wasseige, D. Devers, P. de Marcken, R. Eba'a Atyi, R. Nasi and P. Mayaux (eds.) *The forests of the Congo Basin: State of the forest 2008*. Luxembourg: European Union.

Edderai, D. and M. Dame (2006) 'A census of the commercial bushmeat market in Yaoundé, Cameroon'. *Oryx* 40(4): 472–5.

Edderai, D. and P. Houben (2002) 'Elevage et performances de reproduction et de croissance de l'athérure africain: Résultats sur l'étude de sa reproduction en captivité'. *Revue d'Élevage et de Médecine Vétérinaire des Pays Tropicaux* 55(4): 313–20.

Ernst, C., P. Mayaux, A. Verhegghen, C. Bodart, M. Christophe and P. Defourny (2013) 'National forest cover change in Congo Basin: Deforestation, reforestation, degradation and regeneration for the years 1990, 2000 and 2005'. *Global Change Biology* 19(4): 1173–87.

Evans-Pritchard, E. E. (1976) *Witchcraft, oracles, and magic among the Azande*. Oxford: Clarendon Press.

Fa, J. E., C. A. Peres and J. Meeuwig (2002) 'Bushmeat exploitation in tropical forests: An intercontinental comparison'. *Conservation Biology* 16(1): 232–7.

Fa, J. E., J. Olivero, M. A. Farfán, A. L. Márquez, J. M. Vargas, R. Real and R. Nasi (2014) 'Integrating sustainable hunting in biodiversity protection in Central Africa: Hot spots, weak spots, and strong spots'. *PLOS One* 9(11): e112367.

Fa, J. E., J. Wright, S. M. Funk, A. L. Márquez, J. Olivero, M. A. Farfán et al. (2019) 'Mapping the availability of bushmeat for consumption in Central African cities'. *Environmental Research Letters* 14: 1–11.

BIBLIOGRAPHY

Fa, J. E., S. M. Funk and R. Nasi (2022) *Hunting wildlife in the tropics and subtropics*. Cambridge: Cambridge University Press.

Fargeot, C. (2004) 'La chasse commerciale en Afrique centrale, I: La venaison ou le négoce d'un produit vivrier'. *Bois et Forêts des Tropiques* 282(4): 27–39.

Fargeot, C., N. Drouet-Hoguet and S. Le Bel (2017) 'The role of bushmeat in urban household consumption: Insights from Bangui, the capital city of the Central African Republic'. *Bois et Forêts des Tropiques* 332(2): 31–42.

Felbab-Brown, V. (2017) *The extinction market: Wildlife trafficking and how to counter it*. New York: Oxford University Press.

Financial Action Task Force (2020) 'Money laundering and the illegal wildlife trade'. Paris: Financial Action Task Force.

Ford, A. T., A. H. Ali, S. R. Colla, S. J. Cooke, C. T. Lamb, J. Pittman et al. (2020) 'Understanding and avoiding misplaced efforts in conservation'. *FACETS* 6: 252–71.

Frazer, J. G. (1957) *The golden bough*. London: Macmillan.

Froment, A., I. de Garine, C. Binam Bikoi and J. F. Loung (eds.) (1996) *Bien manger et bien vivre: Anthropologie alimentaire et développement en Afrique intertropicale, du biologique au social*. Paris: L'Harmattan/ ORSTOM.

Gallagher, S. (2008) 'The bushmeat crisis in Africa: Policy choices, economic incentives and behavioural change'. Unpublished Master's thesis, Fletcher School of Law and Diplomacy, Tufts University.

Geist, H. J. and E. F. Lambin (2002) 'Proximate causes and underlying driving forces of tropical deforestation'. *BioScience* 52(2): 143–50.

Geschiere, P. and F. Nyamnjoh (1998) 'Witchcraft as an issue in the "politics of belonging": Democratization and urban migrants' involvement with the home village'. *African Studies Review* 41(3): 69–91.

Gondola, D. and A. Lauro (2021) 'A social virus: The emergence of HIV-1 in colonial Kinshasa, 1900–1960', in W. H. Schneider (ed.) *The histories of HIVs: The emergence of the multiple viruses that caused the AIDS epidemics*. Athens, OH: Ohio University Press.

Gore, M. L., R. Mwinyihali, L. Mayet, G. D. Makaya Baku-Bumb, C. Plowman and M. Wieland (2021) 'Typologies of urban wildlife traffickers and sellers'. *Global Ecology and Conservation* 27: e01557.

BIBLIOGRAPHY

Gryseels, S., P. Mbala-Kingebeni, I. Akonda, R. Angoyo, A. Ayouba, P. Baelo et al. (2020) 'Role of wildlife in emergence of Ebola virus in Kaigbono (Likati), Democratic Republic of the Congo, 2017'. *Emerging Infectious Diseases* 26(9): 2205–9.

Guyer, J. (1995) 'Wealth in people, wealth in things: Introduction'. *Journal of African History* 36(1): 83–90.

Haider, L. J., W. J. Boonstra, G. D. Peterson and M. Schlüter (2018) 'Traps and sustainable development in rural areas: A review'. *World Development* 101: 311–21.

Hall, R. C. W., M. D. Hall and M. J. Chapman (2008) 'The 1995 Kikwit Ebola outbreak: Lessons hospitals and physicians can apply to future viral epidemics'. *General Hospital Psychiatry* 30(5): 446–52.

Hardin, G. (1968) 'The tragedy of the commons'. *Science* 162(3859): 1243–8.

Hardin, R. and P. Auzel (2001) 'Wildlife utilization and the emergence of viral diseases', in M. I. Bakarr, G. A. B. da Fonseca, R. A. Mittermeier, A. B. Rylands and K. W. Painemilla (eds.) (2001) *Hunting and bushmeat utilization in the African rain forest: Perspectives toward a blueprint for conservation action.* Washington, DC: Conservation International.

Harms, R. (1987) *Games against nature: An eco-cultural history of the Nunu of Equatorial Africa.* Cambridge: Cambridge University Press.

Heath, E. (2010) 'Urbanism and urbanization in Africa', in K. A. Appiah and H. L. Gates (eds.) *Encyclopedia of Africa.* Oxford: Oxford University Press.

Herbst, J. (2000) *States and power in Africa: Comparative lessons in authority and control.* Princeton, NJ: Princeton University Press.

Hickey, L. with G. Mbayama (2008) 'Bushmeat consumption in Kinshasa, Democratic Republic of Congo: Analysis on the household level'. Unpublished report, World Bank and Wildlife Conservation Society.

Hintjens, H. (2006) 'Conflict and resources in post-genocide Rwanda and the Great Lakes region'. *International Journal of Environmental Studies* 63(5): 599–615.

Hladik, C. M. and A. Hladik (1990) 'Food resources of the rain forest', in C. M. Hladik, S. Bahuchet and I. de Garine (eds.) *Food and nutrition in the African rain forest.* Paris: UNESCO.

BIBLIOGRAPHY

Hoffmann, W. A., B. Orthen and P. K. Vargas do Nascimento (2003) 'Comparative fire ecology of tropical savanna and forest trees'. *Functional Ecology* 17: 720–6.

Hooper, E. (2000) *The river: A journey to the source of HIV and AIDS.* Boston: Back Bay Books.

Igugu Murula, O. (2019) 'Déterminants sociaux de la consommation du gibier à Yangambi et Kisangani dans la province de la Tshopo'. Unpublished Master's thesis, University of Kisangani.

Ingram, D. (2020) 'Wild meat in changing times'. *Journal of Ethnobiology* 40(2): 117–30.

Inogwabini, B. (2014) 'Bushmeat, over-fishing and covariates explaining fish abundance declines in the Central Congo Basin'. *Environmental Biology of Fishes* 97: 787–96.

International Union for Conservation of Nature and Natural Resources, United Nations Environment Programme, World Wildlife Fund, Food and Agriculture Organization of the United Nations and UNESCO (1980) *World conservation strategy: Living resource conservation for sustainable development.* Gland (Switzerland): IUCN.

Jackson, R. O. (2014) 'The failure of categories: Haitians in the United Nations Organization in the Congo, 1960–64'. *Journal of Haitian Studies* 20(1): 34–64.

Janson, H. W. with D. J. Janson (1967) *History of art: A survey of the major visual arts from the dawn of history to the present day.* Englewood Cliffs/New York: Prentice-Hall/Harry N. Abrams.

Johnson, C. K., P. L. Hitchens, P. S. Pandit, J. Rushmore, T. S. Evans, C. C. W. Young and M. M. Doyle (2020) 'Global shifts in mammalian population trends reveal key predictors of virus spillover risk'. *Proceedings of the Royal Society B* 287(1924): 20192736.

Johnson, M. (1992) *Lore: Capturing traditional environmental knowledge.* Ottawa: Dene Cultural Institute/IDRC.

Jones, K. E., N. G. Patel, M. A. Levy, A. Storeygard, D. Balk, J. L. Gittleman and P. Daszak (2008) 'Global trends in emerging infectious diseases'. *Nature* 451(7181): 990–3.

Jori, F., M. Lopez-Bejar and P. Houben (1998) 'The biology and use of the African brush-tailed porcupine (*Atherurus africanus*, Gray, 1842) as a food animal: A review'. *Biodiversity and Conservation* 7(11): 1417–26.

BIBLIOGRAPHY

Kabuyaya, N. and T. Trefon (2007) 'Projet AMINEKIN, rapport socio-économique'. Unpublished feasibility study, Brussels.

Kambala Luadia Tshikengela, B. (2018) 'Pratiques et gestion locales des ressources naturelles autour du Parc National de la Salonga en territoire de Monkoto', in A. Ansoms, A. N. Bisoka and S. Vandeginste (eds.) *Conjonctures de l'Afrique centrale*. Tervuren/Paris: AfricaMuseum/ L'Harmattan.

Khonde, S. (2020) 'La moto comme innovation sociale dans la Réserve de Biosphère de Luki (RDC)'. Unpublished Master's thesis, University of Liège.

Kourouma, A. (1998) *En attendant le vote des bêtes sauvages*. Paris: Editions de Seuil.

Kümpel, N. F. (2006) 'Incentives for sustainable hunting of bushmeat in Rio Muni, Equatorial Guinea'. Unpublished PhD thesis, Imperial College London/Zoological Society of London.

Kümpel, N. F., A. Quinn and S. Grange (2015) 'The distribution and population status of the elusive okapi *Okapia johnstoni*'. *African Journal of Ecology* 53(2): 242–5.

La Cerva, G. R. N. (2015) 'Devouring the Congo'. *Tropical Resources* 34: 52–61.

Laugrand, F. and J. G. Oosten (2015) *Hunters, predators and prey: Inuit perceptions of animals*. New York/Oxford: Berghahn.

Lee, R. B. (1969) 'Eating Christmas in the Kalahari'. *Natural History* 78(10): 14–24.

Lemarchand, R. (2002) 'The tunnel at the end of the light'. *Review of African Political Economy* 29(93–4): 389–98.

Lescuyer, G. and R. Nasi (2016) 'Financial and economic values of bushmeat in rural and urban livelihoods in Cameroon: Inputs to the development of public policy'. *International Forestry Review* 18(Supplement 1): 93–107.

Linder, J. M. and J. F. Oates (2011) 'Differential impact of bushmeat hunting on monkey species and implications for primate conservation in Korup National Park, Cameroon'. *Biological Conservation* 144(2): 738–45.

Lindsey, P., W. A. Taylor, V. Nyirenda and L. Barnes (2015) 'Bushmeat, wildlife-based economies, food security and conservation: Insights into the ecological and social impacts of the bushmeat trade in African savannahs'. Harare, Zimbabwe: FAO/Panthera/Zoological Society of London/SULi.

Lombard, L. (2020) *Hunting game: Raiding politics in the Central African Republic.* Cambridge: Cambridge University Press.

Lucas, A., C. Kumakamba, C. E. Lange, E. Obel, G. Miningue, J. Likofata et al. (2020) 'Serology and behavioral perspectives on Ebola virus disease among bushmeat vendors in Equateur, Democratic Republic of the Congo, after the 2018 outbreak'. *Open Forum Infectious Diseases* 7(8).

Ludwig, D. and P. Macnaghten (2020) 'Traditional ecological knowledge in innovation governance: A framework for responsible and just innovation'. *Journal of Responsible Innovation* 7(1): 26–44.

Luiselli, L., E. M. Hema, G. H. Segniagbeto, V. Ouattara, E. A. Eniang, M. Di Vittorio et al. (2017) 'Understanding the influence of non-wealth factors in determining bushmeat consumption: Results from four West African countries'. *Acta Oecologica* 94: 47–56.

Luiselli, L., E. M. Hema, G. H. Segniagbeto, V. Ouattara, E. A. Eniang, G. Parfait et al. (2018) 'Bushmeat consumption in large urban centres in West Africa'. *Oryx* 1–4.

MacGaffey, W. (1970) *Custom and government in the Lower Congo.* Berkeley: University of California Press.

MacKinnon, J., C. Aveling, R. Olivier, M. Murray and C. Paolini (2016) *Larger than elephants: Inputs for an EU strategic approach to wildlife conservation in Africa; Regional analysis.* Brussels: European Commission.

Maffi, L. (2005) 'Linguistic, cultural, and biological diversity'. *Annual Review of Anthropology* 34: 599–617.

Maisels, F., E. Keming, M. Kemei and C. Toh (2001) 'The extirpation of large mammals and implications for montane forest conservation: The case of the Kilum-Ijim Forest, North-West Province, Cameroon'. *Oryx* 35(4): 322–31.

Malinowski, B. (1955 [1925]) *Magic, science and religion and other essays.* Boston: Beacon Press.

Mandillah, K. L. L. and G. I. Ekosse (2018) 'African totems: Cultural heritage for sustainable environmental conservation'. *Conservation Science in Cultural Heritage* 18: 201–18.

BIBLIOGRAPHY

Marijnen, E. (2018) 'Public authority and conservation in areas of armed conflict: Virunga National Park as a "state in a state" in the DR Congo'. *Development and Change* 49(3): 790–814.

Martin, G. H. G. (1983) 'Bushmeat in Nigeria as a natural resource with environmental implications'. *Environmental Conservation* 10(2): 125–32.

Matthysen, K., L. Hoex, P. Schouten and S. Spittaels (2019) 'Mapping artisanal mining areas and mineral supply chains in eastern DRC: Impact of armed interference and responsible sourcing'. Antwerp: IPIS/DIIS. https://ipisresearch.be/wp-content/uploads/2020/10/1904-IOM-mapping-eastern-DRC.pdf.

Mauss, M. (1966) *The gift: Forms and functions of exchange in archaic societies.* London: Cohen and West.

Mavah, G., B. Child and M. E. Swisher (2021) 'Empty laws and empty forests: Reconsidering rights and governance for sustainable wildlife management in the Republic of the Congo'. *Journal of African Ecology* 60: 212–21.

Mavakala, K. (2021) 'Covid-19 in Kinshasa: Trust and distrust in government'. Unpublished report, Kinshasa: TradeHub-GCRF/ERAIFT.

Mayaux, P., J.-F. Pekel, B. Desclée, F. Donnay, A. Lupi, F. Achard et al. (2013) 'State and evolution of the African rainforests between 1990 and 2010'. *Philosophical Transactions of the Royal Society* 368(1625): 20120300.

Mbete, R. A., H. Banga-Mboko, C. Ngokaka, Q. V. Bouckacka III, I. Nganga, J.-L. Hornick et al. (2011) 'Profil des vendeurs de viande de chasse et évaluation de la biomasse commercialisée dans les marchés municipaux de Brazzaville, Congo'. *Tropical Conservation Science* 4(2): 203–17.

Mbete, R. A., H. Banga-Mboko, P. Racey, A. Mfoukou-Ntsakala, I. Nganga, C. Vermeulen et al. (2011) 'Household bushmeat consumption in Brazzaville, the Republic of the Congo'. *Tropical Conservation Science* 4(2): 187–202.

McCall, D. F. (1973–74) 'The prevalence of lions: Kings, deities and feline symbolism in Africa and elsewhere'. Frobenius Institute.

McDonald, B. (2001) 'Considering the nature of wilderness: Reflections on Roderick Nash's "Wilderness and the American mind"'. *Organization and Environment* 14(2): 188–201.

McNamara, J. (2013) 'The dynamics of a bushmeat hunting system under social, economic and environmental change'. Unpublished PhD thesis, Imperial College London.

McNamara, J., J. M. Kumisi, J. M. Rowcliffe, G. Cowlishaw, A. Brenyah and E. J. Milner-Gulland (2015) 'Long-term spatio-temporal changes in a West African bushmeat trade system'. *Conservation Biology* 29(5): 1446–57.

McNamara, J., E. J. Z. Robinson, K. Abernethy, D. Midoko Iponga, H. N. K. Sackey, J. H. Wright and E. J. Milner-Gulland (2020) 'Covid-19, systemic crisis and possible implications for the wild meat trade in sub-Saharan Africa'. *Environmental and Resource Economics* 76: 1045–66.

Mendelson, S., G. Cowlishaw and J. M. Rowcliffe (2003) 'Anatomy of a bushmeat commodity chain in Takoradi, Ghana'. *Journal of Peasant Studies* 31(1): 73–100.

Merson, S. D., L. J. Dollar, P. J. Johnson and D. W. Macdonald (2019) 'Poverty not taste drives the consumption of protected species in Madagascar'. *Biodiversity and Conservation* 28: 3669–89.

Milbank, C. and B. Vira (2022) 'Wildmeat consumption and zoonotic spillover: Contextualising disease emergence and policy responses'. *Lancet Planetary Health* 6(5): e439–e448.

Milner-Gulland, E. J. and H. Resit Akçakaya (2001) 'Sustainability indices for exploited populations'. *Trends in Ecology and Evolution* 16(12): 686–92.

Milner-Gulland, E. J., E. L. Bennett and the SCB (2003) Annual meeting wild meat group, 'Wild meat: The bigger picture'. *Trends in Ecology and Evolution* 18(7): 351–7.

Ministère du Plan et Suivi de la Mise en œuvre de la Révolution de la Modernité (MPSMRM), Ministère de la Santé Publique (MSP) and ICF International (2014) 'Democratic Republic of Congo Demographic and Health Survey 2013–14: Key findings'. Rockville, MD: MPSMRM, MSP and ICF International.

Mogomotsi, G. E. J. and P. K. Madigele (2017) 'Live by the gun, die by the gun: An analysis of Botswana's "shoot-to-kill" policy as an anti-poaching strategy'. *South African Crime Quarterly*, no. 60: 51–9.

Monroe, B. P., J. B. Doty, C. Moses, S. Ibata, M. Reynolds and D. Carroll (2015) 'Collection and utilization of animal carcasses associated with zoonotic disease in Tshuapa District, the Democratic Republic of the Congo, 2012'. *Journal of Wildlife Diseases* 51(3): 734–8.

Moore, J. (2004) 'The puzzling origins of AIDS'. *American Scientist* 92: 540–7.

Morcatty, T. Q., K. Feddema, K. A. I. Nekaris and V. Nijman (2020) 'Online trade in wildlife and the lack of response to Covid-19'. *Environmental Research* 193: 110439.

Morisho, N., S. J. Park, J. Kalubi and M. E. Lubula (2020) 'The response to the Ebola virus disease in the eastern Democratic Republic of Congo: The twists and turns of an unexpected failure'. Goma: Pole Institute.

Morrison-Lanjouw, S. M., R. A. Coutinho, K. Boahene and R. Pool (2021) 'Exploring the characteristics of a local demand for African wild meat: A focus group study of long-term Ghanaian residents in the Netherlands'. *PLOS One* 16(2): e0246868.

Morsello, C., B. Yagüe, L. Beltreschi, N. van Vliet, C. Adams, T. Schor et al. (2015) 'Cultural attitudes are stronger predictors of bushmeat consumption and preference than economic factors among urban Amazonians from Brazil and Colombia'. *Ecology and Society* 20(4): 21.

Nana, E. D. (2021) 'The paradigm of conservation in Central Africa is failing: An analysis of the current situation'. *Academia Letters*, article 3349.

Nasi, R., D. Brown, D. Wilkie, E. Bennett, C. Tutin, G. van Tol and T. Christophersen (2008) 'Conservation and use of wildlife-based resources: The bushmeat crisis'. Montreal/Bogor: Secretariat of the Convention on Biological Diversity/Center for International Forestry Research (CIFOR).

Nasi, R., A. Taber and N. van Vliet (2011) 'Empty forests, empty stomachs? Bushmeat and livelihoods in the Congo and Amazon basins'. *International Forestry Review* 13(3): 355–68.

Nelson, A. and K. M. Chomitz (2011) 'Effectiveness of strict vs. multiple use protected areas in reducing tropical forest fires: A global analysis using matching methods'. *PLOS One* 6(8): e22722.

Nelson, R. H. (2003) 'Environmental colonialism: "Saving" Africa from Africans'. *Independent Review* 8(1): 65–86.

Nganga, I., D. Massamba, F. Mbemba, G. Makosso Vyeiyes, A. R. M'bete and T. Silou (2013) 'L'hygiène dans l'approvisionnement et la distribution de la viande de brousse à Brazzaville-Congo'. *Journal of Applied Biosciences* 61: 4448–59.

Noss, A. J. (1995) 'Duikers, cables, and nets: A cultural ecology of hunting in a Central African forest'. Unpublished PhD dissertation, University of Florida.

Nuwer, R. L. (2018) *Poached: Inside the dark world of wildlife trafficking.* New York: Hachette Books.

Nzalalemba, S. K., D. K. Das and D. Simatele (2016) 'Some happy, others sad: Exploring environmental justice in solid waste management in Kinshasa, the Democratic Republic of Congo'. *Local Environment* 22(5): 595–620.

Ordaz-Ne'meth, I., M. Arandjelovic, L. Boesch, T. Gatiso, T. Grimes, H. S. Kuehl et al. (2017) 'The socio-economic drivers of bushmeat consumption during the West African Ebola crisis'. *PLOS Neglected Tropical Diseases* 11(3): e0005450.

Padilla-Iglesias, C., L. M. Atmore, J. Olivero, K. Lupo, A. Manica, E. Arango Isaza et al. (2022) 'Population interconnectivity over the past 120,000 years explains distribution and diversity of Central African hunter-gatherers'. *Proceedings of the National Academy of Sciences* 119(21).

Pembela Ekwamba, V. (2015–16) 'Consommation et commercialisation de la viande de brousse à Kinshasa'. Unpublished Bachelor's thesis, University of Kinshasa.

Persyn, P. and F. Ladrière (2004) 'The miracle of life in Kinshasa: New approaches to public health', in T. Trefon (ed.) *Re-inventing order in the Congo: How people respond to state failure in Kinshasa.* London: Zed Books.

Polanyi, K. (1944) *The great transformation.* New York: Farrar and Rinehart.

Polepole, P., R. Mwinyihali and D. Kurirakwinja (2021) 'Cadre légal et institutionnel du trafic de la viande de brousse en République Démocratique du Congo: Cas de la ville de Kinshasa'. Unpublished report, Kinshasa: Wildlife Conservation Society.

Poulsen, J. R., C. J. Clark, G. Mavah and P. W. Elkan (2009) 'Bushmeat supply and consumption in a tropical logging concession in northern Congo'. *Conservation Biology* 23(6): 1597–608.

BIBLIOGRAPHY

Powell, B., J. Hall and T. Johns (2011) 'Forest cover, use and dietary intake in the East Usambara Mountains, Tanzania'. *International Forestry Review* 13(3): 305–17.

Prince, T., S. L. Smith, A. D. Radford, T. Solomon, G. L. Hughes and E. I. Patterson (2021) 'SARS-CoV-2 infections in animals: Reservoirs for reverse zoonosis and models for study'. *Viruses* 13(494).

Quammen, D. (2012) *Spillover: Animal infections and the new pandemic.* New York: W. W. Norton and Company.

Rackley, E. B. (2006) 'Democratic Republic of the Congo: Undoing government by predation'. *Disasters* 30(4): 417–32.

Randolph, S. G. (2016) 'The social, economic and cultural dimensions of bushmeat consumption in Yaoundé, Cameroon'. Unpublished PhD thesis, Stanford University.

Redford, K. (1992) 'The empty forest'. *BioScience* 42(6): 412–422.

Reed, J., L. Deakin and T. Sunderland (2015) 'What are "integrated landscape approaches" and how effectively have they been implemented in the tropics: A systematic map protocol'. *Environmental Evidence* 4(2).

Riddell, M. A. (2011) 'Hunting and rural livelihoods in northern Republic of Congo: Local outcomes of integrated conservation and development'. Unpublished DPhil thesis, Oxford University.

Ripple, W. J., K. Abernethy, M. G. Betts, G. Chapron, R. Dirzo, M. Galetti et al. (2016) 'Bushmeat hunting and extinction risk to the world's mammals'. *Royal Society Open Science* 3: 160498.

Robinson, J. G. and E. Bennett (2002) 'Will alleviating poverty solve the bushmeat crisis?' *Oryx* 36(4): 332.

Rodary, E. (2008) 'Développer la conservation ou conserver le développement?' *Mondes en Développement* 36(1): 81–92.

Rose, A. L. (2001) 'Social change and social values in mitigating bushmeat commerce', in M. I. Bakarr, G. A. B. da Fonseca, R. A. Mittermeier, A. B. Rylands and K. W. Painemilla (eds.) *Hunting and bushmeat utilization in the African rain forest: Perspectives toward a blueprint for conservation action.* Washington, DC: Conservation International.

Russell, D., P. Mbile and N. Tchamou (2011) 'Farm and forest in Central Africa: Toward an integrated rural development strategy'. *Journal of Sustainable Forestry* 30(1–2): 111–32.

BIBLIOGRAPHY

Saylors, K., D. J. Wolking, E. Hagan, S. Martinez, L. Francisco, J. Euron et al. (2021) 'Socializing One Health: An innovative strategy to investigate social and behavioral risks of emerging viral threats'. *One Health Outlook* 3(11).

Schenck, M., E. Nsame Effa, M. Starkey, D. Wilkie, K. Abernethy, P. Telfer et al. (2006) 'Why people eat bushmeat: Results from two-choice, taste tests in Gabon, Central Africa'. *Human Ecology* 34(3): 433–45.

Schneider, W. H. (ed.) (2021) *The histories of HIVs: The emergence of the multiple viruses that caused the AIDS epidemics.* Athens, OH: Ohio University Press.

Scholte, P., J.-P. Agnangoye, B. Chardonnet, H.-P. Eloma, C. Nchoutpouen and T. Ngoga (2018) 'A Central African perspective on delegated protected area management'. *Tropical Conservation Science* 11: 1–10.

Schure, J., V. Ingram, M. S. Sakho-Jimbira, P. Levang and K. F. Wiersum (2013) 'Formalisation of charcoal value chains and livelihood outcomes in Central and West Africa'. *Energy for Sustainable Development* 17(2): 95–105.

Shandra, J. M., E. Shor, G. Maynard and B. London (2008) 'Debt, structural adjustment, and deforestation: A cross-national study'. *Journal of World-Systems Research* 14(1): 1–21.

Shapiro, D. (2012) 'Women's education and fertility transition in sub-Saharan Africa'. *Vienna Yearbook of Population Research* 10: 9–30.

Simone, A. (2004) *For the city yet to come: Changing African life in four cities.* Durham, NC: Duke University Press.

Sirén, A. and L. Machoa (2008) 'Fish, wildlife, and human nutrition in tropical forests: A fat gap?' *Interciencia* 33(3): 186–93.

Soewu, D., D. J. Ingram, R. Jansen, O. Sodeinde and D. W. Pietersen (2020) 'Bushmeat and beyond: Historic and contemporary use in Africa', in D. W. S. Challender, H. C. Nash and C. Waterman (eds.) *Pangolins: Science, society and conservation.* London: Academic Press.

Solly, H. (2002–3) '"Vous êtes grands, nous sommes petits": The implications of Bulu history, culture and economy for an Integrated Conservation and Development Project (ICDP) in the Dja Reserve, Cameroon'. Unpublished PhD thesis, Université Libre de Bruxelles.

BIBLIOGRAPHY

South, N. and T. Wyatt (2011) 'Comparing illicit trades in wildlife and drugs: An exploratory study'. *Deviant Behavior* 32(6): 538–61.

Souto, W. M. S., R. N. Lima and B. F. C. F. Sousa (2019) 'Illegal bushmeat hunting and trade dynamics in a major road-hub region of the Brazilian mid north'. *Indian Journal of Traditional Knowledge* 18(2): 402–11.

Spira, C., A. Kirkby, D. Kujirakwinja and A. J. Plumptre (2019) 'The socio-economics of artisanal mining and bushmeat hunting around protected areas: Kahuzi–Biega National Park and Itombwe Nature Reserve, eastern Democratic Republic of Congo'. *Oryx* 53(1): 136–44.

Stearns, J. K. (2022) 'Rebels without a cause: The new face of African warfare'. *Foreign Affairs* 101(3). https://www.foreignaffairs.com/articles/africa/2022-04-19/rebels-without-cause.

Steel, C. (2008) *Hungry city: How food shapes our lives*. London: Vintage Books.

Symes, W. S., M. Rao, M. B. Mascia and L. R. Carrasco (2016) 'Why do we lose protected areas? Factors influencing protected area downgrading, downsizing and degazettement in the tropics and subtropics'. *Global Change Biology* 22: 656–65.

Timberg, C. and D. Halperin (2012) *Tinderbox: How the West sparked the AIDS epidemic and how the world can finally overcome it*. London: Penguin Books.

Trefon, T. (2002) 'Changing patterns of solidarity in Kinshasa'. *Cadernos de Estudos Africanos* 3: 93–109.

Trefon. T. (2006) 'Industrial logging in the Democratic Republic of Congo: Is a stakeholder approach possible?' *South African Journal of International Affairs* 13(2): 101–14.

Trefon, T. (2009) 'Public service provision in a failed state: Looking beyond predation in the Democratic Republic of Congo'. *Review of African Political Economy* 36(119): 9–21.

Trefon, T. (2010) 'Administrative obstacles to reform in the Democratic Republic of Congo'. *International Review of Administrative Sciences* 76(4): 702–22.

Trefon, T. (2011) 'Urban–rural straddling: Conceptualizing the peri-urban in Central Africa'. *Journal of Developing Societies* 27(3–4): 421–43.

Trefon, T. (2016) *Congo's environmental paradox: Potential and predation in a land of plenty*. London: Zed Books.

BIBLIOGRAPHY

Trefon, T. and L. Defo (1999) 'Can rattan help save wildlife'. *Development* 42(2): 68–70.

Trefon, T. and P. de Maret (1999) 'Snack nature dans les villes d'Afrique centrale', in S. Bahuchet, D. Bley, H. Pagezy and N. Vernazza-Licht (eds.) *L'homme et la forêt tropicale*. Travaux de la Société d'Ecologie Humaine. Châteauneuf de Grasse: Editions de Bergier.

Tshikung, K. M., S. E. W. Pongombo, L. Roland and J. L. Hornick (2019) 'Consumption of bushmeat in Lubumbashi/DR Congo: Sociocultural approaches'. *Journal of Health Science* 7: 79–88.

Tyukavina, A., M. C. Hansen, P. Potapov, D. Parker, C. Okpa, S. V. Stehman et al. (2018) 'Congo Basin forest loss dominated by increasing smallholder clearing'. *Science Advances* 4(11).

USAID (2017) 'Evaluation. Midterm evaluation of phase III of the USAID Central Africa Regional Program for the Environment'. Washington, DC: United States Agency for International Development (USAID). https://carpe.umd.edu/sites/default/files/documentsarchive/2017_USAID_Midterm%20Eval%20of%20Phase%20III%20of%20USAID%20CARPE.pdf.

Valimahamed, A., G. Lescuyer and R. Nasi (2017) 'Contributions de la chasse villageoise aux économies locales et nationales au Congo et en République Démocratique du Congo', in N. van Vliet, J. C. Nguinguiri, D. Cornelis and S. Le Bel (eds.) *Communautés locales et utilisation durable de la faune en Afrique centrale*. Libreville/Bogor/Montpellier: FAO/CIFOR/CIRAD.

Van Bockhaven, V. (2009) 'Leopard-men of the Congo in literature and popular imagination'. *Tydskrif vir Letterkunde* 46(1): 79–94.

Van Boekstael, S and K. Vlassenroot (eds.) (2012) *A farmer's best friend? Artisanal diamond mining and rural change in West and Central Africa*. Ghent: Academia Press.

Van Schuylenbergh, P. (2006) 'De l'appropriation à la conservation de la faune sauvage: Pratiques d'une colonisation; Le cas du Congo belge (1885–1960)'. Unpublished PhD thesis, Catholic University of Louvain.

Van Schuylenbergh, P. (2009) 'Entre délinquance et résistance au Congo belge: L'interprétation coloniale du braconnage'. *Afrique et Histoire* 1(7): 25–48.

BIBLIOGRAPHY

Vansina, J. (1990) *Paths in the rainforests: Toward a history of political tradition in Equatorial Africa*. Madison, WI: University of Wisconsin Press.

van Vliet, N. and R. Nasi (2017) 'Viandes sauvages et sécurité alimentaire dans le cadre des systèmes d'alimentation durable en Afrique centrale', in N. van Vliet, J.-C. Nguinguiri, D. Cornelis and S. Le Bel (eds.) *Communautés locales et utilisation durable de la faune en Afrique centrale*. Libreville/Bogor/Montpellier: FAO/CIFOR/CIRAD.

van Vliet, N., C. Nebesse and R. Nasi (2014) 'Bushmeat consumption among rural and urban children from Province Orientale, Democratic Republic of Congo'. *Oryx* 49(1): 65–174.

Verbrugge, B. and S. Geenen (2019) 'The gold commodity frontier: A fresh perspective on change and diversity in the global gold mining economy'. *Extractive Industries and Society* 6(2): 413–23.

Verissimo, D. and A. K. Y. Wan (2019) 'Characterizing efforts to reduce consumer demand for wildlife products'. *Conservation Biology* 33(3): 623–33.

Vermeulen, C. (2000) 'Le facteur humain dans l'aménagement des espaces-ressources en Afrique centrale forestière: Application aux Badjoué de l'Est Cameroun'. Unpublished PhD thesis, Faculté Agronomique de Gembloux.

Vermeulen, C. and A. Karsenty (2017) 'Towards a community-based concession model in the DRC'. *International Forestry Review* 19(2): 80–6.

Vermeulen, C. and F. Lanata (2006) 'Le domaine de chasse de Bombo Lumene: Un espace naturel en péril aux frontières de Kinshasa'. *Parcs et Réserves* 61(2): 4–9.

Vorster, H. H., A. Kruger and B. M. Margetts (2011) 'The nutrition transition in Africa: Can it be steered into a more positive direction?' *Nutrients* 3: 429–41.

Wauchope, H. S., J. P. G. Jones, J. Geldmann, B. I. Simmons, T. Amano, D. E. Blanco et al. (2022) 'Protected areas have a mixed impact on waterbirds, but management helps'. *Nature* 605: 103–7.

White, B. W. (2004) 'The elusive *lupemba*: Rumours about fame and (mis) fortune in Kinshasa', in T. Trefon (ed.) *Re-inventing order in the Congo: How people respond to state failure in Kinshasa*. London: Zed Books.

BIBLIOGRAPHY

Wieland, M. (2008) 'Wildlife conservation in social, economic, and ecological contexts: Multiple stakeholders and extraordinary resource value in a Congolese national park'. Unpublished PhD thesis, University of Minnesota.

Wilkie, D. S. and J. Carpenter (1999) 'Bushmeat hunting in the Congo Basin: An assessment of impacts and options for mitigation'. *Biodiversity and Conservation* 8: 927–55.

Wilkie, D. S. and R. A. Godoy (2000) 'Economics of bushmeat'. *Science* 287(5455): 933.

Wilkie, D. S. and R. A. Godoy (2001) 'Income and price elasticities of bushmeat demand in lowland Amerindian societies'. *Conservation Biology* 15(3): 1–9.

Wilkie, D. S. and R. J. Lee (2004) 'Hunting in agroforestry systems and landscapes: Conservation implications in West-Central Africa and Southeast Asia', in S. J. Scherr and J. A. McNeely (eds.) *Farming with nature: The science and practice of ecoagriculture*. Washington, DC: Island Press.

Wilkie, D. S., M. Starkey, K. Abernethy, E. Nstame Effa, P. Telfer and R. Godoy (2005) 'Role of prices and wealth in consumer demand for bushmeat in Gabon, Central Africa'. *Conservation Biology* 19(1): 268–74.

Wilkie, D. S., M. Starkey, E. L. Bennett, K. Abernethy, R. Fotso, F. Maisels and P. Elkan (2006) 'Can taxation contribute to sustainable management of the bushmeat trade? Evidence from Gabon and Cameroon'. *Journal of International Wildlife Law and Policy* 9: 335–49.

Wilkie, D., E. Shaw, F. Rotberg, G. Morelli and P. Auzel (2008) 'Roads, development, and conservation in the Congo Basin'. *Conservation Biology* 14(6): 1614–22.

World Bank (2008) 'Democratic Republic of Congo: Growth with governance in the mining sector'. Washington, DC: World Bank.

World Commission on Environment and Development (1987) *Our common future*. Oxford: Oxford University Press.

Wright, J. H. (2018) 'Bushmeat consumption across the cities of Pointe-Noire, Brazzaville and Kinshasa'. Unpublished report, Kinshasa: Wildlife Conservation Society.

Wright, J. H. (2021) 'Livelihood interventions in conservation: Expectations and reality around protected areas in Cameroon'. Unpublished PhD thesis, Imperial College London.

INDEX

INDEX

INDEX

INDEX

INDEX

INDEX

INDEX

INDEX

INDEX

INDEX

INDEX